INTERNATIONAL

COMMUNITY POWER

STRUCTURES

INTERNATIONAL COMMUNITY POWER STRUCTURES

Comparative Studies of Four World Cities

DELBERT C. MILLER

INDIANA UNIVERSITY PRESS

Bloomington / London

To

M IKE *and* T RUDY

and to all of the new generation

who seek to understand

community power

CONTENTS

vii

LIST OF FIGURES

LIST OF TABLES

ACKNOWLEDGMENTS

MY DEBT FOR ASSISTANCE IS GREAT, and many specific instances of that assistance are noted in chapter footnotes. Here I want to express my appreciation particularly to the many individuals who have contributed to the development of the research process and to interpreting the results. In Cordoba, Argentina I received counsel and guidance from Juan Carlos Agulla, Alfredo Poviña, and Alfredo Critto of the Institute of Sociology of the University of Cordoba. In Lima, Peru faculty members Aníbal Ismodes Cairo and José Mejía Valera of the Sociology Department at the University of San Marcos and Manuel Román de Sirgado of Catholic University gave counsel and advice.

I owe a special debt of gratitude to my Latin American research assistants, Eva Chamorro Greca at Cordoba and Patricia Frankman at Lima. They worked with me daily and constantly guided me in everything from the pronunciation of difficult Spanish words to gaining access to available documents in local archives and providing interpretation of research data and local customs. The graduate students in sociology at the University of Cordoba and the University of San Marcos are due a special vote of thanks for their participation and assistance.

I am grateful to the editors and publishers who have granted me permission to reprint or adapt previously published materials. These sources are noted at the appropriate chapters.

I wish to express my appreciation for financial assistance received from the graduate schools of the University of Washington and Indiana University, from the Social Science Research Council, and from a Ford Foundation grant to Indiana University in April 1961. Two sabbatical years and a Fulbright fellowship also helped make these studies possible.

Floyd Hunter and Peter H. Rossi have rendered me an especial service by reading the manuscript and providing many suggestions for its improvement. Naturally, I take full responsibility for the finished product.

PREFACE

THE COMPARATIVE STUDY OF INTERNATIONAL COMMUNITY POWER STRUC-
tures is one of the most challenging frontiers for future research. The
growing ties between nations place an increasing importance on understanding different power structures at both the national and the community levels. The central questions with which the social scientist must
deal are: What *generalizations* may be drawn about leadership and decision making within different types of social and political structures?
What is the *significance of the differences* within each of the various
socio-political systems for leadership and decision making?

I began asking myself these questions about community power structures in 1953 when I lived in Seattle, Washington and was teaching at
the University of Washington. Community power research as we know
it today was just beginning. Floyd Hunter published *Community Power
Structure*, his path-breaking study of Atlanta, in that year. The challenge
to compare Seattle with Atlanta prompted me to begin a comparative
research program which ultimately included studies of four world cities
and extended over fifteen years. The cities were studied in the following
order: Seattle, 1953–54 and 1955–57; Bristol, England, 1954–55; Cordoba, Argentina, 1963–64; and Lima, Peru, 1965–66. This book is a report
on that research. The title *International Community Power Structures*
must be regarded as more suggestive than definitive. These four studies
do not span the full range of institutional power structures in the communities of the world, but there is reason to believe they represent major
city types within Western and Latin American civilization. Both of the
Latin American cities are under military control today. During my
studies one—Lima—was a democracy and one—Cordoba—was under military control. This typical variation is captured in the Latin American
research.

At the beginning of the research there were no studies to provide experience and guidance in the design of comparative community power
research. Even today only a few exist. Most research has been done in
the United States where more than one hundred and sixty systematic
studies of the community power structures of American cities have been
carried out during the past fifteen years.[1] In all of Latin America,
Norman E. Whitten, Jr., by pulling together studies that described

power elements in their structure, was able to find studies of seventeen communities.[2] Almost all of these were made by anthropologists interested in general ethnographic description; the studies by sociologists usually failed to employ systematic techniques of community power analysis.[3] The research literature shows a paucity of material on communities in Europe, Africa, and Asia. There are studies of national power and observations about power structures in communities also exist, but most data are capable neither of being compared nor of being brought into a cumulative pattern.

I was acutely aware that I faced a danger of gathering data lacking in comparability. Comparative research requires similar criteria for the selection of cities, similar hypotheses, and a common methodology. The four cities were selected so that they would be similar in population size, in degree of industrialization, and in economic base. I believed that the city should be of sufficient size to have fully structured institutional sectors in all areas of social life and to reveal issues common to modern, industrialized cities. Cities in the 500,000 to 2,000,000 population range fulfill this requirement and can be studied by available techniques. To assure that each was an industrial city, a requirement was imposed that 20 percent or more of the labor force be engaged in manufacturing. A further mark of a mature industrial city is a diversified economic base with a balanced distribution of manufacturing, wholesaling, and retailing. Generally, in such a community no single economic firm can dominate community decision making.[4]

After ensuring the comparability of the cities, I constructed a system model of community power analysis to provide a theoretical framework for a test of a number of hypotheses. A central set of steps was employed in all four cities to gather comparable data.

Three major comparisons are made to focus attention upon the differences in institutional power base. Seattle and Bristol are first compared because they represent the traditions of Western culture. They share a common heritage of democracy, language, industrial technology, and many similar social customs. These two cities were carefully selected in order to hold constant as many social and economic factors as possible. Atlanta as studied by Floyd Hunter has been brought into the comparison of the Western cities because of its similar economic and social base.

Cordoba and Lima are then compared. They are excellent urban examples of Latin American civilization. Both trace their origins back to the sixteenth century when South America came under Spanish rule. They also share a common language, religion, and extended family system. Finally, the four cities are compared together in order to discover whether the Miller-Form system model of community power will explain the types of groups and leaders which arise in all four cities.

It is hoped that this report will take its place in the growing body of comparative community power research and that it will stimulate interest in the problems of methodology and comparative design. In each of the cities I have not hesitated to explore new research opportunities which were relevant to that city and its community power structure. The reader will find special studies that elaborate the central effort. In Seattle a study was made to ascertain the social and educational backgrounds and career patterns of the city's business leadership. Also in Seattle a new theory to predict issue outcome was applied to the controversial right-to-work initiative placed on the ballot in 1956. In Cordoba the community power perspectives and role definitions of North American business executives were explored and compared with those of the top influentials of Cordoba. In Lima special attention was given to the analysis of cliques and power blocs. Top influentials were studied to determine the bases of their power and influence and power profiles were developed for them.

In my search for a base of decision-making norms which could be said to characterize Latin American civilization I developed a battery of scales to measure international patterns. Finally, I have outlined the frontier of comparative community power research to present fruitful directions for future investigation. All of these supplementary efforts were pursued to add depth to the comparative findings and to encourage scholars to use or challenge the methodological techniques presented.[5]

I have written this book with three audiences in mind: my older fellow scholars who may be familiar with my earlier work and who may have an interest in examining the newer unpublished research as it is brought into an integrated comparative framework; younger scholars who have never observed the evolution of a body of comparative community power research; and those enquiring readers who, though in neither of these groups, may gain a greater understanding of community power structures under different socio-political conditions. It has been commonly observed that one comes to understand his own country and community best as he contrasts it with others. The central challenge is to interest all readers in the substantive findings as the four cities are compared with each other. I hope to show readers in the United States what it means for a city to function under socio-political systems not found in their country. I am trying to interpret the two Latin American cities so South Americans will better understand the nature of their own cities and those of the so-called mature democracies. For social scientists everywhere I seek to draw attention to the significance of differences in institutional power bases that provide the values, the tradition, and the power which shape the influence system of a given community.

DELBERT C. MILLER

Bloomington, Indiana
June 1, 1969

INTERNATIONAL

COMMUNITY POWER

STRUCTURES

Program, Theory,
and Method
in Comparative Analysis
of Community
Power Structures

CHAPTER 1

THEORETICAL POSITIONS,

OPERATING ASSUMPTIONS,

AND METHODOLOGICAL DECISIONS

EACH RESEARCHER OF COMMUNITY POWER STRUCTURES can today draw upon a wide range of theoretical ideas and methodological techniques. As an empirical area of study this specialized field is scarcely fifteen years old. Sociologists and political scientists have been giving almost equal time to testing and contesting. The controversy over method is one of the most vehement in the general field of sociology. There are constant demands that researchers reformulate their definitions of power, influence, authority, leadership, and other basic concepts of the field. Critics often complain that the research has missed a vital part of the power structure or distorted it by the method employed. In a summary paper Terry N. Clark sets out sixteen differing conceptions of power and shows how each concentrates attention upon a specific aspect, often to the neglect of all the others.[1]

In the midst of this highly pluralistic—or perhaps anarchic—state of theory and methodology the researcher must constantly re-evaluate his concepts and his techniques. He must then make operating choices. In order to do long-range programming for comparative analysis, he must freeze his theory and methodology sufficiently to permit generalization from one case study to the others. But he must allow himself the option of adding new techniques, hypotheses, and theoretical concepts as discoveries demand. Some of these new ideas emerge from the growing literature, others develop out of his own work. New concepts of theory or methodology are always challenging. As Abraham Kaplan points out, the function of scientific concepts is to mark the categories which will tell us more about our subject matter than any other categorical sets. They identify modes or junctions in the network of relationships, termini at which we can halt while preserving the maximum range of choice as to where to go next.[2]

The concepts are selected and defined because of certain presuppositions drawn from earlier inquiries, from other sciences, from everyday knowledge, from the experiences of conflict and frustration which motivated our inquiry, from habit and tradition, from who knows where. Methodology does not rob us of our footing; it enjoins us, rather, to look at it.[3]

In this chapter we shall look at the concepts and theoretical positions chosen as guides and describe the operating assumptions and methodological decisions for the studies that comprise this research.

Theoretical Position with Reference to the Generalized Concept of Power

INDIVIDUALS, GROUPS, AND INSTITUTIONS are able to command compliance by means of power, influence, and authority. Peter H. Rossi has distinguished between power and influence by saying that "power" implies a relationship in which actor or organization A affects the behavior of actor or organization B because B wishes to avoid the sanctions which A would employ if B did not comply with his wishes, and "influence" implies alteration of behavior without perceived sanctions.[4] "Authority," then, may be viewed as institutionalized power that can command obedience by the use of either manifest or latent sanctions. But it may also be viewed as a status relationship in which a person may influence the behavior of others without the employment of sanctions.

The impetus to alter behavior may be a compound of power, influence, and authority with stimuli so subtly intermingled that it is impossible to separate them. The field researcher will do well to ignore the theoretical distinctions and proceed to identify those acts and forces in the social system that affect issues, projects, or individual decisions of general import to the community. He should recognize that power can be latent as well as overt. The military force of the armed services or the economic force of a union can secure compliance even while held in reserve. The church can bring moral force to bear at strategic moments and upon certain issues though it may appear impotent and moribund for long periods of time. Latent power is the most puzzling of all forces operating in community power structures and most studies have not dealt with it directly. The major emphasis has been put upon the identification of influential positions, leaders, or overt acts during relatively short periods of time. Longitudinal studies of power are few.

OPERATING ASSUMPTION. Power and influence are generated in many different ways and the terms can be used interchangeably in research operations. It has been suggested that the bases of power rest on control over wealth and other resources such as banks, land, industries; control over mass communications media, including newspapers, radio and television stations, and magazines; control over solidary groups represented by organized groups or cliques that can provide support or threaten sanctions; control over cultural, educational, and moral values; control over prestigeful interaction in desirable social circles.[5]

These bases of power may be elaborated into ten types of mutually exclusive forms of power that are easily distinguishable:

Economic power. Holder may wield power through his command of money and credit, control over jobs or conditions of work, ability to buy and sell freely, and a willingness to employ his economic power as a sanction or an inducement.

Political influence. Holder may control party and governmental policy making, jobs, and votes.

Governmental authority. Holder may wield the formal power designated by his office and the informal influence emanating from his command of rewards and penalties.

Moral and religious persuasion. Holder may control political, economic, and general cultural influence by control over moral values and moral support of such highly solidary groups as the church and the middle class.

Social prestige. Holder may control access to prestigeful interaction—be able to provide access to desired social and business circles and secure entry for himself and others to highly desired segments of the marriage market.

Means of communication. Holder may command access to mass communications media by ownership or by personal influence, advertising, being relative or friend of owner, etc.

Specialized knowledge and skill. Holder has knowledge or skill that gives him ability to command decision making—lawyer, engineer, city planner, public health specialist, military expert, etc.

Military support. Holder enjoys confidence of the military and can use support as positive influence or negative sanction as needed.

Very well-liked personality. Holder can use his personality as a source of influence.

Superior qualities of leadership. Holder can command influence be-

5

cause of his ability to organize, implement, articulate, or function in some manner that mobilizes persons and groups to action.

Community power may be defined as the network of influences that bear upon all decisions that have a general effect upon the community. Community decisions of general importance occur around issues and projects and around status and power allocations in voluntary, political, and governmental organizations, in work organizations, and in decisions regarding land use. These may be arranged in various visibility levels and by magnitude as shown in Figure 1. This figure attempts to

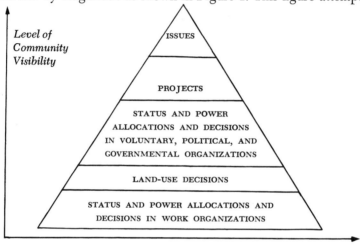

FIGURE 1. *A Depiction of the Decisional Areas That Have General Importance to the Community*

depict two dimensions which give a pyramidical character to the decisional areas. The vertical dimension is an arrangement of areas by level of community visibility. Issues and projects have the highest visibility because they are given the greatest publicity by the mass communications media. Status and power allocations in voluntary, political, and governmental organizations refer to the winning of positions, authority, and resources in such organizations as chambers of commerce, central labor councils, political parties, and governmental offices. Land-use decisions involve the expansion of factories, the erection of new shopping centers, the removal of slums, etc. Ordinarily, these decisions are made quietly and executed with little publicity; if they are contested their visibility rises. Finally, status and power allocations in work organizations refer to winning of positions, authority, and resources within various organizations including bank, factory, store, school, church, and

6

hospital. The incumbent in an important position can transfer his status within the organization to a standing in the community and thus have potential or actual influence.

The horizontal dimension of magnitude is simply a recognition that the greatest number of events occurs at the base of the pyramid and that magnitude is inversely related to visibility. Nearly all research in community power structures has been concerned primarily with issues and projects to the neglect of the other three areas. Actually, however, community leaders are those who draw influence and power in varying degrees from most of the five areas. The potential influence of reputed leaders in all these areas is especially important because top leaders assess each other's overall or potential influence on the community. For this reason a broad conception of decisional areas and of community power is appropriate.

Theoretical Position in Reference to Positional, Reputational, and Issue-Decisional Levels of Power

POWER OPERATES on three major overlapping levels: positional, reputational, and issue-decisional. Specific types of influence on each level can be ascertained only by employing appropriate techniques.

Positional power refers essentially to the formal power of authority —power of unilateral decision such as often occurs in decision making within firms, labor unions, institutions, public agencies, and even political parties.

Reputational power refers to power and influence imputed to persons and organizations in both private and public decision making. It is commonly observed in community decisions where voluntary organizations and top leaders of the community are involved either in issues or projects.

Issue-decisional power refers to power exerted in the resolution of public issues requiring approval of public officials and community leaders.

All these types of power are represented by leaders and organizations as shown in Figure 2. Positional power leaders are ascertained by identifying the formal positions that are considered most important in power and authority and designating the incumbents as positional or potential power leaders. Reputational leaders are identified by judges as those most influential in the community life of the city. Issue-decisional leaders are those who have demonstrated activity in salient issues of high community concern. In varying degrees each group of leaders reflects a continuum of power ranging from latent to manifest.

7

Type of Power	Conception of Power	How it is Described	Techniques Employed	Principal Products of Research
Positional Power (*Structural*)	Power that can be mobilized if available resources are used. Ordinarily employed in private decisions.	Identification of the institutions, organizations, and offices in the community that have potential power.	Documents. Informants.	List of persons in the most influential offices. Resources of persons and organizations. Records of results achieved.
Reputational Power (*Sociometric*)	Power that is imputed to persons and organizations and institutions. Employed variously in both private and public decision making.	1. Identification by judges of the most influential leaders, organizations, and institutions. 2. Description of roles played by influential leaders.	Interviews with panel of judges, informants, and with influential leaders.	List of leaders considered most important, and their participation patterns.
Issue-Decisional Power (*Issue-Relevant*)	Power that can be assigned to persons, organizations, and institutions through the debate of public issues or promotion of public projects. Employed mainly in decisions on public matters.	1. Identification of recent issues that are considered most important in the life of the community. 2. Identification of the persons and the roles they played in resolving issues or projects.	Interviews with persons associated with issues or projects during decision making. Attendance and recording of decision making meetings.	List of most influential leaders in recent issues. Analyses of roles played.

FIGURE 2. *Positional, Reputational, and Issue-Decisional Definitions of Power and the Accompanying Research Techniques*

Community power structure research seeks those aspects of social structure which are relatively stable and exhibit recurring regularities in community decison making. The search for such stable characteristics should take precedence over the examination of *power arrangements* indicated by the study of single issues. We accept the assumption that discrete private and public decision-making systems tend to exist simultaneously. Economic leaders tend to dominate essentially "private" types of decisions that entail the use of nongovernmental resources. Political leaders generally control "public issues" requiring the expenditure of public funds. "Welfare oriented" leaders have only marginal power and prestige with respect to private and public decisions; they are rarely nominated as influentials nor do they characteristically prove to be active in more than one major issue. Economic, political, and welfare-oriented leadership groups play different roles in different communities and they may be in competition.

Communities with many leaders and abundant internal resources will probably be dominated by economic leaders, whereas communities with limited leadership and economic resources are more likely to be dominated by political leaders. Over an extended period of time economic leaders will probably exert the most power in community affairs because their characteristic bases of power are more stable than those of the political leaders.[6]

OPERATING ASSUMPTION. All levels of power—positional, reputational, and issue-decisional—are important in delineating a community power structure. Leadership concepts appropriate to the various power levels should be applied to understand both latent and manifest exercise of power, to provide basic information for mapping the total influence pattern and decision-making processes, and to predict the resolution of community issues.

The positional power approach focuses on those dominant leaders who possess resources, skills, and formal authority in economic, political, military, labor, and religious institutions. The ranking of dominants by their potential reveals the latent force of the leaders in each sector. Tracing the interaction between these leaders reveals also the regularized pattern of potential power of combined sectors. Often such leaders work behind the scenes making decisions quietly. For example, economic dominants can change the land-use pattern of an entire city in a relatively short time by their control over property. They can alter the political character of a community by their control over political leaders and parties.

The reputational approach identifies leaders according to the influence they are imputed to have. Such leaders can be ranked in influence as key influentials and top influentials. Their type of power and patterns of participation can be mapped at a current time and also in historical perspective.[7] Bonjean and Noland have recently developed a new typology of leadership based on the reputational rankings of top leaders as they are ranked by top leaders.[8] Those persons receiving a significantly higher rank position from top-ranking leaders than from lower-ranking leaders were designated *concealed leaders*. It was believed that their influence was greater than most leaders and the general community recognized. Those persons receiving a significantly higher rank position from the lower-ranking leaders than from top-ranking leaders were designated *symbolic leaders*. The symbolic leaders probably did not wield as much influence as the lower-ranking leaders and the community at large believed they did. *Visible leaders* were so designated when both top- and lower-ranking leaders agreed on the degree of influence exerted by these leaders. It was believed that the roles played by these visible leaders were perceived and known by the community at large.

Characteristics which can be associated with each type of reputational leader include occupation, political affiliation, possession of wealth, participation in voluntary organizations, and activity in the Chamber of Commerce. The patterned differences revealed for each of these three types of reputational leaders provide greater understanding of the roles and behaviors of leaders in the resolution of community issues and projects.[9]

The issue-decisional approach focuses clearly upon roles played in the resolution of community-relevant issues. *Generalist leaders* are those who participate extensively in many but not in all issue areas. The *issue specialists* participate regularly in one particular issue area, but are not active in other aspects of the community. *Meteors* or *irregulars* are those who participate sporadically in a few issues. *Apathetics* or *inactives* are recognized potential or occupational leaders who do not participate directly in projects or issues of the community.[10] Wildavsky says the reason so many issue leaders are left out of the reputational elites is that most issue leaders are "meteors."[11] The roles played by these different kinds of leaders provide new insights into the leadership structure of the community. Willingness to take an active role in community issues is an important criterion of leadership in a society like that of the United States, where citizen participation and voluntary organizations are considered important. In Latin American societies participation is exercised more commonly inside bureaucracies, political parties, and large family kinship systems.

It is not unexpected to find some degree of overlap among the leaders identified with the three types of power. This is shown in Figure 3. It is well known that the activity of community leaders fluctuates. Such phases of activity and inactivity are clearly seen in observing issue-decisional leaders. However, a leader's inactivity on issues does not necessarily mean that his influence in community decision making has vanished. Reputational leaders are commonly active in civic projects, in influencing policies in voluntary associations, in land-use decisions, and within their own work organizations where community-oriented decisions are made. And, as shown in Figure 1, positional leaders may function throughout all five decisional areas although their most frequent impact is through decisions affecting the community which they make within their own work organizations. The president of a large organization who does no more than insist that his executives and managers par-

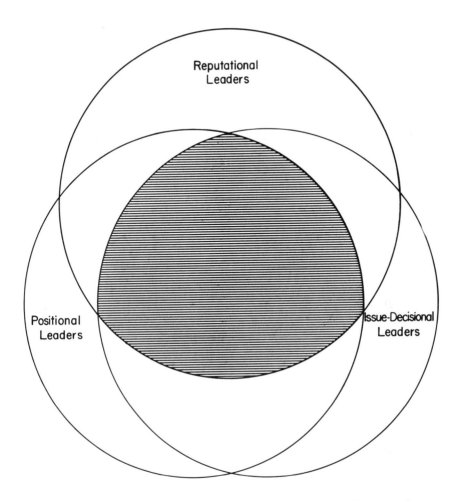

FIGURE 3. *The Overlapping Character of Leadership Findings Employing the Positional, Reputational, and Issue-decisional Techniques*

ticipate actively in community life can have a great influence in converting positional leaders into community leaders.

This research study will employ all three approaches to leadership identification and will investigate the degree of overlap among leaders, but the primary concern will be with the total community power structure. The reputational leadership structure will be given primary attention in this study. This decision is based on the belief that the reputational leadership structure is made up of leaders who have demonstrated community activity and influence over a relatively long period of time

11

and thus combine the highest manifest and latent power. It is based also on the belief that their influence extends over the widest range of decisions which affect the community. On these counts, it is assumed that an analysis of reputed influence of leaders, organizations, and community institutions will reveal those aspects of social structure which are *relatively stable and exhibit recurring regularities.* This is another way of affirming that a community power *structure* is a reality and not a metaphysical fiction. Moreover, we agree with Rossi that the reputational method "yields data of significance, lending itself to systematization, and for these reasons is the appropriate tool for comparative studies."[12]

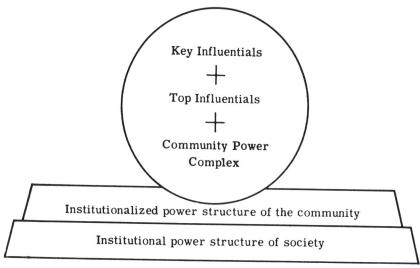

FIGURE 4. *The Five Components of Community Power Structure*

Theoretical Position with Reference to Composition of the Community Power Structure: Community Power System Model

THE COMMUNITY POWER STRUCTURE is a pattern of interacting parts. To illustrate, Form and Miller have outlined a system model (see Figure 4) and have defined five component parts as follows:

1. The *institutional power structure of the society* refers to the relative distribution of power among societal institutions.
2. The *institutionalized power structure of the community* refers to the relative distribution of power among local institutions.
3. The *community power complex* is a power arrangement among temporary or permanent organizations, special-interest associa-

tions, and informal groups emerging in specific issues and projects.

4. The *top influentials* are those persons who are reputed to exert the most influence and power in community decision making.

5. The *key influentials* are acknowledged leaders among the top influentials.[13]

Each part is believed to be interrelated with and to influence the nature of each successive part. This means that the entire structure is greatly influenced by the nature of the institutional power structure of the society. Institutional dominance may vary among such sectors as *business and finance, government, labor, military, religion, society and wealth, independent professions, education, mass communications, recreation, social welfare,* and *cultural and artistic* institutions. In general, the power pattern of the society puts its stamp on the institutional power structure within the community. In turn, organizaions and leaders draw their power and influence from the institutional power structure of the community.

The validity of the model rests on the following assumptions:

1. In the institutional power structure of society, influence is derived from dominant values which are exercised by certain social institutions. The power of these institutions is due to their resources, the rate at which they use their resources for political influence, and the efficiency with which they use their resources.

2. The institutional sectors of the local community reflect the institutional power structure of the society (nation) because of high interrelationships of economy, communication, and transportation.

3. Organizations composing the community power complex have identifiable interest groupings anchored in institutional sectors.

4. Top influentials will occur in number and influence proportionate to the power distribution of institutions in the institutionalized power structure of the community.

5. Key influentials reflect top influentials in attitude and behavior but are selected out more rigorously because of their higher power ranking and their leadership abilities.

Partial breakdowns of these assumptions are known to take place. This study of four cities was designed to test the model and determine the points of divergence and the degree of dispersion. A prediction instrument to forecast the outcome of issues is community decision making was constructed and applied to ascertain validity of the theory.

OPERATING ASSUMPTION. All five components of the community structure are identifiable and their quality and intensity can be measured. Such measurement focuses attention upon structural aspects and reveals the most stable elements in the structure. It prevents community power structure analysis from degenerating into leadership or issue analysis. Leadership is important, but it represents only a part of the total analysis. The focus on structure forces the social scientist to study the economic base, social composition, and power base of the community in both cross-sectional and historical dimensions. In the next chapter a framework of comparative analysis is outlined to provide theoretical and research guides to these essential parts of the community.

Theoretical Position with Reference to Range and Types of Community Power Structure

COMMUNITY POWER STRUCTURES range from monolithic or oligarchic to pluralistic or amorphous. Figure 5 illustrates five types of power structure models.

A number of patterns will appear along a continuum ranging from extreme monolithic power (one-man or one-party rule) to extreme pluralism (a multi-party system of balanced and/or unstable forces). Industrialization accompanied by such democratic guarantees as the right to a secret ballot and the right to organize political parties, pressure groups, and other voluntary associations tends to have the effect of restructuring community power toward more pluralistic patterns. In this connection, Rossi states that a monolithic power structure tends to accompany a very subordinate position for public officials and labor unions, while a prominent position for public officials and labor unions implies a polylithic (pluralistic) patterning.[14]

OPERATING ASSUMPTION. All cities can be classified by power types if their structures are identified. The number of top influentials will vary from small (10–15) to large (50–100) as community power structures range from monolithic to polylithic. Large pools of fluid leadership in pluralistic structures tend to harden into small and exclusive cliques in monolithic ones. Decision-making processes reflect these structural differences.

METHODOLOGICAL DECISIONS

A NUMBER OF METHODOLOGICAL PROBLEMS presented themselves in all four of the studies reported here; each reduced to the evaluation of the efficiency of the alternative methods that could be utilized for tests of the major hypotheses.[15] The hypotheses required a search for the pattern of power distribution in each community and the character of the

FIGURE 5.   *Five Types of Community Power Models*

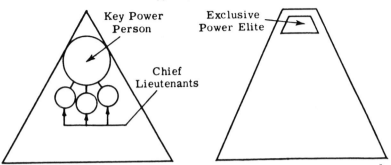

MODEL A. Pyramidical structure centering in one person. Example: one-industry town with no form of countervailing power. See *Middletown* (Lynd).

MODEL B. Pyramidical structure centering in an aristocracy. Characterized by small, tightly knit group at top; other interests capable of challenging those in power; no single group owning the whole town. Example: *Middletown in Transition.*

First- Rate	Industrial, commercial, financial owners and top executives of large enterprises.
Second- Rate	Operations officials, bank vice-presidents, public relations men, small businessmen, top ranking public officials, corporation attorneys, contractors.
Third- Rate	Civic organizations personnel, civic agency board personnel, newspaper columnists, radio commentators, petty public officials, selected organization executives, and small business proprietors.
Fourth- Rate	Professionals such as ministers, teachers, social workers, personnel directors, and such persons as small business managers, higher-paid accountants, and the like.

MODEL C. Stratified pyramidical structure. Characterized by top policy makers drawn largely from a social aristocracy built on class values. Industrial, commercial, financial owners and top executives of large enterprises dominate distinguishable strata of second, third, and fourth rate leaders of influence. Example: Atlanta, Georgia (Hunter).

15

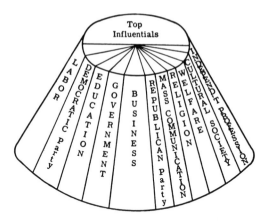

MODEL D. Ring or cone model. Characterized in many modern communities by heterogeneous business sector; countervailing powers (labor, church, second political party); autonomy of institutional sectors. No single focus of decision making. Example: Bristol, England (Miller).

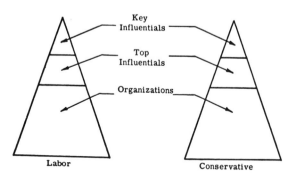

MODEL E. Segmented power pyramids. Characterized by political parties forming clearly opposing blocs; community power breaking cleanly among party lines (extreme right and extreme left parties in power conflict). Example: Various Latin American cities.

individual and group interaction through which decision making took place. Research was directed at seven objectives: identification of the influential leaders, organizations, and institutional sectors and their degree of influence; selection and application of appropriate tests of validity for the above; determination of the presence or absence of policy-maker cliques and the degree of solidarity and extent of conflict among top influentials; detection of institutional linkages and development of a technique for mapping them; selection and depiction of appropriate community power models; measurement of the patterns, norms, and values which affect decision making; and interpretation of the larger social system in cross-sectional and historical terms.

Identification of the Influential Leaders, Organizations, and Institutional Sectors and Their Degree of Influence. The decision to combine the positional, reputational, and issue-decisional methods was made because of the growing consensus among researchers that no single method is best since it will reveal but a specific aspect of the power structure.[16] The reputational technique was given priority because it identifies leaders who are most likely to demonstrate stable, repeatable patterns of community leadership since they have gained repute because of their interest in community activity or they have won the confidence of other leaders over relatively long periods of time. The identification of positional leaders presents a potential power structure and is a useful check on the list of reputational leaders. Most reputational leaders are also positional leaders, although not all positional leaders are reputational leaders.

Criteria of selection are very important in detecting influential leaders. Hunter introduced a selection criterion stressing influence, acceptability, and cooperativeness. "If a project were before the community that required *decision* by a group of leaders—leaders that nearly everyone would accept—which ten on the list of forty would you choose?" All of the studies in this monograph have used this criterion, but it has been shown to have limitations. Rossi has said it stresses influence centered about private nongovernmental decisions resolved in voluntary organizations and suggests that it identifies a civic elite. Such a list of civic elite often fails to match closely a list of issue-decisional leaders since it tends to exclude loners, controversial leaders, "meteors," and leaders interested in governmental issues. Other reputational criteria can be used to block these gaps. A criterion used in the Lima study states: "Without taking into account what you may think of them or their ideas, select fifteen persons from the list that are the most powerful in regard to the *initiation, support,* or *prohibition* of acts that have influence over issues or events that have general importance to the community." This more general criterion permits identification of many powerful persons previously omitted who play roles in many of the five decisional areas set out in Figure 1. Results indicate that this "power" criterion yields a higher overlap with issue-decisional leaders than did Hunter's "acceptability" criterion. The degree of overlap is a useful index, but it is not as important as the *validity of the methods* and the *extent to which stable regularities can be ascertained.*

In this research the reputational technique was applied not only to the study of leaders, but to the study of organizations and institutions as well in order to seek roots of influence in the social structure of the community. Judges and top leaders were asked to evaluate the organizations they believed supported or opposed "with the most effort and influence a project or issue that is placed before the community for decision." For a determination of the institutional power ranking they were asked to rank each of the institutional sectors of both the nation and the community "for its relative power or influence in getting the things it wants done and for its influence within the community when issues and projects are debated and decided." These studies represent the first effort to apply the reputational technique to institutional ranking.

Selection and Application of Appropriate Tests of Validity. Since many critics declare that reputational findings are not an actual demonstration of influence, the reputational technique must be buttressed with tests of validity. A large number of these tests may be made. The reputed leader's formal position and its ranking within the institutional sector to which it pertains can be determined. A history of the reputed leader can be traced by observing his participation in issues, projects, land-use decisions, and other decisions influencing community life. Also useful is a record of the reputed leader's current participation on committees or as an officer in civic, social, and professional organizations. The bases of a reputed leader's institutional power should be determined, including political influence, economic power, governmental authority, military support, means of communication, and moral and religious persuasion. This should be coupled with a determination of the leader's personal power including qualities of leadership, the esteem in which he is held, social prestige, special knowledge and skill. The combined validity of a leader's organizational, institutional, and personal influence can be tested by the prediction of issue outcome. Sociometric analysis of visible, concealed, and symbolic leaders will provide evidence for the true nature of each top influential's role.

The Determination of the Presence or Absence of Policy-Making Cliques and the Degree of Solidarity and Extent of Conflict among Top Influentials. This is unquestionably the most difficult problem facing the community power researcher. An abundance of hearsay evidence must be sifted in order to make an accurate determination.

The open-end probing question is most appropriate and should be asked of top leaders and specially qualified informants. The typical probe begins: "It is often said that there is a crowd that pretty well runs things in this city. Is it true or false? Why?" The researcher asks for details: "What issue was decided? By whom? Where? What others were brought in?"

In Lima and Cordoba another question was used: "In your opinion what groups are most important for assuring support of a project or issue that has general community importance? Who are the key persons to see in these groups?"

In all four city studies top leaders were ranked by one another for their mutual acquaintance on a schedule that ranged from "don't know, heard of, know little" to "know well, know socially (exchange home visits or see each other socially)." Participation patterns in business, social, civic, and professional organizations were carefully examined for overlapping patterns. Informants were asked to describe decision-making patterns of key leaders.

The Detection of Institutional Linkages and Techniques of Mapping Them. In the Latin American studies the institutional linkages were of great importance because of the alleged interlocking of church, military, and large economic interests. Many advised a study of family structure to find the interrelations of large kinship ties across different institutional sectors, since, it was said, the pattern of reciprocal support among family members would forge effective links for powerful "old families." Because of this advice, family patterns were analyzed and father-son chains were examined. Military positions were also ranked by informants for their relative influence, and channels of communication were mapped. In a similar fashion labor and church hierarchies were examined. Large land holders were given special attention and their overlapping positions in banks, industries, investment houses, and real estate were diagrammed. Political and governmental ties were studied and communication links given attention. All of these studies used documents, books, newspapers, and interviews. Especially useful were the interpretative interviews carried out when differing facts or opinions had been assembled and the researcher was trying to interpret the results. Informants who had special knowledge and experience were able to be unusually effective when the researcher asked them focused questions to gain understanding of a puzzling aspect of the power structure. The worth of such interviews has convinced me that *the results of a study should be written during the stay in the site city.*

Selection and Depiction of Appropriate Community Power Model. An overall knowledge of the community power structure is essential for diagramming a community power model. The researcher must know the relative power of the institutional sectors, the degree of solidarity of top leaders, and the nature of institutional linkage. The community power models set out earlier were used as standards to fit each study to its appropriate model. In the final chapter a quantitative measure of the degree of fluidity existing in each city is presented. I hope that succeeding researchers will use, test, and refine this measure.

Measurement of the Patterns, Norms, and Values which Affect Decision Making. The student of comparative community power structures has great need of a scaling instrument that will reveal cross-national cultural differences. Ideally, such an instrument should show those important variations in cultural patterns that make significant differences when problems and issues are being debated or resolved in the decision-making process within the community. Fifteen scales were constructed for this purpose and have met tests of reliability and validity. They delineate some of the significant parameters of community decision making, especially belief in a democratic political system, consensus over the general philosophy and objectives of the society, labor's orientation to the prevailing economic and social system, civic participation and voluntary activity, class structure and class consciousness, confidence and trust in others, and definition of the role of private and public ownership of property.

I am seeking in future work to include more scales dealing with degree of honesty and integrity of government; degree of nepotism in business, government, and organizational life; extent of expected reciprocity of favors and rewards; acceptance of foreign enterprise; and degree to which foreign enterprise is believed to influence the existing government. Always the search is for the pivot on which the minds of leaders turn as influence and pressure bring about a critical decision. I anticipate that some of the patterns tapped by the present scales are background factors and others are critical determiners. It is my intent to discover the differences and to allocate the old and new scales to appropriate dimensions.

Interpretation of the Larger Social System Involving the Community Power Structure. To understand a given community power structure the researcher must eventually come to grips with the larger social system of which it is one part. Certain questions press for an answer. In Seattle one asks why the mayor's office and the city council do not attract key leaders. In Bristol one asks why the labor organizations were able to develop a political party that could gain power. In Cordoba one asks why military juntas can seize power when the military is so cordially disliked. In Lima one asks why people will not cooperate in voluntary organizations and why they have so little trust in one another. These are only a few of the questions that continually arise and for which there are no answers except as the researcher studies the history, government, and social institutions in depth. In the analysis of the four cities the larger social system is sometimes viewed as two parts, one including modern, economically developed countries (United States and England) and, in contrast, the other enclosing economically underdeveloped countries (Argentina and Peru). Moreover, it proved fruitful to view Seattle and Bristol as Western English-speaking cultures in contrast with Cordoba and Lima as products of Spanish Colonial culture. Such perspectives focused attention on contrasting economic, social, and cultural factors and often opened up interpretations that illumined the community power structures.

The method required here is social and historical analysis searching in time depth for answers revealed in culture pattern and tradition. Repeatedly, this method of cultural appraisal is needed to make interpretations. Sociologists are now discovering what anthropologists have long known . . . that in comparative research, cultures must be understood as wholes. The following chapter describes a framework to guide cultural and historical analysis.

CHAPTER 2

A FRAMEWORK FOR
COMPARATIVE ANALYSIS OF
COMMUNITY POWER STRUCTURES

THE COMMUNITY POWER RESEARCHER has two purposes: to depict accurately the structure of community power and to show how the power structure functions and why it acts as it does. The first is accomplished by the use of relatively standard techniques; the second requires careful cross-sectional and historical analysis of the community and society.

The theoretical framework upon which I have drawn for explanatory insights during the course of these studies postulates that the community functions as a social unity through the interaction of its economic and governmental base, its social base, and its power structure. Figure 6 indicates the principal factors which interact within power processes affecting the community. To understand how economic power operates, the student of power structure must assess the composition, locus, and organization of economic power and must understand how government and labor function in relation to industry. When these factors have been identified, it is necessary to relate them to the social base of a given community. The factors of principal concern in the social base are the social stratification pattern, the degree of access to community power, the scope of the community interests and activities of various institutional sectors, and the central values determining leadership representation and issue outcome.

Factors Explaining the Appearance of Different Community Power Structures and Functions within Industrialized Cities

THE ECONOMIC FACTORS seem especially significant in describing variations. Each may be considered a quantitative variable that may be scaled on a continuum. The economic base for various communities can vary greatly in the amount and the distribution of manufacturing, wholesaling, retailing, and the supporting economic activities. It can vary

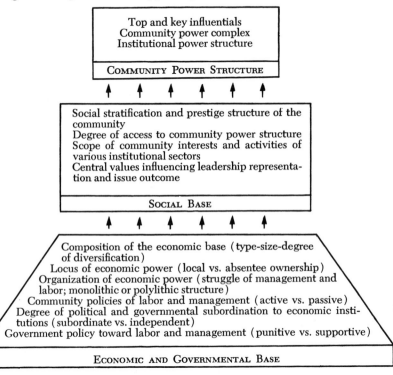

FIGURE 6. *Framework of Community Variables Showing the Interaction of the Economic and Governmental Base, Social Base, and Community Power Structure*

greatly in its ownership pattern. The one-industry town may be considered to be at one pole, the highly diversified multi-industry town at the other. In the former, economic power is usually highly concentrated; in the latter, economic power tends to be much more diffuse.

Local ownership and operation may be contrasted with absentee ownership and operation by transient managers. When local ownership is dominant, the top influentials represent a highly stable group. Under absentee ownership, managers have high occupational mobility and cannot be counted upon as permanent residents with deep roots in the community. Moreover, managers are often given instructions to avoid involvement in the controversial issues of the community and always to check with headquarters when in doubt.

Economic power may be highly organized in both management and labor groups. These twin pyramids of economic power may range from highly rigid and exclusive domains to fluid, interacting structures integrated with other institutions of the community. Strong unions provide countervailing power, strengthen weak political parties, and create greater pluralism in the community power structure.

The community policies of management and labor may vary from active participation to aloof withdrawal. Participation may be broad in scope, including interest in the welfare activities of the community, the school, politics and government, and civic improvements generally. The degree of participation is important in determining whether potential economic (or union) power is translated into active influence in community decision making.

Among the political factors the degree of political and governmental subordination to economic institutions is extremely important in ascertaining the degree of fluidity in a community power structure. In communities where the political institutions are independent, a representative expression of the community may be secured. Under these conditions democracy is a powerful instrument: a free election puts decision-making power in the hands of the majority of the people. When political institutions are dependent, business classes tend to dominate and a status quo is entrenched. Government policy toward labor and management is always important. A strong local government may act as a punitive agent or a supportive body as it relates to labor and management. It can mediate the distribution of power between labor and management in a balanced or disproportionate manner. All organs of the government are important—the mayor, the city council, the courts, and the police. Legal protections are vital to the preservation of the power of labor.

Social factors in the community may also explain differences in community power structures. Most important are the social stratification and prestige pattern, the degree of access to community power structures, the scope of community interests and activities of various institutional sectors, and the central values determining leadership representation and issue outcomes.

A social stratification pattern depicts the relative size of different social classes and represents the potential voting and political influence of each class. Social classes reflect economic interests. Conservatism is usually displayed by upper-class members, progressive policies of social security and reform are supported by middle classes, and radical and leftist movements secure adherents in the lower class. The middle class is often viewed as a moderate and moderating influence in the society; its size is of especial significance for this reason. Absence of this class can mean that the schism between rich and poor breeds continuous latent or actual conflict. The nature and number of political parties is influenced by the stratification pattern. It must also be recognized that a prestige structure develops from and tends to parallel the existing stratification pattern. The ability of a leader to command influence is commonly conditioned by the prestige of his occupation, income, and general social status.

The degree of access to a community power structure is often related to the existing stratification pattern. Admission to the community power structure may vary from free access to rigid exclusion. In a relatively stable economic system with a high degree of occupational inheritance, the transmission of property from father to son (or sons) may build rigid elements in the community power structure. This can be seen most clearly in one-industry towns, but it is equally visible in multi-industry communities where a few families have come to dominate the economic life. South American and European nations are the most likely locales for a high degree of industrial inheritance because the social system reinforces power and control within a family line. However, restricted access may be found anywhere the social system has been congenial to the growth of a social aristocracy and where business control has a history of hereditary succession. Indeed, Hunter points out that for Atlanta only fifteen of the top forty policy leaders gained positions of prominence on their own. Each of the others inherited his father's business or was helped by the wealth and connections of his father.[1]

The scope of community interests and activity of various institutional sectors is a significant determinant of the fluidity of a community power structure. The noneconomic institutional sectors such as education, church, welfare, political parties, mass communications, and government may exercise great influence on the character of the community, depending on the range of their involvement. What is significant about these sectors is their potential influence: all can command substantial numbers of adherents and resources—at least enough to influence the balance of power. Robert A. Dahl points out that the potential influence of a group or individual depends upon possession of resources that might be converted into political influence. The actual influence of the group or individual depends, however, first upon willingness to employ these resources or the rate at which the resources are used and second upon the efficiency with which these resources are used.[2] Therefore, to gauge the influence of any institutional sector one must apply the equation: Potential Power = Resources $\times$ Rate of Use $\times$ Efficiency. Dahl distinguishes between tight and slack systems of power. Tight systems are those in which all contestants employ close to their maximum resources for purposes of political influence. A slack system is one in which contestants use only a small part of their available resources. The noneconomic sectors are like sleeping giants. They lack activation and cohesion and usually operate as a slack system, but when they are activated by a relevant issue, these sectors can be powerful forces in community decision making. In fact, the only clear distinction that can be observed among community power structures in the United States is between systems in which only business exercises significant power and those in which business shares power with other sectors.

Ideologies, values, and belief systems are the levers which trip decisions in given directions. The outcome of a decision often rests upon the nature of the values placed in conflict. New and emerging values must have exceptional political influence generated behind them if they are to win out over traditional values. The values that count are those that cluster around property, taxes, the role of government in business, expansion of public services, civil rights, power of unions, and land-use controls.

All of the above factors are useful in a cross-sectional analysis of a community power structure. If the researcher seeks to understand changes that take place in the structure over a period of time, he needs to be aware of those forces which commonly bring about change.

Historical Factors Explaining Changes in Community Power Structures

THE SOCIAL FACTORS which have special significance in initiating community change are growth and decline of business, business centralization and decentralization, government centralization and decentralization, transfer of ownership, rise of new organizations and functions, diffusion and discussion of new ideas, and breakdown of traditional values. Examples drawn from Bristol will be used to illustrate the significance of these factors.

26

Growth and decline of business is a major factor in any community. One worker added to a production industry can mean an average increase of from six to nine people in the community. When a basic industry expands, a magnified population effect can be thrust upon the community affecting schools, churches, doctors, stores, recreation, homes, traffic, etc. In Bristol the growth of the Bristol Airplane Company from its initial development in World War I has had major consequences in adding new wealth and new people to the community. The managing director of the company is now a key leader in the city overshadowing the leaders of the tobacco manufacturing industry, which prior to World War II was the major industry.

When a business centralizes its offices in a community, its major owners or executives come to reside there and their concern for the community is heightened. The central offices of the Charles Hill Shipbuilding Company, the Robinson Paper Company, the Imperial Tobacco Company, and the Bristol Airplane Company have this effect in Bristol. The philanthropy of the Wills family, whose fortunes came from tobacco, has played a large role in the development of the University of Bristol and in numerous charities. The engineering interests of the Bristol Airplane Company are effective reasons for its support of the rapidly expanding engineering college at the University.

Decentralization has an opposite effect. Bankers are respected, but not a single banker is regarded as a top leader in Bristol. This is because most of the bankers are managers of branches whose main offices are in London. (In contrast, among the top leaders in Seattle there are six bankers; each leads a bank whose central offices are in Seattle.) Numerous other illustrations could be given to show that executives of decentralized businesses do not have sufficient prestige to appear as top community leaders. Among the businesses so affected in Bristol are large retail stores, insurance, chocolate, and smelting.

The national government's policies regarding centralization and decentralization can also affect the power structure of a community. The British national government can withdraw power from a community by withdrawing an administrative function and centralizing it in London. Bristol, on the other hand, has many regional offices of the national government as the result of the decentralization of electricity, gas, the British broadcasting system, and hospital administration. In addition, the city receives direct national assistance for schools, housing, city planning, docks, public health, and children's welfare and maintains local control as long as it conforms to national requirements. The distribution of control between local and national authorities is a direct index of the local influence of the political leaders and government heads.

Ownership may be transferred from private to municipal, or the reverse; from private to national, or the reverse. When private ownership is replaced by municipal or national ownership, the displaced owners tend to be eliminated as top leaders of influence. The new government managers are either required or expected to play neutral roles. Moreover, their career orientation is often toward advancement outside the community. The community knows this and regards them as "temporary" or at least "contemporary." It is very common in Bristol for even prominent citizens to be unable to name the regional manager of the gas or the electric board. Yet within their organizations the regional managers carry a very large measure of responsibility over the lives of everyone in the community.

The effect of the rise of new organizations and functions is illustrated by the role of the Labour party in Bristol's community power structure. Since 1926, when Labour became the leading party, the power of labor leaders over the affairs of the city has become increasingly greater. The establishment of comprehensive schools can be traced directly to their influence. High, progressive income taxation and real estate rates have reduced the land-holding aristocracy. The industrial, labor, and governmental managers have replaced the "peers of the realm" in a bloodless social revolution.

Diffusion and discussion of new ideas can also bring about change. The Labour party discusses further socialization of such industries as the chemical and heavy manufacturing industries. It presses for comprehensive schools and the progressive elimination of grammar schools. These changes, if made, would alter the nature of leadership within the affected industries and schools.

With the rise of the laboring groups and the decline of the aristocracy, many traditional values are breaking down. This is affecting the social status formerly accorded the military officer and the ministry. Secondary and university education are no longer associated only with the well-to-do. New leaders are rising in labor, in government, and in business. Old, wealth-holding leaders of society and of the industrial and merchant classes are passing, and new kinds of managerial leadership are rising.

No one factor taken alone will give an accurate explanation of the changes occurring in the community power structure in a given community. On the contrary, all factors interact and produce a wide range of variation. However, when data have been accurately collected on each of the seven social factors, the changes in the community power structure may be depicted with a high degree of accuracy.

A number of concluding statements can now be made about comparative analysis:

Power relations are rooted in the economic, governmental, and social base of the community and society.

The explanation of community power structures requires both cross-sectional and historical analysis.

Differences in community power structures can be increasingly explained and predicted with a limited number of economic, political, and social factors.

The community power researcher can achieve a greater degree of understanding and a higher level of generality if he uses a comparative framework to guide him.

PART II

*Comparative Analysis
of the Western Cities:
Seattle, Washington
& Bristol, England*

THE RESEARCH FINDINGS FOR THE TWO WESTERN CITIES, *Seattle and Bristol, are reported here, and Atlanta, studied in 1950–51 by Floyd Hunter, is used to broaden the comparative analysis. Thus, the three cities provide a unique power triangulation. There are many similarities among these cities, and an initial guess would be that they would share highly similar community power structures. Investigation shows, however, that certain factors bring about large differences in their prevailing power structures. In the search for these factors, the positional, reputational, and issue-decisional leaders of Seattle and Bristol are studied.*

The role and influence of the business leader receives high attention in this section. His influence in the community power structures of the three cities is estimated. The backgrounds and general social participation of Seattle business leaders are studied. The clique behavior of all reputed influentials in Seattle and Bristol is carefully appraised. The prediction of issue outcome is demonstrated as a validation of a community power structure in action.

CHAPTER 3

SEATTLE AND BRISTOL: *A Comparison*

of Community Power Structures Contrasting

Private Enterprise and Democratic Socialist

Political Ideologies

SEATTLE IS A NEW, FRONTIER CITY marked by an open class system and a rapidly expanding population and economy, while Bristol is a very old city with a hereditary upper class and a long industrial and commercial tradition. Both cities, however, have stable, democratic political structures and mixed economies of government and private industry. Seattle has a strong ideological commitment to private enterprise; Bristol is committed to the gradualist tradition of English democratic socialism. Of all the cities of England, Bristol most closely matches Seattle in population, nature of its largest basic industry, social composition, position as a regional trade center, and location on the main lanes of ocean commerce. Atlanta is an older city with a more rigid class system than that of Seattle, but it is in transition to the modern technology of an industrial society. All three of these cities have enjoyed stable governments and their people have a deep commitment to the democratic way of life.

At the time of study, Seattle was governed by a Republican mayor and a city council with a Republican majority. Their philosophy was to keep the city government out of any activity that private enterprise could and would undertake. They were for a "tight" budget on public spending for services except those which they could justify as absolutely necessary for the health and safety of the city. They pledged to support the growth and development of private industry. Democrats who had come to power in earlier years did not deviate greatly from these same principles. It is interesting to note that the most powerful labor leader of the city, Dave Beck of the Teamsters, supported the Republican administration during this time.

In Bristol the Labour party emerged as the largest political party in the city in 1918,[1] and it has dominated the city council and its important committees continuously since 1926. The Labour party platform repeatedly has called for nationalization of many basic industries, including steel, transport, and utilities. Party leaders have worked for a growing range of services including national health services. The heart of the Labour party strength derives from the trade unions which are powerful and well organized. Many Labour party leaders are trade union leaders. All of them affirm that they adhere to democratic socialism.

In the contrast of these two political ideologies the role of business leaders becomes a critical factor in ascertaining the leadership structure of a community and the accompanying decision-making processes. Why do business leaders take an active interest in community affairs? What is the extent of their influence in the community? How do they exercise this influence?[2] These questions have been asked by sociologists and political scientists who have sought the answers by conducting research on both the community[3] and the national levels.[4] However, political sociology as a field of knowledge still has wide areas in which research data are lacking.[5]

It has been repeatedly asserted that business men—manufacturers, bankers, merchants, investment brokers, and large real estate holders— exert predominant influence in community decision making. This is the central hypothesis under test. The purpose of this chapter is to describe and analyze the characteristics of decision makers in an American and an English city.

The research was designed so that the system model of community power structure reported in Chapter 1 might be applied. The model required the identification of the institutional power structure of the nation and the community, the community power complex, and the top and key influentials in Seattle and Bristol.[6] Comparisons were made with Atlanta when comparable data were available. Seattle, Bristol, and Atlanta qualify under the Harris classification as "diversified economic types."[7] The following summary shows the close similarity of the three cities.

Seattle had a population of 468,000 in 1950. It is the commercial, financial, and distributive center for the Pacific Northwest. Major transportation lines are centered in the city, and it has a fine port. Among its major manufactures are aircraft, ships, and paper. The city is the largest educational center of the region with a state university and many small colleges.

Bristol, also a regional city, serves as the commercial, financial, and distributive center of the west of England. Its population in 1950 was 444,000. The major manufactures are airplanes, ships, beer, cigarettes, chocolate, machinery, and paper. It has an ocean port. The city houses a provincial (state) university and many private grammar schools.

Atlanta in 1950 had a population of 331,000. It serves as the commercial, financial, and distributive center for the southeastern section of the United States. Its manufactures include aircraft, textiles, and cotton waste products. It is a transportation center of rail, air, bus, and truck lines. The city is a center of education, having a large university and many small colleges.

Method

LISTS OF LEADERS were secured from organizations and informants in nine institutional sectors: business and finance, education, religion, society and wealth, political and governmental organizations, labor, independent professions, cultural (aesthetic) institutions, and social welfare. These initial lists of reputed leaders included a total of 312 names for Seattle and 278 for Bristol.

In each city a panel of ten experts was selected on the basis of their thorough knowledge of the leaders in one specific institutional sector, their broad knowledge of the community, and their many contacts with community leaders. Individuals meeting these qualifications are commonly found among public relations officials, newspaper reporters, association and government officials. Panel members were asked to rate each person on the initial lists as *most influential, influential,* or *less influential* on this specific criterion: "Person participates actively in either supporting or initiating policy decisions which have the most effect on the community." Those nominated most frequently as most influential were selected for interviewing.[8] These panels of experts were also asked to make ratings of the relative power of institutional sectors in the nation and in the city and to identify the most influential organizations.

Personal interviews were held with a 50-percent stratified random sample of 44 top influentials in Seattle and 32 top influentials in Bristol. The sample had been stratified according to the nine institutional sectors enumerated above, and corresponding proportions of leaders from each sector were interviewed. During the interview each top influential was asked the following question: "If you were responsible for a major project which was before the community that required decision by a

35

group of leaders—leaders that nearly everyone would accept—which ten on this list would you choose, regardless of whether they are known personally to you or not? Add other names if you wish." Responses to this question identified the key influentials of the community.

Each respondent was asked to check a social acquaintance scale for all top influentials by "don't know, heard of, know slightly, know well, know socially (exchange home visits)." He was also asked to check each top influential with whom he had on committees during the past two years. (See Appendix II.)

The interview included questions on current issues, on the role played by respondent, and on persons and organizations that worked for and against issues. Ratings of influential organizations and associations in the community were also secured. The interview concluded with this question: "There are several crowds in Seattle that work together and pretty much make the big decisions. Is this true or false?" The responses were probed.

At the time of interview each respondent was given a questionnaire which asked for background data, career history, participation in business other than his own, and social, civic, and professional participation. These questionnaires were later collected through the mail or by a personal visit.

Newspaper accounts during the period of the study were used to learn about activities of top influentials, committee appointments of top influentials, activities of their wives, community issues, and interactions between various institutions and the community.

Informants were interviewed to validate findings on clique behavior and to describe activities of top influentials and the community power complex in the resolution of current issues.

To summarize, evidence for the test of the hypothesis that businessmen exert a predominant influence in community decision making was secured from four major sources: interviews, questionnaires, newspapers, and informants.

Indentification of Reputational Leaders

TABLE 1 shows the institutional affiliation of the top influentials as selected by the panels of raters in the three cities. Business has the largest representation among the top influentials: 33 percent in Seattle, 34 percent in Bristol, and 58 percent in Atlanta. However, there is considerable representation of other institutional sectors. A chi-square test applied to the frequency distribution failed to reveal any significant variation in the sectors represented by the top influentials selected by the rating panels in the three cities.

TABLE 1. *Top Influentials of Seattle, Bristol, and Atlanta by Institutional Affiliation as Selected by Rating Panels*

INSTITUTIONAL AFFILIATION	SEATTLE (N=44)	BRISTOL (N=32)	ATLANTA (N=40)
Business	33%	34%	58%
Labor	14	19	5
Education	10	9	5
Government	17	9	5
Independent professions	12	13	15
Religion	7	9	0
Society and wealth	0	7	12
Social welfare and cultural leaders (combined)	7	0	0
Totals	**100%**	**100%**	**100%**

Significant differences were found, however, when the key influentials were selected by the top influentials.[9] Table 2 shows the 12 key influentials for each of the three cities. In Seattle and Atlanta business representation dominates among the key influentials, with 67 percent and 75 percent respectively. Representation of other sectors is limited in Seattle to government, education, religion, and independent professions. In Atlanta the only other sectors represented are independent professions and government. Bristol, on the other hand, has wide representation, with key influentials representing education, political parties, government, labor, religion, independent professions, and society. The key influentials play major roles in the community power structure. They are "generalist leaders"—leaders others turn to for the initiation and sanction of major projects and policies. As a result, they may greatly influence the values which dominate in decision making.

The marked difference between the kinds of key influentials found in Seattle and Atlanta and those in Bristol raises questions about community organization. Why should two labor leaders be among the outstanding leaders in Bristol while not one labor leaders appears among the key influentials of the two American cities? Why do political parties play so large a role in Bristol and not in Seattle and Atlanta? These and other questions will be explored after more findings have been introduced. We must first determine if evidence can be secured to validate the reputed rankings of influence imputed to the top influentials.

The correlations shown in Table 3 demonstrate that a definite correlation between influence and performance exists in both Seattle and Bristol. The highest correlation is between the influence rankings of top influentials and their committee participations (.84 for Seattle and .67 for Bristol). High correlations are also shown between leaders' influence rankings and their participation in other businesses, in social clubs, in civic organizations, and in professional or trade associations.

TABLE 2. *Key Influentials as Selected by Top Influentials in Each City and Ranked as Influential Policy Makers*

SEATTLE	BRISTOL	ATLANTA
1. Manufacturing executive	1. Labor party leader and Councilman	1. Utilities executive
2. Wholesale owner and investor	2. University president	2. Transport executive
3. Mercantile executive	3. Manufacturing executive	3. Lawyer
4. Real estate owner-executive	4. Bishop, Church of England	4. Mayor
5. Business executive (woman)	5. Manufacturing executive	5. Manufacturing executive
6. University president	6. Citizen party leader and Councilman	6. Utilities executive
7. Investment executive	7. University official	7. Manufacturer-owner
8. Investment executive	8. Manufacturer-owner	8. Mercantile executive
9. Bank executive-investor	9. Labor leader	9. Investment executive
10. Episcopal bishop	10. Civic leader (woman)	10. Lawyer
11. Mayor (lawyer)	11. Lawyer	11. Mercantile executive
12. Lawyer	12. Society leader	12. Mercantile owner
Business representation: **67 percent**	**Business representation:** **25 percent**	**Business representation:** **75 percent**

TABLE 3. *Spearman Rank Order Correlations between Influence Rankings of Top Influentials and Ranking on Various Measures of Community Behavior*

Influence Rankings of Top Influentials compared with:	SEATTLE (N=44)	BRISTOL (N=32)
Committee appointments accepted during past two years, as shown by newspaper reports	.51	.43
Committee participation for two-year period, as designated by top influentials on the interview schedule	.84	.67
Newspaper mentions of community activities of and statements about top influentials	.15	−.31
Participation in other businesses as owner or director	.53	.33
Participation in social clubs	.51	.47
Participation in civic organizations	.58	.43
Participation in professional organizations	.45	.34
Total social participation in business, social, civic, and professional organizations	**.59**	**.48**

Among these leaders, those with the highest influence rank—the key influentials—are especially active in community affairs. The similarities in participation exhibited by the top and key influentials in the two cities suggest that there are many common role patterns. It would appear that such leaders could exchange positions with their counterparts in other American or English cities and function effectively.

There are some differences in degree between the patterns of leadership behavior in Seattle and Bristol. In general, as Table 3 shows, there is more participation of all kinds by top influentials in Seattle than by the top influentials of Bristol. In Seattle more top influentials are identified with business and finance so that more activity is centered upon business itself; in addition, memberships in voluntary organizations are more important in generating influence in community decision making. In Bristol, there is a negative correlation between the influence of the key influentials and newspaper mentions. Influentials receive less newspaper publicity because there is a social convention that "first-rate leaders" do not seek publicity. In fact, a deliberate effort is made by many top influentials in England to keep their names from the newspaper as a role requirement of their social class.

Differences in Business Dominance in Seattle and Bristol

THE HYPOTHESIS THAT BUSINESSMEN exert a predominant influence in community decision making in Seattle (and in Atlanta) is now held to be partially validated. At this point we base this conclusion on the large number of key influentials who are identified with business and finance. Further evidence will be assembled in Chapters 4 and 6, where we shall explore the extent to which the decision-making structures are fluid or rigid in character and give special attention to the role of tightly organized cliques in decision making. In Bristol the hypothesis of business dominance is rejected since only 25 percent of the key influentials come from business and finance and there is a representation of seven other institutional sectors of community life.

Two major factors seem to explain much of the difference between the American cities and the English city. The first of these factors is the difference in occupational prestige values in the United States and England. In contrast to the United States, where business leaders enjoy high esteem, "the social status of industry in England, and so of its captains, is low by comparison with the law, medicine, and the universities."[10] In England top business managers are recruited from the universities (and upper-class families) where liberal education traditionally predominates, emphasizing humanistic values and minimizing the specialized training that characterizes the curriculum of the typical American school of business. Many top business leaders, educated at Oxford and Cambridge, reported during interviews that they regarded business as a very useful activity but did not view it as occupying the whole man. They reserved their highest respect for scholarly pursuits. Indeed, in the English university specialized courses in business administration are very few, and the tradition continues that business management is learned by experience within the firm. This value system affects the selection of community leaders in Bristol just as emphasis on the prestige of business and finance influences the selection of community leaders in the two American cities.[11]

The second major factor is the difference in structure of city government. In Seattle, the city council is composed of nine members elected at large on a nonpartisan ballot. In 1956 the occupational composition of the Seattle city council was:

Newspaper owner-editor (subcommunity)	Business
Merchant	Business
Merchant	Business
Newspaper owner-editor (subcommunity)	Business
Merchant	Business
Merchant	Business
Housewife (formerly teacher)	Professional
Jeweler (and labor officer)	Skilled worker
Bus operator	Semiskilled worker

A background of small business predominated. None of the council members was chosen as a top influential by the panel of raters or by top influentials. There was every indication that the top community leaders did not regard the council as a strong center of community power. The council tended to make decisions on community issues after a relatively long period of debate and after power mobilization had taken place in the community. During this period such groups as the chamber of commerce, labor council, municipal league, parent teacher association, and council of churches would take stands. Council members might be approached and appeals made to them. Newspaper editors would write articles. Key influentials might make open declarations for or against the current issues and use their influence with the "right" persons or groups. The mayor, as administrative head and an elective official, was relatively powerful as patronage dispenser and, at the same time, was exposed to pressure from citizens to whom he might be indebted for either his past or his future position. Rossi has reported on this pattern:

> Another striking characteristic of the American community of today, in contrast to that of the past, is the status gap between the personnel of local government and the local elites of wealth, intellect, and staus. The local echelons of the party organizations and the elective offices of municipal, county, and even state governments are manned by persons whose social positions are often many levels below the denizens of the Country Club, Rotary Club, and the Chamber of Commerce. The City Fathers and the county commissioners are recruited, at best, from among local lawyers of somewhat uncertain income and miscellaneous clientele, and more likely from among small proprietors or professional politicians. Money, status, and intellect seem to be in one place and political control in another. Such anomalies lead to the hypothesis that somewhere there are strings by means of which local government is guided from without.[12]

In contrast to this pattern, Bristol has a city council composed of 112 members selected by 28 wards. Each ward selects four members. When the council is organized, members are appointed to committees that meet once or twice a week. Issues that arise in any part of the community are quickly brought to the council's attention. The city clerk, a civil servant appointed by the council on the basis of his administrative ability, is the nonpolitical administrative head of the city government. The members of the council are released from work by their employers for committee and council meetings. They are paid a stipend by the local government for time lost from work and for any personal expenses incurred in attending meetings within or outside the city. Table 4 shows the occupations of the members of the Bristol city council in 1955.

The council membership is rather evenly divided among trade union members (32 percent), business group members (30 percent), and other community members (37 percent). Five of the 12 key influentials of the community are council members and play major roles in their

TABLE 4. *Occupational Compensation of Bristol City Council in 1955*[°]

TRADE UNION MEMBERS	BUSINESS GROUP MEMBERS	OTHER COMMUNITY SECTORS
2 Foremen	4 Manufacturers	2 Solicitors
16 Skilled workers	7 Wholesale and retail	1 Physician
5 Semiskilled workers	owners	1 Dentist
8 Clerical workers	1 Cinema owner	1 Engineer
4 Trade union officials	4 Contractors	1 Accountant
2 Unskilled workers	8 Company directors	1 Auctioneer
	and secretaries	1 Teacher
	1 Bank official	2 Ministers
	8 Insurance officials	3 Political party organizing
		secretaries
		3 National government officials
		12 Housewives
		12 Retired workers
Totals 37 (32%)	33 (30%)	40 (37%)

° Two of the 112 seats were vacant.

respective parties. The council is the major arena of community decision. Issues reach it directly, are investigated by council committees, and are decided upon by a vote taken in the full council. Community organizations play important roles in debating the issues, but these are definitely secondary or supplementary activities. The community value system condemns any pressure tactics on the council as "bad taste." However, in the council a caucus of elected party leaders is held and a position taken before any important vote. The "whip" is applied and members are expected to vote as instructed. Such action is rationalized as necessary for responsible party government. The Labour party as the majority party expresses its strength through its labor leaders who act as influential party and council leaders. A large number of labor union members are also council members.

In Seattle (and in Atlanta) business leaders are reputed to be powerful by leaders in all sectors of community life. Arnold Rose explains this high repute by pointing out that in the United States business influence is exercised by

business leaders using lobbyists, "business representatives" in legislatures, contributions to campaign funds, publicity designed to influence public opinion, the "political strike," and other lesser techniques to influence government. Businessmen influence government more effectively than most non-businessmen—not only because they can afford lobbyists, advertisements, and other costly techniques—but also because they are more educated, more knowledgeable, more articulate, and more activist than average citizens. The latter qualities give them an advantage quite compatible with a democratic society.[13]

CHAPTER 4

POSITIONAL, REPUTATIONAL,

AND ISSUE-DECISIONAL LEADERS

IN SEATTLE AND BRISTOL

It has been pointed out that leaders can be identified by positional, reputational, and issue techniques. We said that each method reveals different facets of leadership and therefore somewhat different lists. The degree of overlap between the lists is always of interest because the greater the overlap, the greater is the scope of influence of a given group of leaders.

Top influentials for Seattle and Bristol have been identified by the reputational technique. This chapter describes the identification of leaders in Seattle and Bristol by the positional and issue-decisional techniques and examines similarities and differences between such leaders and the reputed influentials.

Identification of Positional Leaders

Persons who occupy positions that control economic resources are of major interest in all influence studies, but many institutional sectors generate influence. Table 5 is a schedule of positions regarded as having potential power in community decision making for Seattle. Each position was selected because of the size of the organization (number of workers), its command of resources, and its authority rank within the institutional sector. The objective is to specify offices in such a way as to make the schedule function in any large American city and, with slight modification, in any industrial city. Note the broad range through busi-

TABLE 5. *Standard Schedule of Potential Power Positions in an Industrial City: Data Supplied for Seattle*

Business and Finance

Presidents of 2 largest manufacturing concerns	President, Boeing Airplane Co.
	President, Pacific Car and Foundry
Chairmen of 2 largest investment houses	Chairman, United Natl. Corporation
	Chairman, United Pacific Corporation
Presidents of 2 largest mercantile stores	President, Frederick and Nelson
	President, Bon Marche
Holder of largest amount of real estate	President, Clise Investments
President or owner of largest hotel	President, Olympic Hotel
President of Chamber of Commerce	President, Chamber of Commerce
Presidents of 3 largest banks	President, Seattle First Natl. Bank
	President, Peoples National Bank
	President, Pacific National Bank
Real estate board chairman	Chairman, Seattle Real Estate Board

Mass Communication

Editors of largest newspapers	Editor, *Seattle Times*
	Editor, *Post Intelligencer*
Owners of largest radio-TV stations	Owner, KOMO
	Owner, KING

Political Party and Government

Mayor	Mayor of City (Republican)
Immediate past mayor	Past Mayor of City (Democrat)
City Council chairman	Chairman of City Council
Chairman, Republican party organization	Chairman, King County Republican Party
Chairman, Democratic party organization	Chairman, King County Democratic Party

Education

Presidents of largest universities	President, University of Washington
	President, Seattle University
School board chairman	Chairman, Seattle Public Schools
School superintendents	Superintendent, Seattle Public Schools
	Superintendent, Seattle Parochial Schools
President of major teachers' organization	President, Association of Classsroom Teachers

Labor

President of central labor council	President, Seattle Central Labor Council
President of 3 largest unions	President, Teamsters' Union
	President, CIO
	President, Aero Mechanics

Religion

Bishop of major Protestant church	Bishop, Episcopal Church
Rabbi of leading Jewish temple	Rabbi, Jewish Temple
Local bishop of Catholic diocese	Archbishop, Catholic Diocese

44

TABLE 5.—*Continued*

Society and Wealth
    Presidents of 4 largest social clubs

President, Rainier Club
President, Washington Athletic Club
President, Seattle Yacht Club
President, Seattle Tennis Club

Independent Professions
    President of central medical society
    President of bar association

President, King County Medical Society
President, Seattle Bar Association

Welfare
    Executive secretary, health and
      welfare council
    Head of welfare department
    Chairman of Community Chest

Secretary, Health and Welfare Council
    of Seattle and King County
Chief, King County Welfare Department
Chief, United Good Neighbor Fund

ness and finance, mass communication, political parties and government, education, labor, religion, society and wealth, independent professions, and social welfare. When such a standard schedule is filled in with the names of the individuals in a specific city who occupy these positions, the list may be presumed to designate the leaders of influence in that community's affairs.

Implicit in the positional approach is the assumption that the leaders' potential for power or influence will be employed in active community leadership. This is a very broad assumption, and research indicates that it is only partially true.

Evaluation of Positional and Reputational Methods

SEVERAL STUDIES indicate that the holders of potential power positions are not necessarily community leaders of influence. For example, Schulze and Blumberg employed alternative methods for determining local power elites in a midwestern satellite industrial city of some 20,000 inhabitants.[1] The method based on position involves selecting certain persons as most powerful and influential on the basis of their official positions in the community. Persons occupying the top formal positions in the major local economic enterprises were designated as the "economic dominants," and 17 persons were listed as occupying major industrial and financial positions. In contrast, the method based on reputation utilizes nominations by panels of knowledgeable local informants. A panel drawn from the voluntary associations of the community nominated 18 local persons as the most influential leaders in community life. There was almost no overlap between the nominated leaders and the holders of major economic positions—the economic dominants; specifi-

45

cally, the 17 economic dominants included only two of the 18 nominated leaders.[2]

In another comparison of position leaders and nominated leaders, Samuel A. Stouffer selected as civic leaders the holders of 14 objectively defined public and civic positions: mayor; president of the chamber of commerce; chairman of the community chest; president of the largest labor union; county chairmen of the Republican and Democratic parties; commander of the largest American Legion post; regent of the DAR; president of the women's club; chairmen of the library and school boards, the parent-teacher association, and the bar association; and the publisher of the largest locally owned newspaper.[3] Applying this definition of civic leaders to the selected community, another study showed only four of the 18 nominated leaders occupied any of the 14 top civic positions in the list.[4]

Similar comparisons were made in Seattle and in Bristol between the holders of the official positions shown in Table 5 and the top influentials of the community as nominated by knowledgeable panels. In Seattle only 17, or 39 percent, of the reputational leaders were also holders of designated power positions. In Bristol 55 percent of the reputational leaders were also positional leaders.

Even though positional leaders often are not designated as reputational leaders, the potential or positional power of economic, political, military, labor, and religious dominants cannot be ignored. Positional leaders are making important decisions within their own organizations which affect the life and growth of the community. They make decisions to expand, cut back, or remove organizations that may supply employment; decisions to buy land or buildings and convert them to residences, stores, or factories, altering the land-use pattern of the community; decisions to marshal and exert political power by influencing the selection and backing of political candidates and to intervene by pressuring the mayor, the council, or the courts of the city; decisions to support various community organizations with money and loan of personnel. Sometimes powerful leaders work behind the scenes and use front men to put over their ideas. Robert Presthus has shown this very clearly in *Men at the Top.* In fact, a wide spectrum of decisions affecting the community in a profound way may be made quietly. A dominant officeholder can be very powerful and still not be identified as a "civic influential."

This level of power is one that community power studies have tended to ignore. The importance of the positional dominants did not become clear to me until my study of the Latin American communities brought this factor into the foreground. In Latin America lack of civic participation is the norm in contrast to the customary pattern that is found among community influentials in the United States and England. In Cordoba and Lima we shall find that positional power becomes more important since community problems tend to go to government bureaucracies rather than to voluntary organizations. New methodological problems arise because the exercise of bureaucratic power is difficult to identify. The exercise of reputational power as shown by structured actions can be fairly well described.

Floyd Hunter has developed useful criteria for determining how reputational leaders exercise power. In their study of Salem, Massachusetts, Hunter and his associates discovered that various influentials spontaneously gave their reasons for choosing and ranking persons as powerful. Notes were kept by the interviewers and a summary of the reasons shows that a man was considered for top billing if:

1. He belonged to a recognized power clique. He is given additional weight if he was a clique leader.
2. He had the will to exercise power and leadership. Many men possessed a potential of power, but they did not choose to exercise this social prerogative.
3. He had a moderate amount of wealth or property. Great wealth did not coincide with power wielding.
4. His relationships with major civic associations was such that either within them he exerted influence or influenced their direction by acting through key leaders within them. Often the top leaders delegated civic associational work to a lesser man within a corporate hierarchy and kept in touch with community affairs through him. This latter fact was well known to the associational personnel, and therefore deference was given the corporate proxy.
5. His community residence was "satisfactory." Newcomers were often subjected to a trial period, and length of residence had some bearing on his acceptance. The place of his residence was also a factor in his social acceptance. Newcomers who settled in the community with high status in corporate enterprises often found ready acceptance in business associations. Their social acceptance tended to follow, in these latter cases, the social position of corporate executives of similar position, and in some cases a man carried his "family background" with him from community to community. Social status, as will be later demonstrated, did not coincide with power standing.
6. He controlled a large number of employees. All other factors equal, the greater the number of employees, the greater was the power of the person.
7. He had "control" of a corporate enterprise. Local control, through ownership first, or management second, helps to raise a man's rating in a power scale. Management of an outside corporation gives the local

manager power in conformity to the size of the enterprise and in relation to the power of decision the local manager possesses.

8. He is of "prime" age. If he is too young, he may be a "comer." If he is too old, he may be discounted in the making of community decisions; however, some men become elder statesmen and are consulted on most matters. As before indicated, the prime age of men of power seems to be, on the average, in the neighborhood of 50 years of age.

9. He is closely allied with major economic or political enterprises. This is particularly relevant for the professional man.

10. He maintains good press relations. This includes the ability to keep out of the press and put others forward as public figures. In the latter case, those "in the know" are aware of the "fronting" situation, and carefully watch the "front man" to ascertain what the "number one man" is doing.

11. His personal qualities are in conformity to standard community conduct. This does not mean that he has to be a paragon of virtue, aggressive, or shy, or of any particular personality stamp, but his general behavior must be accommodated and accepted.

12. His social clubs and church affiliations are in conformity with his life station. These factors are subject to wide latitude, but they remain factors and are more important in some communities than in others. Hobbies and types of recreation may have some bearing on a man's acceptance by other leaders. Yachting, for example, in Salem is considered far superior to other types of recreation and many of the leaders engage in the sport. It is not a primary requisite to leadership, but it seems to help establish some of the leaders and is symbolic of prowess.

13. He has an adequate rate of interaction with other community leaders. The "lone wolf" enterpriser might be a powerful individual within a particular industry or business establishment, but if he has no interaction with community leaders on civic matters, his own community power of decision is delegated, per se, to others. Many men were of considerable independence in matters of decision, even on community affairs, but there had to be some give and take in arriving at action decisions, and if a man was too biased or stubborn in most situations, he finally was disregarded or largely discounted in community issues or projects.[5]

The findings reported for the Seattle and Bristol top influentials conform closely to many of Hunter's criteria. A description of Seattle business leaders (Chapter 5) will validate many of these characteristics.

Use of Issue Analysis to Identify Leaders

ISSUES PROVIDE CONCRETE POINTS of power conflict, and the identification of issue leaders and value conflicts provides another means of understanding power structures. Organizations often take sides and entire institutional sectors may become active participants. For example, when the business and the labor sectors find themselves in conflict on an issue, they organize themselves cohesively and other institutional sectors may align themselves with one or the other group. Major issues of community conflict present the best opportunities for study because individuals and groups identify their interests and their support.

The ideal issue would be one that activated all parts of the institutional and organizational structure of the community. In on-going community life this almost never happens. Community researchers report that in some small communities no issues have been raised publicly in years.[6] When community issues do arise the community power researcher must be sensitive to the saliency of an issue or decision. It is believed that issue saliency ranges over the following levels of intensity:

Level 1—Routine administrative decision: close the West End garbage dump; promote a police lieutenant to captain; make Broadway Avenue a one-way street.

Level 2—Adaptive decision caused by ecological forces: build a new school; open new streets; direct city planners to prepare comprehensive plan; install sewers.

Level 3—Introduction of new instrumentalities or new rules: new procedures of public safety; reorganize budget procedures; increase rates of firemen.

Level 4—Maintenance of institutional or associated authority when status quo is threatened: right-to-work initiative; abolition of city planning department; firing of top governmental administrators over policy disagreement; annexation of county land by the city.

Level 5—Increase of authority in some institution or association giving it greater control of some operations in the community: real estate personnel are packed on city planning commission; labor personnel dominate private welfare agencies; plan for a metropolitan government.

Level 6—Established authority challenged by revolt: violence against police and nonstrikers on picket lines; civil rights marchers challenge police authority in violent contacts; black power leaders use armed forced to gain immediate demands.[7]

Individuals who rise to lead highly salient issues are undoubtedly persons who warrent attention. They may be well-established leaders or may be meteors who rise with one issue and then disappear. They may be generally respected or may be controversial. Certainly issue analysis will identify controversial leaders who might be overlooked if civic leaders only are studied. Civic leaders are often reluctant to engage directly in controversy, preferring to get behind "projects"—these are "safer" to handle and less threatening to their personal status and that of the organizations with which they are affiliated.

Comparison of Issue and Reputational Results

IN SEATTLE AND BRISTOL judges were used to identify major issues and projects currently before the community or that had been important in the previous two years. The resulting list was presented in the interview of top influentials and each respondent was asked: "In which of these have you taken a part? Kindly select an issue in which you have had a high interest. What part did you take or are you now taking? What persons and organizations are working for the issue or project? Against?" Individuals who received the highest participation rankings —"for" or "against"—were called issue-decisional leaders. The correspondence between the highest ranked reputed leaders and the issue-decisional leaders was 58 percent in Seattle and 49 percent in Bristol.

These results compare closely with those reported by Robert Presthus in *Men at the Top*. His carefully developed separate lists of reputed influentials and decisional leaders showed 66 percent overlap in "Riverview" and 43 percent in "Edgewood."[8] Presthus points out that a higher overlap might have been reported if the covert roles of reputed leaders were better known. Some worked quietly behind the scenes giving money and personal support. Others maintained a quiet but active management of their interest and used "leg men" to provide the public leadership.

Another factor accounting for some of the variance between reputed and issue leaders is the criterion, "leaders that nearly everyone will accept," by which the reputational leaders have been selected. This criterion automatically rejects many controversial influentials who are issue leaders; it tends to ignore newly emergent leaders who are often younger and have not yet won their place among the better-known, well-established leaders; it often fails to award a place to lower-status persons, especially government officials, small owners and managers, and clerical personnel. The mayor is often regarded as a top influential, but he may be considered as "temporary" and not a free agent.

The charge is often made that reputed leaders have nothing but "hollow" reputations. Sometimes it is charged that they are status leaders but not decision-making leaders. Polsby called for a burial of the reputational approach when he found little overlap between leaders in three issues resolved in New Haven, Connecticut.[9]

We have pointed out that evidence can be gathered in many ways to determine if reputed leaders actually perform important roles in community decision making. Their participation both in issues and projects should be discovered. A question commonly asked of respondents is: "In most cities, certain persons are said to be influential 'behind the scenes' and to have a lot of say about programs that are planned and about projects and issues that come up around town. What persons are influential in this way in this community?" A relatively long list of persons is suggested by top influentials and other informants. I have found this a useful but not highly valid effort. Too often the names are based solely on hearsay evidence. The lack of consensus on names does not invite confidence. A more valid approach is to seek reputational leaders who are believed to have effective influence in specific situations by asking top influentials: "To what persons should the community turn for leadership when the economic welfare of the community is threatened? When a civic project needs to succeed? When political influence or power is needed?" (See Appendix II.)

Many top influentials will support projects, but are cautious about jumping into controversial issues, where their participation is often covert—the most common pattern is quiet, personal support or rejection. They may encourage participation by other influentials and understructure personnel or discourage them from further effort. Their influence reaches into the many organizations to which they belong. In addition, many are making important decisions in their own firms or organizations which may profoundly affect the community.

William Gamson has recently reported that 82 percent of the reputational leaders were active on at least one issue within the 18 New England communities in his study. He finds that when the reputational leaders are both active and united, they are on the winning side of controversial issues three fourths of the time. Their proportion of victories is equally high even when their support is not visible. Further, the side supporting change wins only 30 percent of the time without the united support of reputational leaders but wins two thirds of the time with it. He attributes this outcome to the sanctioning influence the reputational leaders possess.

It is not difficult to conceive of sanctioning resources of high stability and generality. A person who holds a position of great potential influence in an elaborate network of institutional and interpersonal relationships possesses a powerful set of inducements. It is virtually certain that there will be some present or future alternative that he can influence that present decision makers care about. Furthermore, it is a valuable political asset to have such a potentially influential person obligated to oneself.[10]

To understand more clearly the sanctioning resources of top influentials I have been exploring the validity of the question: "Whom do you regard as the chief community spokesman for merchants, manufacturers, bankers, labor, University, society and wealth, social welfare, local government, religion, Republican party, Democratic party; the best local contact man with state officials (besides local members of legislature); the best local contact man with federal officials in Washington (besides legislators); the spokesmen for cultural and artistic interests, local newspapers, doctors, lawyers, and public school teachers?" Two kinds of analysis have been used upon the data secured, ascertaining first, the degree of consensus on nominees in these areas, and second, the correspondence between the highest ranked nominees and the list of reputed key influentials. These tests show that the chief spokesmen are selected primarily from those individuals reputed to be top influentials and that the chief spokesmen who receive high consensus tend to come from the ranks of key influentials. Perhaps this is to be expected, but such tests are very important if a hard determination of influence and consequences is to be made between reputed influentials and active participation in decision making.

More confidence can be placed in organization participation patterns of top influentials. Participation of top influentials in civic and professional organizations should be carefully examined since many express their support of controversial issues in active participation within organizations—businessmen in a powerful chamber of commerce and labor men in their central labor council or powerful union locals. Their friendship patterns often reveal clues to their alignments on issues and their strategies for protecting interests that concern them.

Predicting and Validating Future Behavior Patterns
of Top Influentials

KNOWLEDGE OF COMMUNITY LEADERS and their organizational bases often provides opportunities to test the effectiveness of leaders and to provide validity for reputational assessments. The community power researcher is often requested by action agencies to recommend leaders for particular projects or policy-making groups. I was asked in Seattle to recommend a committee of influential leaders for a governor's advisory group on reform of the state's institutional program. These were to be persons who could receive training and be of such influence that they could rally support behind the governor when reform proposals were submitted.

Another request involved the naming of a policy committee that would assure support of an organization that wished to present a TV forum dealing with controversial public questions. The policy committee was to be named so that its separate members could legitimize and interpret the forum to each of the important organizations in the city, especially those likely to cause trouble. In this instance, the American Legion, the Chamber of Commerce, the Urban League, American Medical Society, and the Teamsters' Union were considered particularly sensitive. It was thought important to have the newspapers represented so a sympathetic press could be assured. Other important organizations were known to be the Municipal League, PTA, American Bar Association, Republican party, Democratic party, and the 97 Social Club. To meet this request, the matrix of social participation among top influentials was examined and nominees were presented so that each represented one sensitive organization, yet interlocked with other important organizations. Table 6 shows this matrix of 30 interlocking memberships produced by the active participation of eight influential persons.

TABLE 6. *Matrix of 30 Interlocking Memberships in Significant Community Organizations Produced by Eight Influential Persons*

	SENSITIVE					IMPORTANT	INFLUENTIAL						
	American Legion	Chamber of Commerce	Urban League	Medical Society	Teamsters' Union	Newspaper Connection	Municipal League	Labor Council	Parent-Teachers Association	American Bar Association	Republican Party	Democratic Party	97 Club
N. R.		X		X			X				X		X
A. L.	X	X								X			X
S. P.					X			X				X	
B. H.	X	X					X						X
P. C.		X	X							X	X		
B. E.	X				X			X					
DR. P. K.				X					X				X
L. C.		X				X	X						X
Total Memberships	3	5	1	2	2	1	3	2	1	2	2	1	5

This social participation matrix is constructed upon accurate knowledge of the current memberships and roles of each member. Table 7 is an example of the individual participation data from which such a matrix is developed. It is the total personal record of the civic, social, and professional memberships of L.C., who has an important newspaper post in Seattle and was placed among the nominees for the policy-making group. His multiple memberships provide a wide scope of personal contact and communication in addition to the range of leaders he may influence through the columns of his paper.

TABLE 7. *The Participation of a Top Influential in Civic, Social, and Professional Organizations*

ORGANIZATION	ATTEND REGULARLY	COMMITTEE MEMBER	OFFICER
Civic Organizations			
Chamber of Commerce	Yes	Yes	Trustee
Pacific Trade Association	Yes	Yes	Past president
Municipal League	No	No	No
Memorial Hospital	Yes	Yes	Trustee
Greater City, Inc.	Yes	Yes	Trustee
Community Development League	Yes	Yes	Past president
War Savings Bond League	Yes	Yes	Chairman
Safety Council	Yes	Yes	No
Social Organizations			
Social Club A	Yes	Yes	No
Social Club B	Yes	Yes	Past president
Golf Club	Yes	Yes	Past president
97 Club	Yes	Yes	Past president
Thunder Country Club	Winter	No	No
790 Club–650 Club	Yes	Yes	No
Quarterbacks	Yes	No	No
Varsity Club	Yes	No	No
Professional and Employee Organizations			
Allied Dailies Association	Yes	Yes	No
Newspaper Association	Yes	Yes	No
National Association of Manufacturers	No	No	No
Better Business Bureau	Yes	No	No

This opportunity to influence nominations gives the researcher a prospective experimental design. Can the behavior of a leader in a specified position be predicted on the basis of his past performance and his participation within an organizational network? This is an intriguing question and offers new research opportunities. Other possibilities for experimental study are presented by issues and the prospect of predicting issue outcome. Each effort is a step toward achieving higher validity. The experimental results reported in Chapter 7, have been very promising.

This endeavor to seek validation or rejection of reputed influentials as major agents in community decision making leads to better ways of identifying the activity of different kinds of leaders and to deeper penetration into all parts of the community power structure as specified by the system model.

CHAPTER 5

THE SEATTLE BUSINESS LEADER[*]

THE BUSINESS LEADER has been shown to play a large role in Seattle, Atlanta, Dallas, El Paso, and many other American cities. Since it is believed that he has such a central importance, a study was undertaken to learn more about him in Seattle. A survey of 36 top Seattle business leaders covered their social backgrounds, their career histories, and their current participation in business, civic, social, and professional organizations. Special attention was given to how they attained a position of influence. Whenever possible the data were compared with the results of a study by *Fortune* magazine of 900 business leaders selected as the top executives in the United States.[1]

A list of 132 important business leaders had been prepared earlier from nominations submitted by the Seattle Chamber of Commerce, the Rotary Club, the Kiwanis Club, and the Personnel Management Association.[2] Eight judges, carefully chosen because of their close acquaintanceship with the business community, were asked to select those leaders they believed to be most influential in the business and community life of Seattle and to explain the bases for their selections. A number of top business leaders reviewed the list. The 49 individuals selected as the top business leaders were sent a questionnaire with a letter describing

* Revision of the author's article of the same title, *Pacific Northwest Business*, XV (February 1956), 5–12.

the study. The report which follows is based on the replies of the 36 individuals (74 percent) who responded.

SOCIAL BACKGROUND. Most Seattle business leaders (52 percent) are between 51 and 60 years of age; 20 percent are over 60 years of age; 28 percent are between 41 and 50 years of age. None is under 40. The "900" top executives in the United States exhibit an older age pattern. (See Table 8.)

TABLE 8. *Age of Seattle Business Leaders Compared with Top 900 Business Executives of the United States*

AGE	Frequencies for Seattle	Percent for Seattle	Percent for the "900"
Under 40	0	0	0
41 to 50	10	28	12
51 to 60	19	52	41
61 to 70	6	17	40
71 and over	1	3	7
TOTALS	36	100%	100%

Most Seattle business leaders (64 percent) were born in the West. The Midwest contributed 22 percent, and 11 percent were foreign-born. No Seattle leaders were born in the East and only 3 percent in the South. Only 6 percent of the "900" top executives were born in the West. (See Table 9.)

TABLE 9. *Regional Birthplaces of Seattle Business Leaders Compared with the Top 900 Business Executives of the United States*

WHERE BORN	Frequencies for Seattle	Percent for Seattle	Percent for the "900"
West	23	64	6
Midwest	8	22	38
South	1	3	17
East	0	0	33
Foreign	4	11	7
TOTALS	36	100%	101% °

° Total is more than 100% because of rounding.

Both in Seattle and nationally most top business leaders were college graduates. Seventy-five percent of Seattle leaders and 81 percent of the "900" group attended or were graduated from college.

(See Table 10.) The most frequent educational interest among Seattle business leaders was business economics: one in three stated that this was his major interest. Approximately one in four gave science and en-

TABLE 10. *Education of Seattle Business Leaders Compared with the Top 900 Business Executives of the United States*

EXTENT OF EDUCATION	Frequencies for Seattle	Percent for Seattle	Percent for the "900"
High school and under	9	25	19
College attendance	7	19	16
College graduation	15	42	43
Post graduate study	5	14	22
TOTALS	36	100%	100%

gineering as his interest, while about one in five listed arts or law. One in four gave no major subject interest. In the "900" study educational interests followed a very similar pattern, but there was greater emphasis on science and engineering. (See Table 11). However, an analysis of those

TABLE 11. *Major Educational Interest of Seattle Business Leaders Compared with the Top 900 Business Executives of the United States*

MAJOR EDUCATIONAL INTEREST	Frequencies for Seattle	Percent for Seattle	Percent for the "900"
Arts	2	6	9
Law	5	14	15
Business economics	12	33	31
Science and Engineering	8	22	46
None specified	9	25	..
TOTALS	36	100%	101% *

* Total is more than 100% because of rounding.

in the "900" study who were under 50 years of age shows an increase of interest in the arts, law, and business economics and a decrease of interest in science and engineering.

In both studies the fathers of most of the business leaders were also identified with business: 56 percent of the Seattle business leaders and 62 percent of the top "900" were sons of businessmen. Fathers of 14 percent of Seattle's business leaders were professional men. Fathers of 14 percent were craftsmen. Sons of laborers and farmers each compose 8 percent of the Seattle business leaders. (See Table 12.) The occupa-

TABLE 12. *Father's Occupation of Seattle Business Leaders Compared with the Top 900 Business Executives of the United States*

FATHER'S OCCUPATION	Frequencies for Seattle	Percent for Seattle	Percent for the "900"	Percent of total U.S. male population in 1920
General professions	0	0	7	
Law	1	3	4	
Engineering	2	6	3	
TOTAL PROFESSIONS	3	9	14	4
General business	13	36	43	
Railroading	1	3	4	
Founder or executive	6	17	15	
TOTAL BUSINESS	20	56	62	9
Farmer	3	8	13	27
Laborer	3	8	8	31
Craftsman	5	14	..	18
Politics and government	2	6	3	1
Clerk or salesman°	..	..	..	10
TOTALS	36	101%†	100%	100%

° This category not used in Seattle and *Fortune* studies.
† Total is more than 100% because of rounding.

tional distribution in 1920 has been chosen as best representing the distribution of occupations when most of the business leaders in both studies were entering upon their careers. If occupations of the leaders' fathers are compared with those of the national labor force, the influence of the fathers' occupations on their sons' careers can be appraised. It is clear that a man's birth into the business and professional echelons enormously increases the probabilities of his subsequently holding a similar position.[3]

The data collected indicate that the Seattle business leaders have spent the greater parts of their lives in the Seattle area. (See Table 13.) In another study, Warner and Abegglen have concluded that territorial mobility, on the whole, seems to be related to retardation of the career: men who have moved about a lot tend to achieve business leadership later than those who stay close to home.[4]

CAREER HISTORY. Roughly seven out of ten Seattle leaders (69 percent) have been with their present companies for more than 20 years. In the "900" study 74 percent have been with their present companies for more than 20 years. (See Table 14.) Only 11 percent of Seattle

TABLE 13. *Years Spent in the Seattle Area by*
Seattle Business Leaders

YEARS SPENT IN SEATTLE AREA	Frequencies	Percentages
Less than 5	0	0
6 to 10	1	3
11 to 20	2	6
21 to 30	8	22
31 to 40	6	17
41 to 50	9	25
51 to 60	8	22
61 and over	2	6
TOTALS	36	101% *

* Total is more than 100% because of rounding.

TABLE 14. *Years Spent with Present Company by*
Seattle Business Leaders Compared with the Top
900 Business Executives of the United States

YEARS SPENT WITH PRESENT COMPANY	Frequencies for Seattle	Percent for Seattle	Percent for the "900"
Under 2	0	0	0
2 to 5	3	8	3
6 to 10	1	3	7
11 to 20	7	19	15
21 to 30	17	47	28
31 to 40	5	14	29
41 to 50	3	8	14
51 to 60	0	0	3
TOTALS	36	99% *	100%

* Total is less than 100% because of rounding.

leaders and 10 percent of the "900" leaders have been in their present companies for 10 years or less.

More than half of the Seattle leaders (58 percent) have been in their present position for more than 11 years. In contrast, only 27 percent of the "900" major executives have held their present positions that long. The difference is probably explained by the smaller size of the Seattle businesses and the fact that some of the leaders own their businesses. All of the "900" are employed as managers. (See Table 15.)

For both Seattle and the "900," the largest proportion of business leaders started to work for their present companies between the ages of 21 and 30. The next largest proportion started work for their present companies between the ages of 31 and 40. It should be noted that only

TABLE 15. *Years in Present Position for Seattle Business Leaders Compared with the Top 900 Business Executives of the United States*

YEARS IN PRESENT POSITION	Frequencies for Seattle	Percent for Seattle	Percent for the "900"
5 or less	8	22	47
6 to 10	7	19	26
11 to 20	16	44	19
21 or over	5	14	8
TOTALS	36	99% °	100%

° Total is less than 100% because of rounding.

a small number of leaders–17 percent in Seattle and 21 percent of the "900"–changed from one firm to another after 40 years of age. (See Table 16.)

TABLE 16. *Age of Seattle Business Leaders when Started with Present Company Compared with the Top 900 Business Executives of the United States*

AGE WHEN JOINED COMPANY	Frequencies for Seattle	Percent for Seattle	Percent for the "900"
20 and under	5	14	8
21 to 30	16	44	48
31 to 40	9	25	23
41 to 50	4	11	·15
51 and over	2	6	6
TOTALS	36	100%	100%

Mobility in younger years is certainly indicated for the majority of Seattle leaders. More than half (53 percent) have worked for three or more other companies. The "900" study shows a less mobile pattern. (See Table 17.) The types of companies represented in the Seattle study are shown in Table 18. Banks were first in number, with manufacturing, real estate and investments, and retail sales tied for second.

The 36 men in the Seattle study reached a high level of occupational status very quickly with few stops along the way. Nine of these business leaders began their careers in high-status jobs as owner, manager, professional, or executive. Ten more achieved such positions after holding just one job at a lower status. The average time it took the Seattle business leader to get his first high-status job was approximately four years. Most men achieved a high-status job within one or two moves or promotions.

TABLE 17. *Number of Other Companies Worked For by Seattle Business Leaders Compared with the Top 900 Business Executives of the United States*

NUMBER OF OTHER COMPANIES WORKED FOR	Frequencies for Seattle	Percent for Seattle	Percent for the "900"
0	5	14	33
1	7	19	26
2	5	14	17
3	6	17	12
4 or more	13	36	11
TOTALS	36	100%	99% °

° Total is less than 100% because of rounding.

TABLE 18. *Types of Companies Represented by Seattle Business Leaders*

TYPES OF COMPANIES	Frequencies	Percentages
Banks	6	17
Railways	1	3
Manufacturing	4	11
Logging	2	6
Communications	1	3
Utilities	3	8
Printing	2	6
Foods	2	6
Real Estate and Investment	4	11
Insurance	1	3
Law	3	8
Retail Sales	4	11
Building Supplies	2	6
Advertising	1	3
TOTALS	36	102% °

° Total is more than 100% because of rounding.

COMMUNITY PARTICIPATION. The "average" Seattle business leader belonged to a total of 17 organizations, with civic organizations leading the list. He had four business affiliations and belonged to six civic, four social, and three professional organizations. Table 19 shows the extent of participation in civic and social organizations; probably no other group of persons in the city would surpass such participation in community organizations.

ACTIVITIES AND THE INFLUENCE OF THE SEATTLE BUSINESS LEADERS. In the composite picture of the social background, career patterns, and com-

TABLE 19. *Seattle Business Leaders' Participation
in Civic and Social Organizations
(Frequencies of 5 or more)*

Civic Organizations	Frequency
Chamber of Commerce	30
United Good Neighbors	17
Rotary Club	13
International Trade Fair	12
Greater Seattle, Inc.	8
Seattle Historical Society	7
Municipal League	7
Community Chest	7
Seattle Symphony Orchestra	7
China Club	6
World Affairs Council	6
Nat. Conf. of Christians and Jews	6
Seattle Foundation	5
Goodwill Industries	5
Social Organizations	
Rainier Club	32
Washington Athletic Club	26
Seattle Golf Club	19
Seattle Tennis Club	9
University Club	8
Broadmoor Club (Golf)	7
Seattle Yacht Club	5

munity participation of top Seattle business leaders the most significant findings seem to center around their high degree of stability and
concentration on a business career. The typical business leader had a father who was a businessman, indicating that the present leader's interest in business was encouraged early in life. He was born in the West—
or in a few cases in the Midwest. He either attended or was graduated
from college, where he concentrated on business or science. He changed
jobs once or twice before settling down at age 30 with his present company, where he has served from 21 to 30 years. He has lived in Seattle
nearly 40 years, is between 51 and 60 years of age, and is an owner, manager, professional man, or executive. It took him, on the average, four
years and less than two moves to get to his first-status job. He is most
likely to be a banker, a manufacturer, a merchant, or a real estate or
investment broker. He belongs to many civic, business, social, and professional organizations.

In order to discover how these top business leaders attained positions of highest community influence, the individuals on the panel
of judges were interviewed as they made their nominations of the most

influential leaders. The specific reasons they gave for selecting each leader were carefully analyzed and interpreted.

The *potential* influence of a business leader is defined by the work position he holds. The top Seattle business leaders occupy the following positions:

Manufacturing Executives	6
Bankers	6
Investment Brokers	4
Manufacturing Owners	2
Merchant Owners	2
Utilities Executives	2
Publishers	2
Mercantile Executives	2
Wholesale Executives	2
Hotel Executive	1
Insurance Executive	1

The *actual* influence of the leaders in these positions derives from their activities within their companies and within the community. If a business leader is to achieve the highest influence, he not only must have secured an important work position, but he must also take an active part in business and civic organizations. Most of these influential business leaders were characterized by at least five of the following six attributes: (1) leads a relatively large or influential company; (2) participates actively either in initiating, sanctioning, or vetoing policy decisions affecting the community; (3) possesses certain identifiable leadership qualities (i.e., ability to plan, organize, and secure collaboration of others); (4) has direct (status) access to other leaders through formal and informal contacts; (5) serves on policy-making bodies of both business and community organizations; and (6) has relatively large income or personal wealth. These characteristics show high agreement with Hunter's criteria of reputed leadership.

Society status, although useful in reinforcing contacts, is not necessary to win high influence in business circles. It is more important to remain active among a wide circle of business and civic associates and within organizations where policy-making decisions are made. The top leaders increasingly add business affiliations to their participation; as directors they command still wider policy-making influence. Business leaders come to know one another well as a result of this pattern of wide participation in business, civic, social, and professional organizations. The better known they become, the greater are the demands for even more participation. To conserve their time and energy leaders in the very top positions tend to accept only those assignments which maximize their policy-making influence. Indeed, other community leaders will often be satisfied if the top leaders will but lend their names to organization letterheads.

The data assembled here build higher confidence in the reputational identification of leaders.[5] We have seen that business leaders share a common pattern of intense community activity. How business and other community influentials make decisions affecting the community is our next concern. The number of participants involved and their informal group relations are of especial significance in judging the fluidity or rigidity of a community power structure.

CHAPTER 6

DECISION-MAKING CLIQUES

AND COMMUNITY POWER STRUCTURES

IN SEATTLE AND BRISTOL*

MOST RESEARCH IN COMMUNITY POWER STRUCTURE has centered about the identification of influential policy makers and the group relationships through which policy makers wield their influence. A considerable body of research deals with identification of the influential persons in the community.[1] Much less is known about decision-making cliques, and techniques for measuring the degree of clique solidarity are especially meager.[2] This study was designed to test the working hypothesis that top influentials in a community influence policy making by acting in concert through cliques.

In his study of Atlanta, Floyd Hunter describes a top group of policy makers drawn largely from the businessmen's class. A pattern of twenty-one clique relationships was shown to exist among the forty top influentials. The most recognized groupings were known as "crowds," which Hunter called the "First State Bank Crowd," the "Regional Gas Crowd," the "Mercantile Crowd," the "Homer Chemical Crowd," the "Grower Bank Crowd," and the like. Each crowd had a leader. "Several of the top leaders within the crowds would 'clear with each other' informally on many matters. . . . Each man at the top of a 'crowd pyramid' depended upon those close to him in business to carry out decisions when made."[3]

Hunter's findings strongly suggest the need for comparative studies

* Adapted from the author's article of the same title, *American Journal of Sociology*, LXIV (November 1958), 299–310.

of community decision making. Behind his research lies the persistent question: to what extent do the findings from this particular southern city permit wider generalization to other cities? Pellegrin and Coates report that the generalization fits (with some variation) another large southern city called "Bigtown," which they studied in 1954 and 1955.[4] And Hunter, Schaffer, and Sheps claim that Salem, Massachusetts presents a pyramid of power dominated by the business and industrial group organized into power cliques with clique leaders.[5] However, less solidary power structures have been reported by Rossi for New England's "Bay City" and by Schulze for midwestern "Cibola."[6] McKee, reporting on his study of Lorain, Ohio, has said that no one group can be labeled as a ruling group. A number of groups have varying effects upon decision making in a given locus. "The pyramidical model is . . . inaccurate and misleading."[7] Among many other community power studies discovering a pluralist distribution of power are those of Dahl in New Haven,[8] Rossi and Dentler in Chicago,[9] Banfield in Chicago,[10] Martin and his associates in Syracuse,[11] Freeman and his associates in Syracuse,[12] and Long in Boston.[13] Perhaps the most comprehensive study is that of Freeman and his associates, who discover no less than nineteen fluid leadership groups active in the thirty-nine issues studied. It can be concluded that there is variety in American leadership structures ranging from high to low degrees of fluidity. What is yet unknown is the extent and types of clique arrangements in American communities, and almost nothing is known about cities in other nations. Of all the mysteries in community power structure none is more hidden than the nature and operation of clique or friendship ties among top influentials.

The identification of clique structures is an extremely difficult undertaking. Many respondents will claim cliques exist simply because they have seen persons together many times or have heard that certain people were good friends. Hunter relied upon the mapping of certain sociometric relationships based on committee choices, on participation patterns of influentials in issues as described by them, and on specific statements of informants. The researcher would like to make direct observations of key influentials when they are acting in relation to community issues or projects and perhaps in other dealings with each other. Since it is almost impossible to enter this "private" world, cumulative indirect evidence is sought.

Method

As REPORTED in Chapter 3, personal interviews were held with a 50-percent-stratified random sample of 44 top influentials in Seattle and 32 top influentials in Bristol. The test of the hypothesis relied upon evidence drawn from interviews, questionnaires, and reports by informants.

In interviews with top influentials the sociometric choices were utilized to determine group cohesiveness. The acquaintance patterns of top and key influentials were analyzed to ascertain social relationships. Committee participation of the top and key influentials was analyzed. And finally, the personal estimates of clique behavior as described by top and key influentials were given high weight.

The questionnaires yielded data on the activity of the key influentials in community organizations and their overlapping memberships in business, social, civic, professional, and trade associations. Selected informants were interviewed and asked to describe how decisions were debated and resolved when community issues arose or projects were undertaken.

Choice Patterns of Top and Key Influentials

TOP INFLUENTIALS may range from a large group of independent persons to a small, autonomous group which is well organized and is actively organizing support of the community power complex. Along the continuum between these two poles, various degrees of solidarity may exist. In testing the hypothesis, the research task is to assemble the best measures to appraise the degree of solidarity. Important evidence gathered in this study (and in Hunter's) is the choice pattern of top influentials who selected ten leaders according to the question: "If you were responsible for a major project which was before the community that required decision by a group of leaders—leaders that nearly everyone would accept—which ten on this list would you choose, regardless of whether they are known to you personally or not? Add other names if you wish." Figure 7 is a sociogram showing the choices made by the key influentials in Seattle who had been identified as the sociometric leaders.

The Criswell in-group preference index was applied to all three test cities to ascertain the extent to which the key influentials chose within themselves in contrast to their out-group choices to all remaining top influentials.[14] In order of intensity of in-group preference, the three cities exhibited the following index numbers: Atlanta, 11.2; Seattle, 5.3; Bristol, 3.0. In-group preference greater than 1.00 shows that the ratio of the key influential in-group choices to their top influentials choices is greater than the ratio of key influential membership to top influential membership. The index scores above indicate a high degree of key influtial in-group preference in all three cities, with an extraordinarily high score in Atlanta. These cross-group comparisons reflect a solidarity of

KEY INFLUENTIALS

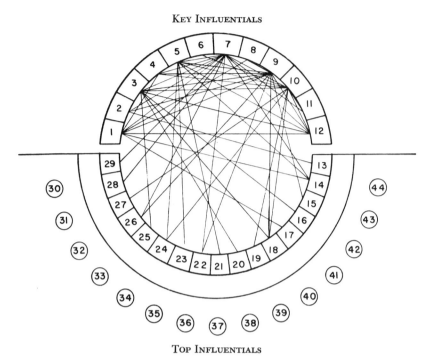

TOP INFLUENTIALS

FIGURE 7.   *Sociogram Showing All Choices of Six Key Influentials of Seattle to Other Key and Top Influentials*

the key influentials in their civic behavior within these cities. However, the index scores are based only on sociometric choices; the actual influence and working relationships are not demonstrated by such data. Acceptance of the hypothesis of clique behavior in community decision making awaits further evidence.

ACQUAINTANCESHIP PATTERN.   The acquaintanceship scores for key influentials and top influentials were derived from the interview schedules, which sought a response from each person as to his acquaintanceship with all other top influentials listed. This schedule asked each respondent to check one of five responses: don't know, heard of, know slightly, know well, know socially (exchange of home visits). Scores of 1, 2, 3, 4, 5 were allocated to these response categories, and a total acquaintance score was derived from each interview respondent. Table 20 shows the mean acquaintanceship scores for Seattle and Bristol for the key influentials and the top influentials and values of *t* for the differences between means. These scores show that in both Seattle and Bristol the key influentials are better acquainted with the total population of

TABLE 20. *Mean Acquaintanceship Scores for Key Influentials and Top Influentials in Seattle and Bristol with t-Tests of Significance for Differences between Means*

TEST CITIES	KI mean score	TI mean score	t	d.f.	P
Seattle	129.7	106.8	2.10	20	$<.05$
Bristol	131.0	107.1	2.21	14	$<.05$

influentials than are the top influentials. This evidence suggests an intensive pattern of social contact among the key influentials.

COMMITTEE PARTICIPATION. Each interview respondent indicated whether he had participated on committees with each of the top influentials during the preceding two years. Each respondent was given one point for each committee contact he reported. The mean score for the key influentials in Seattle was 18.8 and for the top influentials was 11.6. This difference was found statistically significant at the 5-percent level in Seattle. In Bristol the mean score for the key influentials was 17.5 and for the top influentials was 12.3; the difference was also statistically significant at the 5-percent level. Again, the evidence points to a high degree of contact and to possible key influential dominance of committees.

The questionnaire which each respondent answered and mailed to us asked about participation in other businesses as a director or owner and participation in social, civic, and professional organizations. Scores were derived from participation in each type of organization[15] and also for total participation. The key influentials were consistently more active than top influentials in both Seattle and Bristol. In Seattle the mean total participation score for key influentials was 69.9 and for top influentials was 46.4. In Bristol the mean total participation score for key influentials was 65.3 and for top influentials was 48.1. In both cities the differences were statistically significant at the .01 level.

Community participation was further analyzed to seek evidence of overlapping memberships, on the assumption that persons participating together in community organizations may use these organizations as communication centers for community decision making or at least as places to reinforce friendships. We asked all top influentials to rate social and civic organizations as to their influence in the community. Selecting the most important organizations, we analyzed the memberships of key influentials to see whether any pattern of common participation could be discerned. Table 21 is a matrix pattern of the overlapping memberships of the key influentials in the business, civic, and social organiza-

TABLE 21. *Matrix of Overlapping Memberships of the 12 Key Influentials in Seattle for Business, Social, and Civic Organizations*

Key Influentials of Seattle	Investment Co. A	Investment Co. B	Insurance Co. A	Insurance Co. B	Real Estate Co.	Bank A	Bank B	Bank C	Social Club	Business Club	Golf Club	Masonic Lodge	University Club	College Club	Golf Club	Tennis Club	Chamber of Commerce	United Good Neighbors	Rotary	Municipal League	Community Chest	World Affairs Council	Orthopedic Hospital	Total no. overlapping memberships in business, social, and civic organizations
D. D.	×	×	×				×	×	×	×	×	×					×	×	×	×	×	×		15
H. E.	×	×		×			×	×	×	×	×	×					×	×	×		×			12
O. R.	×			×			×		×	×	×	×	×				×	×	×		×			11
T. S.									×	×	×	×	×				×	×	×		×	×		10
L. A.									×	×	×	×		×			×	×				×		8
R. F.			×						×	×		×		×			×	×	×					8
B. B.	×			×					×	×					×		×				×			7
A. Y.		×		×					×	×					×		×							6
C. S.		×			×				×	×						×	×							6
E. L.					×											×	×			×	×			5
L. C.						×														×			×	3
W. O.						×							×							×			×	3

Total number overlapping memberships in business organizations = 21
Total number overlapping memberships in social organizations = 37
Total number overlapping memberships in civic organizations = 36

Grand total all overlapping memberships = 94

tions of Seattle. This table shows that mutual contact is established between the key influentials in business, social, and civic organizations, but that the common participation established by the small group who interact in the business sector may be the most significant. Among those most active in the business sector are three of the key influentials who have been designated as meeting together when there is a serious financial crisis or money-raising need.

There is a grand total of 94 overlapping business, social, and civic memberships among the 12 key influentials. The rank order correlation between the sociometric influence rankings and rank position based on the overlapping membership is .42. This indicates that a moderate correlation exists and suggests that group interaction may build common ties and leadership reputations.

DIRECT TESTIMONY FROM INTERVIEWS. All this indirect evidence points to an underlying pattern of common participation and friendships, but it does not tell us whether the key influentials actually form crowds and make decisions about community affairs in concert. We decided to ask all top influentials in the sample and certain selected informants in Seattle about community decision making by putting this point-blank statement in front of them: "There are several crowds in Seattle that work together and pretty much make the big decisions." They were asked to say whether this was true or false and to comment. The answers of the top influentials interviewed in Seattle are shown in Table 22.

TABLE 22. *Answers by 22 Top Influentials to Statement "There are several crowds in Seattle that work together and pretty much make the big decisions."*

	KI	TI	TOTAL
True	4	11	15
False	2	4	6
Don't know	..	1	1

Fifteen of the 22 respondents believed that "crowds" existed in Seattle. The Fisher exact probability test was applied (ignoring the "don't know" category) to find out whether there were any significant differences between the replies of the key influentials and top influentials. No statistically significant differences were shown.[16] Both groups of influentials believed that crowds exist and work together. However, these replies must be interpreted with great caution. The term "crowds" does not evoke a common meaning for all respondents.[17]

Fluid Coalition and Clique Patterns

Focused interviews of approximately one hour were conducted with each top influential and key influential and with some carefully selected informants to probe for the bases of their opinions. Two patterned groupings emerged as the principal referents: *a general pattern of fluid coalition among influentials is discerned about most issues;* and *clique relations are observed around a set of specific situations.* A few interview comments are quoted to show these two patterns as they were observed in Seattle.

INTERVIEW EVIDENCE FOR A GENERAL PATTERN OF FLUID COALITION: SEATTLE

There are no crowds as such. There are perhaps ten main leaders and the majority of them must be behind any major controversial issue in Seattle to make it successful. There are probably thirty more persons, less active and less influential, who contribute their time and energy. I am not aware of any subgroups within this group of forty that cling together on issues generally.   University president (ki)

There are no crowds as such, just fluid coalitions. I want to judge a case on its merits, and I refuse to bind myself to any reciprocal *quid pro quo* agreements.   Utility executive and former president of Chamber of Commerce (ti)

There are no "cliques" or "crowds." However, every group has their leaders; there are probably five from industry, five from labor, and five from lay groups who lead in their respective groups. If they can be "sold" the others will generally follow.   Labor leader (ti)

There is a group of about thirty men who are primarily responsible for the major decisions in Seattle. Quite frequently they are the "second men" in important organizations who have both the approval of the top men and the youth and time to spend a large amount of time and energy on civic work. Many of the decisions are formulated informally in groups of two or three at social functions.   ·Physician (ti)

Seattle has no rigid structure of leadership. No one person or group runs the city. As issues appear, various persons take sides and push for their view. Different coalitions appear on the issues. However, there is a small core of four leaders, all of them are good fund raisers and people and groups turn to them.   Veteran newspaper writer (informant)

INTERVIEW EVIDENCE FOR CLIQUE RELATIONS: SEATTLE

There are probably four groups in Seattle who are stable and act as a group. The most influential one is the businessmen's group, who are largely

Republicans, active in both city and state affairs, members of the Chamber of Commerce, Municipal League, and active in school-board elections. The second is the labor groups, who act together on some issues. There is a third group which is composed mainly of Democrats. They have their own money. There is also a fourth group which unofficially stems from the Council of Churches but influences mainly through individual Protestant ministers. They are interested in the character of various political candidates and boosted the last Governor.   REPUBLICAN PARTY LEADER (TI)

There is no one crowd, but a key leader works through friends whom he respects and with whom he can get things done. Take yesterday afternoon. The President of the Symphony Board wanted help on the symphony drive. I met with E.B. and S.B. and L.B. [all KI] in L.B.'s office. We sat around and talked about who should head up the drive. B.G.'s name was suggested. I was tagged to go with E.B. and hang the job on him. That's the way things get done—informal meetings.

Now in politics, there are ten of us who have gotten together and tried to see that a good man was selected for mayor. We picked T.N., and you could have gotten one hundred to one that he would have been licked, but he won. Now I haven't been in the mayor's office since. We don't dictate.   BUSINESS LEADER (KI)

There are several recognizable blocs that usually present the same front. The Chamber of Commerce is probably the most important bloc both in initiating and influencing. Labor is generally well organized. Educational groups are usually united on issues such as passage of school bond levies but are too divided to present any solid influential body. Welfare agencies shy from expressions of opinion and are not opinion molders. Newspapers and radio are not influential in local issues.   RELIGIOUS LEADER (KI)

There are ten to twelve in the elite that make the big decisions. They are primarily in the business field, and they work in cliques, the cliques being formed with a member of this ten or twelve and they delegate authority down to lesser influentials in their areas.

SOCIAL WORK LEADER (TI)

There are five or six "big men" who make most of the decisions; they are important through private and corporate wealth and property. They are socially cohesive, stable, and mostly Republicans, but that is not an important factor. They vote consistently together on issues and are mainly interested in only the important decisions . . . "top level" operators. There is a second-level group of about twenty-five who are mainly from business. Both the small and large groups are Chamber of Commerce members in part.   LAWYER AND FORMER MAYOR (TI)

The above comments do not indicate general agreement, but a scrutiny of all the behavioral and attitudinal evidence for Seattle leads us to reject the working hypothesis for the following reasons: 1. Key influentials do not repeatedly act in concert, utilizing subordinate groups.

There is no "crowd" pattern in Seattle such as Hunter reports for Atlanta. Atlanta had a more structured organization of the top influentials with ties to subordinate groups. 2. There are key leaders who bring various other influentials around them when they are responsible for getting a civic project carried out. These groupings do have a pattern and they tend to be repeated because key leaders find that they can work best with certain leaders and can get the job done. However, there is a significant degree of fluidity. Various leaders may be called upon for the responsible direction of policy making, and different key influentials and top influentials may be drawn in. Seattle shows a fluid core of from 12 to 15 key influentials, with up to 150 top influentials. Different combinations appear with different issues. No one person or group dominates.

The evidence leads to acceptance of the working hypothesis in the following respects: 1. Relatively stable groups of leaders are identified with certain institutional sectors of the community—business, labor, political party, education, and religion—through which they express common interest. 2. Solidarity of the key influentials is revealed in the group of 10 key influentials who in Seattle came together when the selection of a (conservative) mayoralty candidate for the primary was a community issue. 3. Certain key influentials in Seattle come together when a very important fund-raising project is before the community or when a very serious financial or civic crisis arises. 4. Key influentials tend to confine their activity to policymaking. Sometimes, they are sought out as advisers, as spokesmen, as fund-raisers or givers, and as nominal administrative heads. Organizations and leaders turn repeatedly to this core group of from 12 to 15 persons. Much of the activity of the key influentials is pursued without publicity and visibility.

In Bristol the interviews with top influentials revealed a very similar set of patterns in community decision making. There is fluidity among the top influentials. Cliques with clique leaders such as Hunter reported for Atlanta do not exist, but powerful leaders do operate in firms, organizations, and the city council in initiating and sanctioning community projects and programs. The following interview quotations reveal the multiple interaction of leaders and groups for many different institutional sectors.

INTERVIEW EVIDENCE FOR A GENERAL PATTERN OF FLUID COALITION: BRISTOL

Labor leaders have grown increasingly powerful. Political power is now almost evenly split between two groups: management and property vs. manual workers with white collar worker support. One hundred years ago the merchants dealing with the West Indies in tobacco, rum, and cocoa held the center of influence. Today, the power of merchants has been diluted by the rise of the aircraft industry and the shift of larger merchant interests outside of the community. There are five groups which hold the power today—political parties, government, industry, labor, and merchants. UNIVERSITY OFFICIAL

Old families mean something here. Most of the top business leaders inherited a family business. Business is powerful but so is labor, government, and education. The University carries a lot of weight. The Church of England has a good deal of influence because of the Bishop and the Dean. Not many professionals are active in community life. They are just too busy with their own work. LAWYER AND CITIZEN PARTY LEADER

Leaders work through committees and organizations. As a labor party leader in the Council when I want to get something done I get a committee together of three or four people. That's plenty. I make sure that labor, business, and education are represented and sometimes the church. During the war we really moved. I was Lord Mayor and had a bipartisan executive group of four. We did things in those days. We didn't worry about a thing being political or not. I used to say we are going to do so and so. Someone would say, "But there is no authority for that!" I would say, "We are going to do it. We shall get the authority later."
LABOUR UNION AND LABOUR PARTY LEADER

Do leaders work together in crowds? No. There are groups and organizations but in the council every man speaks for himself. If he says, "I speak for the Allied Grocers," then he is a dead duck. We won't give attention to that kind of talk. It is when we say "I believe" that we listen. It is a protection of independence. MINISTER AND COUNCILMAN

INTERVIEW EVIDENCE FOR CLIQUE RELATIONS: BRISTOL

The important committees of the city council hold the political power. It is supposed that five or six aldermen run the show but the chief officers of the government departments do exercise much power. The mayor is a figurehead. ECONOMIST

Banks, large retail stores, and even newspapers are controlled from London. The local establishments are substantially branches run by branch managers. Electricity, gas, radio broadcasting, unemployment and health administration have passed from local government to regional offices of the national government. But this does not mean a local power structure is not powerful. The city council is the center of a government that owns and operates housing estates worth 26 million pounds, docks and facilities (valued at 13½ million pounds), highways, sewers, and parks (8¼ million pounds), civic buildings (4¾ million pounds), schools (4¾ million pounds), and redevelopment area (3¼ million pounds.) That's where the power is.

PUBLIC RELATIONS OFFICER IN INDUSTRY

We are always in the public eye. We get more requests for community help. The usual pattern is for someone who wants to get something done to call here, then check with Robinson's [containers], Fry's [chocolates] and Wills' [tobacco—all three are old-family, locally-owned manufacturers]. If it will go with these people, then they know they can move the projects.

PRESIDENT OF THE LARGEST LOCALLY-OWNED MANUFACTURING PLANT

Who makes decisions, you ask, and by what or whom are they influenced? Now to us, I think the answer is that the city council makes decisions on all matters affecting the community as a unit. We are not conscious of their being influenced by any external person, or body of persons. We tend to think of the government, whether local or central, as an impersonal "they" and to feel that "they" are all-powerful, difficult to approach, and almost impossible to persuade. The idea that policy may be affected by some hidden hand, not belonging to "them," is not a natural one to us. If we try to analyze "them," we may say that in a democracy it is the majority that holds the power, the party which is "in" at the time. If we are addicted to political speculation, we may even go as far as pinning ultimate "power" or policy making on the long-suffering civil service—our permanent officials. Of course, the Labor party is always open to the charge of being in the Trade Union pocket, and the Conservatives are always the suspect "Slaves of Big Business." But I fancy that these ideas are not taken very seriously, being regarded as so much party propaganda. It is very difficult for us to believe that majority decisions may have been taken as a result of the economic power of Imperial Chemicals, or Bristol Aeroplane Company, or the industrial pressure of the Transport and General Workers, or the social prestige of the Duke of Beaufort. We like to believe that government, whether local or national, is affected by the uninhibited operation of political institutions alone. Of course there are many influences that can affect the individuals which comprise a majority.

UNIVERSITY OFFICIAL

Power Structures of Seattle, Bristol, and Atlanta

SEATTLE, BRISTOL, AND ATLANTA are alike in many ways. There is a vigorous business leadership in all three cities. There is a hierarchy of civic leadership in which various key influentials and top influentials have a "place." There are friendship groupings and patterns of common social and civic participation which bring people together. In all three cities there are a large number of top influentials (up to 100–150) who have a standing in the eyes of the total community and may be called upon for leadership services when a project is before the entire community. However, the three cities are different in significant ways. Bristol does not look to its business leaders as much for civic leadership as do the two American cities. The business representation among the key influentials in Seattle is 67 percent; in Atlanta, 75 percent; in Bristol, 25 percent. The solution of civic problems is carried on more directly by the city council in Bristol, while voluntary organizations are more fluid and there is less solidarity among the key influentials in both Bristol and Seattle than in Atlanta.[18]

These phenomena of community power raise the question of what models might be appropriate to describe the power structures of Seattle and Bristol. For Atlanta, Hunter has described a stratified pyramid with a broad base of leadership centering in a top group of policy makers drawn largely from the business class. (See Figure 5.) At the top of the pyramid are found the industrial, commercial, and financial owners and top executives of large enterprises. I believe that this model emerges sharply in Atlanta because it is an older, established community where the social system has been congenial to the growth of a social aristocracy and where business control has a history of hereditary growth. It should be recalled that only 15 of the 40 top policy leaders in Atlanta gained a position of prominence on their own. Each of the others inherited his father's business or was helped by the wealth an connections of his father.

The stratified pyramid model is not appropriate for Bristol. While it applies to Seattle for a wide range of issues and projects, it does not apply during many political campaigns when coalitions form and often defeat the leaders who are ranked according to the stratified model. For example, it did not explain the defeat of the right-to-work issue in Seattle in 1956 as will be described in the next chapter.

An institutional ring or cone model best fits the pattern of community power as observed in political contests and as seen in certain issues. It reflects a number of current social forces in large industrial cities as shown by three major characteristics: increasing heterogeneity of interests within the business sector, the rise of new power structures, and a growing autonomy and heterogeneity of interests in all institutional sectors.

Increasing heterogeneity of interests within the business sector is manifested by the following characteristics: certain manufacturers and merchants view expansion as a threat to labor supply and wage level; the rise of managers brings a new caution and results in many leaders playing a neutral role;[19] and financial and property ties grow more complex as outside interests enter. Branch businesses increase; community improvements seem to some to be assets, to others to be tax liabilities.

The rise of new power structures can be observed when labor leaders become ever stronger agents of their own organizations and labor becomes more educated and participates more broadly in community organizations, especially in political parties, government, and welfare organizations; citizens of low status more easily attain a share in decision making in the community; political and government leaders exercise greater influence over more activities of community life; military leadership has been given ever greater responsibility; educational leaders command greater attention as the need for specialized personnel increases; major business leaders are being recruited from managerial talent rather than from hereditary and exclusively educated classes.

Autonomy in all institutionalized sectors is increasing and large-scale organization is growing in all sectors. This is accompanied by increased specialization of functions and growing professionalization, especially in government, education, and welfare. The power of administration and policy making is increasingly concentrated within the specialized personnel of the organization.

Figure 8 is a graphic illustration of those individuals in Bristol who were ranked as having the highest personal influence over policy making affecting the community. The ring structure shows the range of institutional representatives. The area of each segment is an approximation of the relative power of that institutional sector as judged by the choice rank of the top influentials and by rating panels who were asked to review the strength of each institutional area in securing desired outcomes on a number of community issues. Those persons whose influence is greatest are shown toward the center of the circle. Note the representatives from the Labour party, the trade union and consumer cooperatives, the Citizens party, business, civic organizations, religion, education, and society. *There is no single solidary elite structure and no hierarchical dominance based on one institutional sector.* There is simply a recognizable leadership pool. The pattern of personal influence is best described as a kaleidoscope of recognizable faces shifting in and out of fluid coalitions as issues and projects change. Leaders play a number of different roles, sometimes taking positive action, sometimes negative, often remaining neutral, and at times even withdrawing completely from various issues.

While the cone or ring model is most appropriate for Bristol, the stratified pyramid, with its solidary top business elite such as Hunter describes for Atlanta is also a useful guide to the power potential in Seattle. However, Seattle shows markedly more fluidity among both the key and the top influentials as issues change. Religion and education have a more influential role: a university president and an Episcopal bishop are among its key influentials.

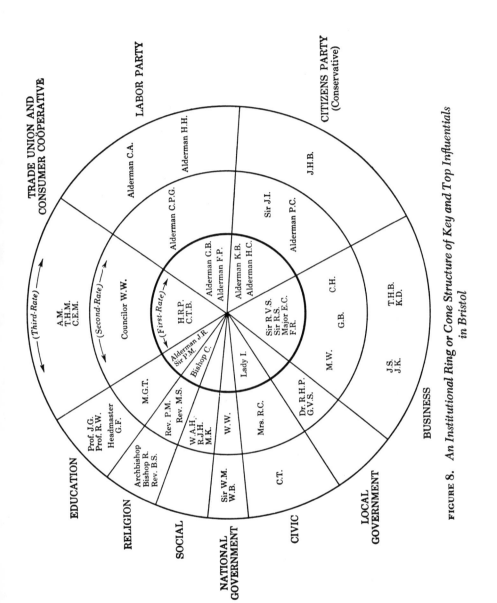

FIGURE 8. *An Institutional Ring or Cone Structure of Key and Top Influentials in Bristol*

For large cities a continuum of community power structures is suggested, ranging from the highly stratified pyramid dominated by a small but powerful business group functioning through cliques of high solidarity to a ring of institutional representatives functioning in relatively independent roles. We have said that Atlanta, Seattle, and Bristol range in the order named along such a continuum.

Assessment of the Comparative Analysis of Seattle, Bristol, and Atlanta

Substantive similarities: Three major factors explain central tendencies in industrializing nations: industrial composition, distribution of private property, and distribution of political power. There is a similarity in the industrial and occupational functions of Seattle and Bristol; relatively strong unions exercise power in both cities; and municipal functions of the two are surprisingly similar. Certainly Seattle, Bristol, and Atlanta are far more alike than different. While there are some basic social and cultural differences, it is firmly believed that top influentials in any of these cities could exchange places with their counterparts in the others without great difficulty since neither language nor custom constitutes a real barrier.

Substantive differences: The framework for comparative analysis lists a number of economic, political, and social factors that explain differences. Two factors have special utility in explaining differences among the three cities. The first of these is the degree of access to community power structures. As a result of the more rigid stratification pattern which governs the political life of Atlanta a higher business representation of "hereditary" leaders were drawn into civic influence in Atlanta than in either Bristol or Seattle. The tight leadership clique of Atlanta coupled with the higher prestige accorded to business leaders in the United States gave impetus to the high business representation and to the exclusiveness of its social participation patterns. The power structure of Bristol has been influenced by the Labour party's long tenure in power (since 1926). What is truly significant is that labor's assumption of power in Bristol has enabled it to make the *structure* of government function so differently. As pointed out earlier the governmental structure in Bristol permits a high representation of many occupational and social classes of the city. Its city council brought many more people into active policy making and increased the scope of representation among the various institutional sectors of the city.

There is some evidence that in the United States local government in the 1960s has been strengthened by many new federally financed but city-sponsored programs. There is still little evidence, however, that top influentials are running for mayor and city council positions. Dahl's historical analysis of New Haven, Connecticut shows clearly that the old families who once accepted responsibility in city government (1784–1842) first abdicated to the new manufacturing group of self-made men of business (1842–1900) and later (1900–   ) to the "ex-plebes" rising out of the working class or lower middle class families of immigrant origins.[20]

Hunter points out that one reason businessmen hesitate to run for office is that defeat brings a loss of status. Another reason is their fear that controversy will hurt their business. Others argue that businessmen believe they can best serve their major interests by overall supervision of the political parties, by financing appropriate candidates, and by control of the press and radio. Whatever may be the reasons, top influentials seldom run for mayor and city council positions in the United States. The result is that the city council is seldom regarded as the center of community power in American cities.[21]

CHAPTER 7

THE PREDICTION OF ISSUE OUTCOME:

*The Right-to-Work Initiative in Seattle**

THE APPEARANCE OF AN ISSUE which concerns the total community may be assumed to indicate a state of conflict and tension between competing groups. These groups may be located anywhere in the institutional or associational structure of the community. An issue comes to be one of central concern as it affects certain vital interests or values. When these interests and values are identified, leaders appear and groups organize to seek a final decision favorable to themselves.

It became apparent in the studies of Seattle and Bristol that a systematic analysis of the institutional power structure of the community and of society should be undertaken. The general assumption of the system model is that the relative distribution of power among societal and community institutions directly influences the character of the community power complex and both the number and the types of top and key influentials. There were no tested techniques to measure the influence of the institutional structure upon community power structures. The theory of issue outcome made possible one such effort.

The prediction of issue outcome is an excellent test of a researcher's knowledge of the community power structure and the decision-making processes within a community. An issue of great concern arouses the community and offers a singular opportunity for determining the network of influences at the time they are presented in a highly activated

* Portions of this chapter have been adapted from the author's article of the same title, *Proceedings of the Pacific Sociological Society* (Research Studies of State College of Washington, XXV, June 1957), 137–47.

state. Such an issue developed when a right-to-work initiative was placed on the Washington state ballot in the November election of 1956. This chapter sets forth a theory of issue outcome and describes an initial test of the theory, utilizing data drawn from the right-to-work issue.[1] The locale of the study is Seattle.

Theory of Issue Outcome

THREE FACTORS DETERMINE THE OUTCOME of a community issue: X_1, the critically activated parts of the institutional power structure; X_2, the power arrangement of the community power complex; and X_3, the solidarity of the top influentials. These three factors are defined as follows.

X_1, the critically activated parts of the institutional power structure, refers to the institutional sectors whose interests are affected and become alerted in whole or in part. Such sectors may include business, labor, education, religion, political parties, government, society, independent professionals, mass communication, recreation, welfare, and cultural institutions. Critical activation occurs in those parts of the institutional power structure which respond with high intensity to an organizational value affected by the issue. Critical activation is identified by analyzing the *substance of the issue* and the *level of the issue*. The substance of the issue refers to the content of the issue and the implications for the various institutional sectors. The level of the issue refers to the "value intensity" exhibited by the affected parties as they appraise the possible impact of the issue outcomes upon their interests.

X_2, the power arrangement of the community power complex, refers to the structure of various individuals, groups, and organizations which mobilize and exert influence either for or against the issue. The arrangements of these influential forces on either side of the issue may be unstructured, semistructured, or a unified coalition. A power arrangement typology of the community power complex is shown in models illustrated in Figure 9. Model A refers to a situation in which important associa-

Model A.
Unstructured

Model B.
Semistructured

Model C.
Highly Structured

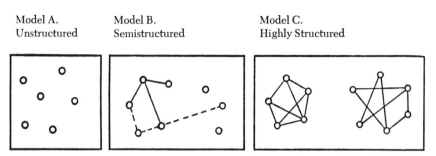

FIGURE 9. *Power Arrangement Models of the Community Power Complex*

tions take a "go it alone" action, avoiding obligations and alliances with other associations. Model B refers to a situation in which some important associations combine in partially cooperative patterns of mobilization while others play independent roles. Model C refers to a power arrangement in which the important associations on either side of an issue form cooperative alliances, pooling resources and leadership.

X_3, solidarity of the top influentials, refers to the degree of cooperative activity evident among the leaders who have major influence in initiating or sanctioning policy-making activities in matters affecting the general community. The top influentials may range from a large group of independent persons to a small autonomous group which is well organized and is actively organizing support of the community power complex. A range of types to represent the possible forms of top influential groupings follows:

Pure democratic type refers to an individuated plural of representative influentials each speaking and acting relatively independently.

Fluid influentials type refers to a large and fluid corps of top influentials surrounded by a large reserve of many other potential influentials who enter as different issues arise.

Core influential type refers to a fairly small group of top influentials surrounded by a small reserve of potential influentials who enter as different issues arise.

Exclusive elite type refers to a stable and unified group of top influentials who repeatedly sanction issues and withhold entry to potential newcomers.

The top influential model sets the bounds to the freedom of action which may be exhibited among the top influentials and the significance of the community power complex. If the top influentials are lacking in solidarity, the community power complex and its leaders become more significant. If the top influentials are inactive on either side of the issue, then the forces are weakened on that side of the issue.

The combined force of these three factors brings about a community decision on a general issue. Issue outcome refers to a final vote by a sovereign body which provides a decision either for or against the issue. Let this issue outcome = y.

$\therefore y = f(X_1{}^I, X_2{}^{II}, X_3{}^{III})$ where the function of issue outcome is recognized as a complex behavioral and algebraic product (with exponents as weightings) since the factors are interactive.

Prediction of Outcome for a Specific Issue

THE FOLLOWING STEPS are required to apply the theory to a specific issue:
  1. Determine the critically activated parts of the institutional power

structure by analyzing substance of issue as seen by affected parties and ascertaining level of issue to each party. If high level, assume relative potential strength of each sector will become manifest. Assign pro and con values of 1 point for each of the critically activated sectors. These values represent the independent influence of each sector represented.

2. Locate most influential organizations by examining the resources, leadership, voting strength, and rank of the institutional sector in the community power profile, and arrange them according to the mobilized relations. Determine the power arrangement type of the community power complex and use the appropriate weight as a multiplier of the total pro and con values respectively. Assign weights as follows to the community power complex multiplier: Model A = 1; Model B = 2; Model C = 3. These values represent the interactive, reinforcing influence of organizations in extending the range of attitude formation and increasing intensity of opinion brought to bear upon the issue.

3. Ascertain the roles of the top influentials. If top influentials act as representative spokesmen or as community power complex leaders, add a weight of 2; if they support with funds or privately sanction the issue but do not take an active part, add a weight of 1; if inactive in the campaign add nothing to total. These values represent the influence of individuals in their ability to project forces of personal persuasion or personal wealth for or against the issue.

4. Determine final total by adding the values for steps 1, 2, and 3. This final total represents the sum of influential forces actively engaged in initiating and ultimately bringing about an outcome of the issue. Predict outcome as passage or defeat of issue, depending upon ratio of the contending forces.

History of the Right-to-Work Initiative in Seattle

DATA ABOUT THE INFLUENTIAL FORCES operating in the community were secured by interviewing the leaders of the major organizations campaigning on both sides of the issue.[2] Certain other informants were also interviewed. Newspapers were carefully followed over a six-month period. The following background is based on these various sources.

Three and a half years before the initiative was placed on the ballot a number of employers found themselves in the midst of a strike. They asked an advertising executive to estimate the cost of launching an "education" campaign against the dangers the strike and organized labor posed for the community. The executive told them that the kind of campaign they had in mind required an issue—one that would direct the attention of the press so that publicity would be focused upon it. The employers told him to get to work on it.

The advertising executive began by studying the closed shop and right-to-work laws aimed at preventing compulsory unionism. He decided that placing an intiative on the ballot would put the issue before the public and give it a great deal of publicity. A professional poll of a sample of citizens in the state showed that a majority were for voluntary unionism. The executive went to a number of employers and asked for support. Many gave contributions, but none would support it with their names. With the contributed funds, he sent out cards to a mailing list and got some 600 signatures of persons who said they would give their support. But when asked later for use of their names in publicity, all except about 25 backed down. It is not fully known why so many refused the use of their names. It is known the unions went to the signers and talked to them about the issue and many asked that their names be removed. Fear of injury to self or property motivated others to withdraw from active support. There were stories alleging damage to automobiles, especially those carrying stickers for the initiative. One man was hit in the nose for distributing literature at a booth on the main street of an inland city. Many threatening "crank calls" were received by the office of the advertising executive.

The executive wrote to trade associations and chambers of commerce seeking support. They often promised financial support but refused to give their official backing. Eventually, 1200 campaign contributions were received, but only 11 contributors permitted the use of their names. An organization called Job Research, Inc. was set up to prepare literature for distribution. The advertising executive proceeded to seek names for a petition. Lacking workers to carry petitions, he resorted to a direct mailing of 800,000 petitions, hoping for a 10 percent return. The return was 64,000 (8 percent), a sufficient number of names to place the initiative on the ballot.

The unions organized to fight its passage. They believed it would take their fullest effort to defeat the measure. Twenty years earlier such a measure had almost passed; they were aware that the Job Research survey had shown majority sentiment for the measure; and they knew that many farmers and business groups would offer strong support for its passage. The city's central labor council set up a special committee and assigned one of its leading officers to direct the campaign. Funds were solicited from individual unions and from internationals. It is alleged each side had a minimum of $175,000 to spend. The union released its officers to give full or part time to the political fight against the initiative. State laws prohibit the use of funds from outside the state in campaigns for state legislation. Each side, however, claimed the other was drawing funds from outside sources. Whatever the facts, both the unions and the

Job Research organization spent large sums on television and newspaper publicity. Informants believe that at least a half million dollars went into the campaign.

Meanwhile, the various political candidates were urged to express their views. All major candidates said they opposed the initiative. The unions rented the armory in the largest city of the state and asked all of the leading candidates to speak out on a radio-television broadcast against the initiative. A professor at a Catholic college was given a prominent place on the speaking panel. The Catholic Church put itself on public record through its archbishop as being soundly opposed to the initiative, and one local priest, with the approval of the Catholic Church, wrote a very scholarly pamphlet with the title: *Right to Work Laws: Public Federal Frauds.* This was widely circulated by a union committee. Job Research, Inc. retaliated with a book written by a Notre Dame professor condemning the closed shop. It was believed that the position of the Catholic Church would be nullified as it commonly was by the position of the Masonic organization.

As the day of election approached, Job Research, Inc. had a very active publicity campaign in operation, but it had no influential spokesman. A Right-to-Work Committee made up of small employers, managers, clerical workers, and housewives was the only group that provided some spokesmen who publicly argued for the initiative. There was evidence that the farmers were going to give strong support, but labor was going to give stronger opposition. Influential labor leaders, political leaders, and a few religious leaders had spoken publicly and solidly against the initiative.

The initiative was to be voted on by the eligible voters of the entire state, but in this research study the test of the theory of issue outcome was restricted to the vote cast in Seattle.

Factors in the Right-to-Work Issue in Seattle

The factors as they were set before the vote on the right-to-work issue are designated for the vote in Seattle only.

Factor 1. Critically activated parts of the institutional power structure

Parts of the power structure involved

Political organizations, business and professional persons, labor, religion.

Substance of issue by values involved

For union leaders and members: power of unions.

To employers: greater employer freedom in employment and collective bargaining.

To professional and white collar groups: threat of higher prices and growth of union power.

Level of issue by values involved

Exceedingly important to labor unions, which believe their present bargaining power may be placed in jeopardy.

Many business people would like to reduce the power of unions as it resides in control of the available work supply and in the bargaining strength inherent in the union or closed shop. Many employers are satisfied with present conditions and believe that labor trouble would result from the passage of the initiative.

A professional-white collar segment believes that unions are now too powerful and that they threaten to hike wage rates out of proportion to their own real earnings.

The Catholic Church is responding to the needs and wishes of many who belong to its faith—a large group of workers are Catholic. The church has defined the issue as a moral one.

The Democratic party gains large support from workers and takes a strong negative stand. Democratic candidates are solidly in opposition and look upon the presence of the initiative on the ballot as helping to bring out a large labor vote.

The Republican party equivocates. It expresses the division of business and conservative interests. Leading political candidates needing labor votes are in opposition and are vocal.

Factor 2. *Power arrangements of community power complex*
Labor

All labor groups are solidly against the initiative. It is agreed that labor is spending a minimum of $175,000 to fight the initiative. Internationals have helped with contributions. The Central Labor Council Committee is the center of funds and leadership. The Democratic party is working in close relationship with the labor unions in a mutual desire to get out the largest possible labor vote. The Catholic Church is offering direct public support by providing moral support, speakers, and literature.

Business and professional

Job Research, Inc. was organized as a corporation in September, 1954 to assemble information on the actual experience of labor and industry under right-to-work legislation. This corporation is the major source of funds for the passage of the initiative, having received over 1200 individual contributions. Some large firms are

known to be among the contributors, but none has officially en-
dorsed the initiative.

The Right-to-Work Committee is made up of small businessmen,
managers, professional-clerical workers, and some dissident labor
members. It has about 1400 members in the state. However, the
members in the city willing to lend their names include only three
small business employers and four managers of small firms. Only
one of them has spoken to a public meeting.

Management and employers are in no sense agreed that right-
to-work legislation is desirable. Many employers report they are
satisfied with the status quo and are not supporting any attempt to
change it. Many employers fail to support the initiative with direct
action because they fear reprisals from organized labor. Major
groups such as the employer organizations refuse to take a stand in
support of the initiative because their membership is divided regarding the issue.

The failure of top influentials to commit themselves has forced
the advertising executive, against his own wishes, to assume active
leadership of the right-to-work advocates. He regards himself as a
professional man providing an advertising service to a client and
wishes to play no other role.

The power arrangement of the community power complex on the pro
side of the issue is shown to be of an unstructured type; on the opposing
side, the arrangement is shown to be of a semistructured type in which
organized labor, the Democratic party, and the Catholic Church are
working in close cooperation; other groups against the measure are acting independently. Some Protestant church groups are giving private
support.

Factor 3. *Solidarity of the top influentials*

The overall model which fits the community top influentials is
that of a fluid group of influentials who are widely split over their
support and their roles in reference to the issue.

The top influentials who are supporting the initiative are not
taking an active part in promoting the issue. Many are contributing
very quietly; some are making contributions under the names of
other people; a few have released the time of their middle management to work for the issue. No top influentials are actively working
or speaking for the measure. As one political writer told us, the attitude of the top influentials is expressed in the phrase, "We will hold
the coat of the advertising executive, but it's his fight."

The top influentials of the opposition are active and vocal. They represent but a small part of the fluid corps of top influentials, but they come from labor unions, the political candidates, lawyers, and the Catholic Church.

APPLYING WEIGHTS TO PREDICTION FACTORS

1. Apply weights for the critically activated parts of the institutional power structure.

For the initiative	Points	Against the initiative	Points
Business owners & managers (as represented by Job Research, Inc.)	1	Organized labor (as represented by the Central Labor Council)	1
Professional, white collar, dissident labor, large and small business (as represented by Right-to-Work Committee)	1	Democratic party (as represented by the party organization and candidates)	1
		Catholic Church (as represented by the archbishop, priests, and members)	1
Total points for institutional power structure	= 2		= 3

2. Type of community power arrangement

Type A. *Unstructured*		Type B. *Semistructured*	
Organizations × weight for type		Organizations × weight for type	
2 × 1		3 × 2	
Total community power structure	= 2	Total community power complex	= 6

3. Solidarity of top influentials

Supportive by funds but inactive in campaign: add	1	Active as spokesmen and leaders in campaign: add	2
Final total of prediction points = 5		Final total of prediction points = 11	

Ratio of support 5:11 (or, 31 percent for; 69 percent against)
Prediction: Defeat for the initiative.

Validation and Evaluation of Prediction Theory

I DID MAKE A VOTING PREDICTION the day before election. Taking into account the electorate represented by the institutional power structure, the type of community power arrangement, and the role of the top influentials, I predicted a heavy vote in Seattle against the initiative, with 60–65 percent against and 35–40 percent for. The actual vote in the city was 67 percent against and 33 percent for the initiative. The issue outcome was correctly predicted. A favorable test of the theory had been demonstrated.

The theory stated here attempts to account for the major influences which bring about an outcome of issues which call for a community decision. The prediction test made in this initial study is probatory evidence that the theory is sound.

It must not be assumed that the theory and the prediction test can supplant public opinion polling. Public opinion polling can make more accurate estimates of the voting percentage. All that the theory of issue outcome attempts is a prediction of passage or defeat of an issue. The weights used in the prediction index are arbitrary and are valid to the extent that they reflect the accumulated influences which bring about a decision. The importance of the theory rests upon its ability to provide an understanding of the community power structure and the decision-making processes within a community. The theory is based on the assumption that the central community power structure is an accurate indicator of the influential forces which are operating to produce a particular decision and that these forces will be reflected in the decision which a community makes on any issue of central concern. It is further assumed that this decision will be accurately reflected whether the decision is made by the voters, the city council, or any public body representative of the community.

Further Validation of the Prediction Theory: Denver

ROBERT C. HANSON applied the prediction theory to two issues in Denver, Colorado in 1958 after refining the methodology to give it a sharper and more rigorous focus. His operational measures provide a much more standardized and reliable treatment. His description of his work follows.[3]

A theory of issue outcome in community decision making formulated by Delbert C. Miller and William H. Form was subjected to an initial test in the November election of 1956, when Miller correctly predicted the outcome of voting for and against a "right to work" initiative in Seattle, Washington. The appearance on the State ballot of a right to work amendment proposal in the November 4, 1958 elections in Colorado provided an excellent opportunity for an independent prediction test of the Miller-Form theory in Denver, where this issue has aroused a high level of interest, publicity, and pre-election activity.

Miller claimed only that the theory of issue outcome would predict passage or defeat of an issue. The model used cannot supplant public opinion polling in arriving at accurate estimates of voting percentages in public elections. In the Seattle case, however, Miller's pre-election analysis yielded a prediction of 31 per cent for and 69 per cent against the right to work initiative. The actual returns were 33 per cent for and 67 per cent against. Such a favorable outcome of the test suggests at least the possibility that, *for certain purposes and under certain conditions,* the Miller-Form model may yield sufficiently accurate quantitative as well as qualitative predictions to justify its use rather than the far more expensive and time consuming public opinion polling procedures. For example, it may be useful for predicting outcome when settlement of the issue involves no public vote, or when very accurate percentage figures are not the most important goal of the study, or when the researcher cannot conduct a public opinion poll because of lack of resources. Yet, as Miller stresses, the major significance of the model rests upon its ability to provide a test of the researcher's knowledge and understanding of the community power structure and the decision making processes within the community. . . .

A SPECIFICATION OF THE FACTORS IN THE MILLER-FORM THEORY

Although Miller provides nominal definitions of the relevant theoretical factors and describes the weighting system to be used when factor values have been determined, he does not specify the procedures to be used in obtaining the data necessary to yield particular values for the factors in the theory. The problem we faced, then, was how to operationalize the concepts in the Miller-Form theory. The solution adopted was to construct a structured interview schedule to be administered to strategically located persons in the subject community who would presumably know the issue situation in their sector and in the community in general. The consensus of their answers to specific questions would provide the basis for the assignment of values to the factors of the theory. The result would be a replicable method for making factor value decisions in using the theory to predict issue outcome.

The twelve sectors named by Miller in his definition of critically activated parts of the institutional power structure were accepted as those which, on one issue or another, may become critically activated. Three presumably knowledgeable persons from each sector (three representing business, three in the field of labor, and so on—a total of 36) were interviewed during the week prior to the election.[4]

The critically activated parts of the institutional power structure. Each respondent was handed a sheet which named and indicated briefly the scope of each of the sectors. (The "political parties" sector was divided into two parts—Republican and Democrat.) Also on the page were the two questions designed to determine, first, the level of intensity of the issue for each sector—the degree of importance of the issue for a sector; and, second, if "important" or "very important," the stand of the sector—for, against, or split on the issue. As they appeared on the page the items were as follows:

Degree of importance for sector interests:
  a. not important—that is, not important enough for their interests to engage in pre-election activity.
  b. important—that is, important enough to engage in at least some pre-election activity.
  c. very important—that is, so important that intensive pre-election activity is necessary.

If important or very important, the stand of the groups involved:
  a. practically all are for the amendment.
  b. a majority are for the amendment.
  c. they are split—about half for and half against.
  d. a majority are against the amendment.
  e. practically all are against the amendment.

Each respondent was asked to estimate the degree of importance of the issue for each sector, and to answer the follow-up question if warranted by the previous response.[5] A summary of the responses of the 36 informants to the degree of importance question in the right to work amendment is presented in Table 23. The outcome of the "stand" question for each activated sector is summarized in Table 26.

TABLE 23.   *Summary of Responses to Questions Determining Critical Activation of Institutional Sectors: Right to Work Issue*

INSTITUTIONAL SECTOR	RESPONSES			
	Not Important	Important	Very Important	Don't Know
Business	1	15	20	0
Labor	0	1	35	0
Mass Communications	2	17	16	1
Religion	17	14	4	1
Welfare	15	13	4	4
Society	11	18	5	2
Independent Professionals	15	20	1	0
Education	13	18	4	1
Recreation	26	6	1	3
Cultural Groups	25	10	0	1
Republican Party	1	15	19	1
Democratic Party	0	9	27	0
Government	5	16	13	2

N = 36

The power arrangement type. The "power arrangement of the community power complex" on either side of the issue was determined by the concensus of responses to the following questions:

Now we are interested in your estimate of the degree of cooperation among those groups and individuals who are working for or against the amendment.

Thinking only of the groups which are *against* the right to work amendment, which of the following arrangements best describes the situation as you see it?

   a. The groups which are against the right to work amendment are going it alone, that is to say, there is little cooperation among them.

   b. Some of the important groups are cooperating, but others have remained independent.

   c. Practically all of the important groups and individuals are united and share resources and leadership in their efforts to defeat the amendment proposal.

What about the different groups of people who are *for* the right to work amendment? Are they working independently, or is there some cooperation, or are they united in their activities for the passage of the amendment?

A summary of the responses to these questions is shown in Table 24.

TABLE **24.** *Summary of Responses to Questions Determining Power Arrangement of the Community Power Complex: Right to Work Issue*

POWER ARRANGEMENT TYPE	For the Amendment	Against the Amendment
Independent (unstructured)	5	0
Some Cooperation (semi-structured)	18	5
United (unified coalition)	13	30
Don't Know	0	1
TOTAL	36	36

Note that the modal categories indicate a united effort against the amendment, but only a semi-structured arrangement for the right to work amendment.

The solidarity and activity of top influentials. Solidarity among top influentials was determined by a modal response to the following question:

Now we would like you to consider only the top 40 or 50 community leaders in Denver. Which of these four alternatives is the case?

   a. All of the top leaders here are for the right to work amendment. (Ask follow-up A only.)

   b. All of the top leaders here are against the right to work amendment. (Ask follow-up B only.)

   c. There is a split among top leaders on this issue. (Ask both A and B.)

   d. None of the top leaders have taken a stand on this issue. (Skip both A and B.)

Depending on the response to this question, two follow-up questions were asked to yield estimates of top influential *activity* for and against the amendment proposal:

A. Among the top leaders who are *for* the right to work amendment, which best describes their degree of supporting activity for the amendment?
   1. Leaders who are for the right to work amendment are *not* supporting it at all.
   2. They are supporting it with contributions, but most of them are not making speeches or publicly demonstrating support.
   3. As a whole, they are supporting it very actively with contributions, speeches, and public appearances.
B. Among the top leaders who are *against* the right to work amendment, would you say that they:
   1. are not fighting it at all.
   2. are only giving contributions, but are not publicly active.
   3. are very active with contributions, speeches, and public appearances.

The summary of responses to the questions concerning the solidarity and activity of top influentials is presented in Table 25. Note again the

TABLE **25.** *Summary of Responses to Questions Determining the Solidarity and Activity of Top Influentials: Right to Work Issue*

SOLIDARITY	Responses	Activity	For	Against
All for	0	Inactive	1	3
All against	1	Supportive	27	4
Split	33	Active	3	27
Uncommitted	2	Don't Know*	5	2
TOTAL	36		36	36

* Or not relevant because of answer to the solidarity question.

consensus of respondents on the greater activity of top leaders against the right to work amendment.

Weighting and analysis of the data, and the prediction. The following weighting system, described and employed by Miller, was used: (1) Each critically activated sector received a value of 1, for or against (or 0 if split, because of cancellation of effect). These weights represent the independent influence of each activated part. (2) Multiplier weights of 1 for unstructured, 2 for semi-structured, and 3 for the unified coalition power arrangement type, on each side of the issue, were assigned, and these weights were used to multiply the pro and con total of the activated sectors. The resulting values represent "the interactive, reinforcing influence of organizations in extending the range of attitude formation and increasing intensity of opinion brought to bear upon the issue." (3) The influence of top influential activity—2 for active, 1 for supportive, 0 for inactive—was added. (4) The final total on each side of the issue—the sum of the critically activated parts, plus the result of the power arrangement type multiplication, plus the top influential activity value—represents the summation of influential forces affecting issue outcome. The outcome was predicted according to the ratio of contending forces.

In our analysis of the data to determine critical activation of sectors, two alternative cutting points were used. Under the more stringent interpretation of activation (Plan I in Table 26), eighteen or more of the re-

TABLE 26. *Summary Table Demonstrating Sector Critical Activation under Two Analysis Plans,*° *Weighting Procedures, and Prediction Ratios Compared with Actual Outcome*

COMMUNITY SECTORS	Not Activated		Split		Activated For		Activated Against	
	I	II	I	II	I	II	I	II
Business					1	1		
Labor							1	1
Mass Communications	0							1
Religion	0							1
Welfare	0							1
Society	0					1		
Independent Professions	0		×					
Education	0		×					
Recreation	0	0						
Cultural Groups	0	0						
Political Parties: Republican					1	1		
Democrat							1	1
Government	0		╲	×				
TOTALS					2	3	2	5

Power Arrangement Type		For		Against	
Unstructured (1)					
Semi-structured (2)		2	2		
Unified coalition (3)				3	3
Summary (power arrangement type × activated sectors)		4	6	6	15
Top Influential Activity					
Inactive (0)					
Supportive (1)		1	1		
Active (2)				2	2
Final Summary (critically activated sector Totals plus power arrangement type Summary plus top influential activity)		7	10	10	22

Ratios and Predictive Percentages	Actual Outcome
Plan I: 7:10 for, or 41 percent for, 59 percent against	For: 56,115 or 34.2 percent
	Against: 108,259 or 65.8 percent
Plan II: 10:22 for, or 31 percent for, 69 percent against	

°Plan I: critical activation—18 or more "very important" responses.
Plan II: critical activation—unless 18 or more "not important" responses.

spondents must have termed the issue "very important" for the interests of the sector.[6] The stand of the sector for or against the issue was determined by inspection of the predominance of responses (collapsing a and b *versus* d and e responses) in the stand question. At least twelve of the 36 respondents must have judged a sector "split" or a clearly bi-modal distribution must have been observed before the split designation of a sector's stand was accepted.[7] Under the more liberal interpretation of critical activation (Plan II in Table 26), a sector was accepted as activated *unless* eighteen or more respondents judged the issue "not important" for a sector's interests.

The designation of the values for type of power arrangement and for top influential activity factors was determined by the modal category of responses on the question inquiring about these variables.

These alternative procedures produced two final ratios, both predicting defeat of the right to work amendment proposal. The more stringent Plan I yielded a predictive percentage of 59 percent against the proposal; the more liberal Plan II percentage was 69 percent against. The actual percentage of the vote against the right to work amendment proposal in Denver was 65.8 percent, a figure bracketed in by our estimates.[8]

A summary of these procedures, the predictions and the actual outcome on the issue is presented in Table 26.

THE CIVIL SERVICE AMENDMENT PROPOSAL

Miller proposed that the predictive model would be valid when the community was highly activated on "an issue of great concern." In order to try to gain some knowledge about the validity of the model over a wider range of issues, an issue of less community concern was included in the test. The issue selected was a civil service amendment proposal which had aroused much less general interest and pre-election activity in Denver than the right to work proposal.[9]

Using the procedures described above, the following results were obtained. Under Plan I, only Government was critically activated, but it was "split" leaving zeros as totals on the critically activated parts factor. Although the power arrangement type values differed (semi-structured *for*, unstructured *against*), the multiplication technique resulted in zero summaries. Finally, the modal response on the top influential activity question was "inactive," or zeros on both sides of the issue. Consequently, the ratio of contending forces amounted to 0:0, or 50/50. Under Plan II, no sectors were activated against. Welfare, Republican Party, and Government were split. Four sectors were critically activated for: Labor, Mass communication, Education, and Democratic Party. Multiplying 4 by the semi-structured power arrangement type weight 2 yielded 8 for to 0 against. Hence our prediction was that the civil service amendment would pass, but the percentage prediction range was as wide as possible—from 50 to 100 percent.

97

Although the civil service amendment proposal failed to pass in the state as a whole, the actual outcome in Denver was 54 percent for and 46 percent against. Again our prediction bracketed in the result. The wide range of the prediction estimate may be interpreted as a consequence of this procedure when the issue arouses relatively little concern. When our confidence in the data decreases it is appropriate that the predictive range of estimates increases. The greater number of "don't know" responses on the civil service questions also supports this interpretation.[10]

Research Assessment

THE PREDICTION OF ISSUE OUTCOME is an important validity test. It provides evidence for the efficacy of the system model of community power structures. All the important factors of the model are part of the prediction theory. It is not important to the community power researcher to predict a percentage for or against an issue. Public opinion polling would seem to be a more appropriate technique for predicting the outcome of public issues and the record of scientific polling is impressive. What the community power researcher wants to know is whether he has isolated the principal factors which generate the influencing forces. If these same factors—(1) critically activated parts of the institutional power structure, (2) the power arrangement of the community power complex, and (3) the solidarity of top influentials–can predict accurate percentage results for highly controversial public issues, then the theory and its validity would be enhanced. However, a number of research problems are present and Hanson has described them succinctly:

A mark for the validity of the Miller-Form theory of issue outcome is the fact that it has been successfully tested independently under different operational procedures. But both tests occurred in large cities and state capitals, and in both cases the outcome on the same kind of issue (the right to work amendment proposal) was decided on the basis of a public election.[11] Evidence from the Denver study on the civil service amendment proposal indicates that less confidence should be placed in a prediction obtained from an application model of the theory when the issue does not arouse a high level of community interest and activity.

Perhaps the major practical research problem is to establish a generally applicable and replicable method for determining sector activation and weighting. Sector definitions should be refined and standardized for different sizes and types of communities, and a theoretically based rationale for whatever weighting system is adopted should be formulated. A procedure for establishing the relative power rank of the sectors, for example, might be developed which could be applied when values are assigned to activated sectors.

Different kinds of situations concerning community issues may require different types of application models. For example, predictive tests of issue outcome might be attempted for cases in which public elections do not determine the outcomes. The problem of establishing the minimum number of respondents needed to secure adequate and reliable information under different situations also calls for exploration. Finally, whether the model is sensitive enough to detect changes in sentiment as an issue approaches its climax is not known at present. As in political polling, a prediction based on the model must assume no significant changes in force alignments between the time of the prediction and the actual outcome.

While it is obvious that application models of the Miller-Form theory rest upon assumptions about the adequacy of information from a small number of respondents, and also upon arbitrary weighting procedures, it is equally apparent that if prediction models consistently "work" they must be tapping real community forces affecting community decisions.

It has been noted that the theory, in effect, ignores the fact or probability of interdependence among the sectors it analyzes as independent "parts" for the purpose of making a prediction. But there is no reason why sector interdependencies cannot be investigated with the present model. It is conceivable that in a given community, certain parts *always* become activated and stand together in the same way, regardless of the issue. Perhaps more probable is a regularity of pattern among certain sectors which vary with the type of issue. On economic issues, for example, one pattern of relationship among sectors may persist, while another may show itself on educational issues. Postulated sector relationship patterns of this kind would likely vary with different types of communities. Clearly, it would require an intensive program of longitudinal and comparative community research to establish such regularities. Moreover, to account for variations in regularities observed in different types of communities demands a more powerful theory of community structure and community decision making than we have available at present.[12]

PART III

---

*Comparative Analysis of
the Latin American Cities:
Cordoba, Argentina
& Lima, Peru*

THE DISTINCTIVE CHARACTERS OF CORDOBA AND LIMA *reflect in a number of ways the political instability of Argentina and Peru just as Seattle and Bristol mirror the political stability of the United States and Great Britain. Although the two Latin American cities are many decades behind the two Western cities in economic development, the economic bases of the four cities are more similar than different. While industrialization is creating homogeneity of culture in large Latin American and Western cities, deep-seated forces of cultural and racial diversity continually change expected behavior in each of them. The differences are sometimes large and obvious, but at other times they are so subtle and concealed as to challenge all efforts at explanation.*

The studies of Cordoba and Lima applied the same basic methods used in the other cities, but more attention was given to the institutional bases of the cities and more intensive analyses of leaders and their interlinkages were undertaken. In Cordoba the community power perspectives of North American executives in the largest automobile manufacturing plant are examined; in Lima special attention is given to the decision-making cliques and power blocs.

CHAPTER 8

CORDOBA AND LIMA: *The Research Setting*

Cordoba was selected for study to fit into the research design that now included Seattle, Bristol, and Atlanta. The Argentine city promised to provide some unique institutional differences. When studied in 1963 it had been under control of a military government for more than a year. The city's mayor-council system had been abolished and a civilian Interventor was governing by appointment of the national military junta. Other local government offices were functioning normally and both national and local elections were held during the period of study. The dominance of military power provided an important new independent factor. Military control, often alternating with democratic governments, occurs so frequently in Latin America as to be a traditional form of governing. Cordoba's 500-year-old history illustrates this pattern. Roman Catholicism is the state religion and the Catholic Church is known to be a most influential institution. The universities have played a long and historic role in the life of the city. The state university was celebrating its 350th year at the time of this study. The Catholic university was growing in size and prestige. Large landholders and a group of wealthy manufacturers and merchants composed the economic sector of the city. Long a commercial center, the city was in the process of rapid industrialization. Since 1945 it had become a leading airplane and automobile manufacturing center with nationalized, private, and foreign ownership—a truly diversified industrial city.

The opportunity to study Lima during 1965–66 opened up the possibility of making a comparative study of two important Latin American cities. Since Lima is also the capital city of Peru, it offered some unique features of social structure. It was the capital of Colonial Spain from which all Spanish possessions were governed for more than 250 years. Many large landholdings have been in the same families since the original grants from the kings of Spain, and an old family elite group holds land and social prestige. Like Cordoba, Lima is experiencing rapid industrialization and at the time of the study was welcoming new assembly plants of Ford, General Motors, Chrysler, and European producers of automobiles. A partial listing of American firms shows 265 wholly American-owned companies operating in Peru, and more than 50 others show a majority ownership by North Americans. Most of these are located in Lima or have their headquarters there.

Lima is one of the most rapidly growing cities of the world, increasing from 520,000 in 1940 to more than 2,000,000 in 1965. The prediction is that this population will double by 1980. Surrounding the city is a ring of barriadas in which an estimated 800,000 people live in little more than huts, some made of grass mats and others of salvaged brick and wood. Most of these people are Indians and Mestizos who come from the farms of the Sierras which cannot support the growing population in that region. The problem of assimilating this agriculturally based, poorly educated group strains the city institutions to the breaking point. Jobs, housing, water and sewage facilities, streets, transportation, police and fire protection, and schools are inadequate, and the quality of service steadily declines while great efforts are made to meet the ever-increasing demands.

The study of the power structure of Lima presented unusual challenges—and was fraught with difficulties. To my knowledge no national capital had been studied previously by modern power structure techniques. The city exhibits highly centralized governmental features arising from its historical traditions and its position as the capital. It is the largest and most important economic center of the nation. There is a direct interrelationship between its own community power structure and the national power structure of Peru, thus making it extremely difficult to draw a line demarking national government from city government although each has formal bodies for administrative, legislative, and judicial functions. Most of the national political and governmental leaders live in Lima, and their decisions usually have the greatest significance for both the city and nation. Their presence nourished the slogan, "Lima is Peru and Peru is Lima."

In Lima, as in Cordoba, the military organization is relatively strong, Roman Catholicism is the state religion, and the oldest university (San Marcos) stands beside many new and rapidly growing universities in the city. But unlike Cordoba, which was under a military government at the time of the study, Lima had a democratic form of urban and national government. Political power was splintered; APRA, the largest party, was not formally in power but had formed a coalition with the Odrista party, giving it greater voting power than the opposing coalition of the Popular Action and Christian Democratic parties represented by the mayor of Lima and the President of Peru. Thus legislative and executive groups faced each other as political opposites. Cabinet members changed frequently (the President in effect was working with his third cabinet in four years) as a result of disagreement over policies.

In summary, in comparing Cordoba and Lima we find their patterns of government power strikingly different. In Cordoba (1963) a military junta exercised supreme power over the municipal government, in contrast with Lima (1965–66), where democracy was operating within a highly divisive political party system. Yet the similarities between the two cities make them easily recognizable products of a Latin American civilization and of industrializing influences. Each has nurtured a large landholding group, become a commercial center, gained independence from Spanish rule, oriented itself toward democratic goals, and become an industrial center. Both cities live in political atmospheres that are precariously balanced between democracy and dictatorship. The military junta is always an imminent force. On June 28, 1966 the military junta again resumed power in Argentina, deposing President Arturo Illia. In Peru, President Fernando Belaúnde Terry won the elections in 1963 and the support of the military junta after it had deposed former President Manuel Prado. Five years later the military gave Belaúnde the same treatment by marching to the presidential palace and removing him.

Richard Patch, the American Universities Field Staff observer in Peru during the regime of the military junta in 1962, made a statement regarding Peru which applies equally to Argentina:

> The situation in Peru may be very disappointing to observers in the United States, certainly to those who interpreted the demise of Getúlio Vargas, the fall of Perón, Batista Perez Jimenez, and Rojas Pinilla, the moderation of Odría, and the death of Trujillo as evidence of a new flowering of democracy in Latin America. That the end of a dictatorship is not the firm foundation for democracy has been amply demonstrated in Cuba, Brazil, and Argentina—and while developments in Peru are a disappointment, they cannot be called surprising. Rather, what is surprising, is that democracy is working in so many Latin American countries which are walking the knife edge between social change and economic order. The

high hopes engendered by the Alliance for Progress must not dull North American realization that the way to functioning democracy in most of the Latin American countries is long and hard with many twistings. The slips backward are not all the fault of small groups of cynical men intent on avoiding a plain and easy path, and their slips will not be remedied by hasty diplomatic and economic chastisement. Latin American countries are still the intellectual and psychological descendants of Spain and Portugal, and this the Alliance for Progress will not change.[1]

It is not our intent, however, to concern ourselves with current events or political tides in either Argentina or Peru. It is important to establish the distinctive character of the two Latin American cities as they contrast with the American and British cities already studied. The economic development of Seattle and Bristol is far more advanced than that of Cordoba and Lima, but there are many similarities in the economic bases of all these cities. Industrialization is weaving a common pattern, and their economic, political, and social life increasingly reflects the recognizable industrial composition of owners, managers, professional and white-collar workers, and manual workers.

NEW RESEARCH CHALLENGES

THE STUDY OF CORDOBA marked an important new step in the research program. Not a single community power structure study of a South American country existed to provide guidance. Two studies report on Ciudad Juarez[2] and Tijuana, Mexico,[3] both near the United States border. Many anthropological studies like Andrew H. Whiteford's *Two Cities of Latin America*[4] are very useful in background materials but do not give appropriate research examples for a community power researcher. Indeed, urban studies of any kind in Latin America are in short supply.[5] Whiteford writes: "Our ignorance of the urban societies of Latin America is almost as great now [1960] as it was ten years ago when the Committee on Latin America of the National Research Council recognized it as a major deficiency in the research and understanding of the area."[6]

In community power research there now exist a field study of San Cristóbal, Venezuela conducted in 1964 by Gary Hoskin[7] and a documentary study by José Lius de Imaz which analyzes leadership backgrounds of the Argentine national ministers, province governers, highest officials of the armed forces, highest leaders of the Catholic Church, and directors of the largest businesses, political parties, and labor organizations.[8] Apart from these studies only a few isolated, often unpublished studies of the military, the church, and political parties may be found. Not much to go on!

The researcher is breaking into new research sites in Latin America, and there is promise and danger. The promise is that new comparative knowledge can be gained; the danger is that it will not be possible to complete a study of power. Pitfalls abound, not the least of them being a growing suspicion that United States researchers are serving the Central Intelligence Agency, the Department of Defense, or simply a foreign "imperialist" country—the economic, military "Colossus of the North." However, these difficulties can challenge, especially if new opportunities are available. The American researcher finds new patterns of institutions in Latin America—patterns never seen in the United States. And always at any given stage new research opportunities emerge from growing research progress. Sociologists and political scientists are continually offering substantial contributions in theory and method.

The test hypothesis for Cordoba and Lima states that the community power structure is a social system with business, military, religious, and political leaders dominating as key influentials at the apex of the structure. The hypothesis grew out of observations made by Latin American scholars and writers. Most of these observers have stressed that those in power are the military, the landowners, and the Roman Catholic Church. Some add political and governmental leaders. Others name industrialists, bankers, and newspaper publishers. A few believe foreign capitalists hold the true reins of economic and political power. Still others say United States government leaders are the real influentials who make the difference in the policies carried out in Latin America since decisions on prices, loans, and investments are made between United States and Latin American governments. These observations are seldom buttressed by a body of verifiable scientific evidence. The scientific study of national and community power structures in Latin America is almost unknown. Yet there seems to be substantial agreement that concentrated and conservative power is shared by the military, business, and landholding groups, the Catholic Church, and the political leaders in power. There is fairly high agreement that government is a subordinate handmaiden to all of the conservative forces. Others say that the military and the church are pawns of the large landowners. The challenge to find the "truth" about these assertions regarding power is compelling. A community power analysis must search for the prevailing power forces, although the difficulties in the Latin American situation are myriad. The focus on a city rather than the nation promised to make the research manageable. Upon this assumption, the hypothesis set out for test what most observers held as fact.

CHAPTER 9

CORDOBA, ARGENTINA
UNDER THE MILITARY JUNTA*

IN 1963 CORDOBA, and indeed all of Argentina, was living under a military government. The military had been in power since the day in 1962 when President Arturo Frondizi had been placed under house arrest because he tried to reincorporate the Peronistas into the political life of the community. The military government had promised general elections in July. There were hopes for peaceful elections, but tension ran high. The Peronistas had been forbidden the right to place their party candidates on the ballot. This denial infuriated the Peronista leaders, and the full police power of the state was brought into protective posture. Army, policy, and firemen were mobilized into a tight pattern of surveillance. An uprising was expected daily. The field work for this study was conducted during these tense days.[1]

Method

IN THE CORDOBA STUDY, care was taken to employ all three of the major approaches to leadership identification—positional, reputational, and a modified issue approach. A positional technique was first carried out. The identification of the most important positions of influence provided a means of discovering whether a standardized schedule of positions

* This study has been published in the Spanish language under the title *De la Industria al Poder*, by Delbert C. Miller, Juan Carlos Agulla, and Eva Chamorro (Ediciones Libera, Buenos Aires, 1966). This chapter is the first published report in English.

could be used for both Western and Latin American cities. It also served to give initial training to a group of 19 Argentine graduate students who served as research associates for the study.[2] The positional identification was followed by a reputational technique seeking nominations of the most influential leaders, organizations, and institutional sectors in city and nation. These nominations were sought to identify generalized leaders ("those who would be most influential in getting things done when projects or issues of general concern to the community were to be carried out or resolved"), specialized leaders ("those who could best represent the interests of their group, bankers, clergy, etc., if they needed to get a project completed or an issue presented"), situational leaders ("those who would be most influential if (a) an economic crisis threatened the community, (b) political influence was needed, or (c) a welfare project was to be supported"). A modified issue approach was also utilized. Important issues and projects were identified and all respondents were asked about those in which they had taken a part and what persons they knew who had also taken a leading part in working for or against the issue or project. These three techniques enabled the researchers to secure much evidence for the appropriate leadership role and influences exerted by those who were identified as top influentials.

Extensive newspaper analysis was employed to gather validating evidence of the community activity of top influentials. Many informants provided additional information about the behavior of organizations and the history of community issues, and they were particularly helpful in providing answers for some of the questions raised by the data.

For the first time the reputational approach was applied to the identification of the institutional power structure of the communiy and the society by securing power rankings from top influentials. Once the power rankings of institutions had been made, it was possible to ascertain more precisely the nature of the interrelationship of the component parts of the system model of community power structure as discussed in Chapter 1.

This study marked the first time that anyone had seriously grappled with the power of all the institutional segments of the community and tried to understand how labor, church, and the military can be observed to be powerful when they lack top influential leadership. This problem has appeared in many American studies which often report with surprise that no labor leader, no religious leader, and often no political or government leader appeared as a key leader, although labor, the church, and government were often considered very powerful. Issue techniques have begun to reveal the importance of political and governmental leaders, but power in voluntary organizations, industrial firms, government agencies, and other institutional bodies, because of its collective and often emergency nature, is difficult to identify with the methodologies employed. In this research the problem appears and is dealt with by a structural functional analysis of the powerful but nonrepresented institutional sector. Documentary materials and informal knowledge were gathered from appropriate scholars and specialists.

IDENTIFICATION OF POSITIONAL LEADERS. The first task was to identify those positions designated as the most powerful official positions in the city. An expert panel of eight raters was selected; a minimum criterion was that they be thoroughly familiar with the community in at least three different institutional sectors. All eight raters met this criterion on the basis of the formal positions they held. As a collective panel, their individual participation patterns show that they had familiarity with all sectors. These raters included the executive secretary of the largest Catholic welfare society (Catholic Action), the executive secretary of the commercial center, a supreme court judge (also a university dean), a province judge and political party leader, the executive secretary of the chamber of commerce, a labor leader (also a labor attorney), a public relations director, and a community relations director.

The panel's rating, on which there was high consensus, revealed the positions of greatest potential influence in community decision making as shown in Table 27.

TABLE 27. *Schedule of Formal Positions of Highest Potential Influence in Cordoba*

	Positions
Business and Finance	
Presidents (directors) of 3 largest Manufacturing plants	
Industrias Kaiser Argentina, S.A. (automobiles)	1
D.I.N.F.I.A. (state owned and operated airplane factory)	1
Corcemar, S.A. (automobiles)	1
Presidents of 2 largest investment houses	2
Presidents of 3 largest banks	3
Largest real estate owner	1
President or owner of largest hotel	1
Owner of largest cinema	1
President of largest association of businessmen	1
Presidents or owners of 2 largest retail stores	2
	14
Political Party and Government	
Governor of the Province (Federal Interventor)	1
Mayor of Cordoba	1
Immediate past mayor	1

TABLE **27.**—*Continued*

Presidents of 4 largest political parties	
Democratic Party of Cordoba	1
Radical Civic Union Party of Pueblo	1
Intransigent Radical Civic Union Party	1
Popular Union Party	1
	7

Education

Presidents (Rectors) of largest universities	
National University of Cordoba	1
Catholic University of Cordoba	1
President of the Provincial Council of Education	1
National inspector of schools	1
President of the teachers' association	1
	5

Religion

Archbishop of Catholic Church	1
Bishop of Catholic Church	1
Rabbi of Jewish Temple	1
	3

Mass Communication

Publisher of largest newspaper	1
Executive director of largest radio and TV station	1
	2

Society

Presidents of 2 largest social clubs	2
Presidents of 2 largest service clubs (Rotary and Lions)	2
	4

Military

Commanders of locally based army and air corps	
Chief, Third Corps of Army	1
Chief, Air Garrison	1
	2

Independent Professions

Presidents of the professional associations	
Law	1
Medicine	1
Engineering	1
	3

Labor

Director, Provincial Department of Labor	1
General secretaries of 3 largest unions	
Association of white-collar workers	1
Association of metal workers	1
Association of auto workers	1
	4

Welfare (subsumed by the Catholic Church)

The Cordoba leadership schedule listing 44 formal positions having the highest potential influence is not markedly different from the schedule used in Seattle and Bristol. The agreement of the South American judges on these positions indicates that a fairly standardized schedule is possible. Variations are introduced by some characteristic differences in social organization or geography. For example, the multiparty system brings four parties to high importance in Cordoba rather than two as in Seattle and Bristol. The fact that Cordoba is also the political capital of the province of Cordoba makes the governor of the province and some state officials like the director of the provincial department of labor important to the city as well. The same pattern appears in education, where the president of the provincial council of education and the national inspector of schools become important offices in the city. The army and air bases are located in Cordoba because of its central position within the nation. The fact that the state religion is Roman Catholic gives the Catholic Church high importance and the Protestant churches an almost negligible influence. No welfare position of importance exists, partly because the Catholic Church takes responsibility for most welfare activities. The recreation and cultural and artistic sectors failed to secure a top position in community decision making.

With all of these differences it is still true that most of the positions important in Seattle and Bristol are important in Cordoba. There are sufficient parallels between the two schedules to say that an adjustment is needed in only eight positions: the governor of the province, leaders of two additional political parties, two military commanders, and the president of the engineering association must be added; a Protestant leadership position and a top position in social welfare were the significant omissions.

The holders of the 44 official positions in the Cordoba schedule of high potential leadership have been identified and a comparison made between them and the reputational leaders and the issue leaders. Each of these comparisons will be discussed after the report on the identification of reputational and issue leaders that follows.

IDENTIFICATION OF REPUTATIONAL LEADERS. Nominees for top influential persons were assembled from the various institutional sectors: religion, education, government, political parties, social welfare, cultural and artistic, business and finance, military, labor, society and wealth, independent professions, mass communication, and recreation. Lists of influential organizations and salient issues were also assembled. These lists of individuals, groups, and issues were prepared by two or more knowledgeable persons selected as the informants for each institutional sector. Then, the expert panel of eight judges made rankings of the most influential persons. Those persons receiving the highest number of nominations were chosen as the top influentials for subsequent interviewing. The public relations and community relations directors (both Argentines) of a large American-owned factory in Cordoba had an elaborate file of community influentials which was used to check the final list.

A total of 210 top influential nominees and 57 organizations were rated for their influence. From these, 37 top influentials and 15 organizations were selected as being most influential in accomplishing things of general concern to the community. The 37 top influentials were found to be associated with all sectors except social welfare (which is almost entirely subsumed by the religious sector), and many of them were identified with two or more sectors.

Interviews were secured with 22 (60 percent) of the top influentials. The respondents represented all the institutional sectors of the city. Fifteen interviews were not obtained because of absence from the city or illness; among these there was only one direct refusal. This single refusal has significance because I was told that the political bias was so strong that every contact would be suspect and that interviewing would be very difficult. All such advance information proved to be incorrect. Letters were sent out to respondents from the Institute of Sociology at the University of Cordoba explaining the study and introducing the Argentine graduate student who was to make the interview. The only difficulties encountered had to do with the frequent absence from the city of top influentials. Also appointments were sometimes not kept with Western punctuality, and students waited hours and even days for appointments to be met. We were to discover that half of these top influentials have two or more positions and lead quite diverse lives.

In Table 28 the top 20 influentials are shown (by fictitious names) according to their reputed rank of influence and are compared with the schedule of official positions previously determined. The comparison seeks to find the correspondence between reputed leaders and the holders of official positions of highest potential influence in community decision making.

The table shows that 10 of the 20 top reputational leaders (50 percent correspondence) hold official positions already identified on our schedule as having high potential influence. This is not to say that the other 10 lack important positions: they are professionals holding high positions in law, education, and engineering; three are vice presidents of businesses and banks. In most cases, they would be considered in the second position of responsibility and authority. Actually, in many cases

TABLE 28. *Comparison of Top 20 Reputational Leaders with Positional Leaders as Shown on the Positional Schedule*

Top influentials by rank of influence	Positional leader as shown on Cordoba schedule	
José Nores	Yes	
Benjamín Orgaz		No
Ramón Novillo	Yes	
Alfredo Rodríguez	Yes	
Hugo Martínez		No
Carlos Allende	Yes	
Félix Ángel	Yes	
Emilio Aguirre	Yes	
Victor Vaca	Yes	
Arturo Toscanini		No
Leandro Manuel	Yes	
Mario Paez		No
Vito Roberto		No
Luis Sánchez		No
Jorge Garzón	Yes	
Ramón Lucrecio	Yes	
Gregorio Remo		No
Armand Sonet		No
Justo Porfilio		No
Pablo Conte		No

they function with a lesser title but exercise the active operating influence in their organizations. A few others of high reputational leadership are owners and managers not listed on the position schedule.[3] It should be understood that in a large metropolis there are literally hundreds of positions which are of high responsibility and authority. Often the difference between a positional leader and a reputational leader is determined by the amount of community activity which potential leaders are willing to give and their ability to function as community leaders. Our informants, the public relations director and the community relations director, used these criteria as they sifted through their own files of over 300 positional leaders. Their independent assessments of the reputational leaders were in close agreement with the nominations of the judges (over 90-percent agreement in each case).

IDENTIFICATION OF ISSUE-DECISIONAL LEADERS. The expert panel of eight judges identified the following as the most salient issues before the community during the previous three years (1960–63): transfer of bus company from municipal ownership to workers' cooperative ownership; transfer of tram company from municipal ownership to workers' cooperative ownership; federal military intervention in the city and province; strike at Kaiser automobile plant; acceptance of new city zoning plan; street illumination; provincial road improvement; bringing television to Cordoba; bringing Eucharistic Congress to Cordoba. The panel was then asked to rank leaders who had been most active in these major issues or in others. The top influentials were then asked to specify their roles in recent issues and to identify all the individuals who participated most actively in either supporting or fighting against recent issues. Leaders were encouraged to think of persons who had veto power and to name such individuals if they were aware that vetoes had been used in any issue context. Forty-nine percent of the top influentials indicated that they had participated in one or more issues.[4]

Table 29 shows the comparison of the key influentials with those

TABLE 29. *Comparison of Key Reputational Leaders and Issue-Decisional Leaders in Cordoba*

Key influentials by rank of influence	Nominations	Issue leaders by rank of influence	Issues	Overlap
José Nores	15	Vito Martinelli	4	No
Benjamín Orgaz	13	Carlos Allende	3	Yes
Ramón Novillo	12	Mario Paez	3	Yes
Alfredo Rodríguez	12	Jorge Fernández	3	No
Hugo Martínez	11	Rudolfo Gonzáles	3	No
Carlos Allende	10	Emilio Aguirre	2	Yes
Félix Ángel	9	José Nores	2	Yes
Emilio Aguirre	8	Christian Indicia	2	No
Victor Vaca	8	Juan Moore	2	No
Arturo Toscanini	7	Jaime Nis	2	No
Leandro Manuel	7	Victor Vaca	2	Yes
Mario Paez	7	Lisardo Bedón	2	No

issue-decisional leaders identified as most active during the previous three years. Five issue leaders appear among the twelve key influentials, or a 42-percent overlap between issue-decisional and reputational leaders. An examination of the issue leaders shows they are primarily political, labor, and governmental leaders. This is significant because it indicates that voluntary organizations do not play a strong role in issue resolution in Cordoba—or, as we shall see, in Lima. In fact, it is expected that issues will be settled by government and the commonly expected channel of resolution is a direct appeal and application of pressure by interested parties to the governmental agency concerned. As was observed in Seattle and Bristol, many issue leaders (meteors) seem to play an important but ephemeral role in community life. This is commonly observed in the role of a mayor whose influence in issues diminishes almost immediately when he leaves office unless he retains influence in his political party.

IDENTIFICATION OF LEADERSHIP TYPES. In order to examine leadership as rigorously as possible, a typology must embrace all levels of power operative in a community power structure. The following typologies combine all the possibilities of leadership identity within the scope of positional, reputational, and issue-decisional levels of power. Seven types of leadership identity can be found:

Leadership identity	Reputational	Issue-decisional	Positional
Type A	×	×	×
Type B	×	×	
Type C	×		×
Type D		×	×
Type E	×		
Type F		×	
Type G			×

A leader of Type A is identifiable as one who exercises power on all three levels. Any one of the three methods of leadership identification will locate him. He can be predicted to be a key influential. All issue leaders of Types A, B, D, or F should be highly visible since issues generally command attention of both leaders and the public at large, and such leaders receive considerable newspaper, radio, TV, and perhaps magazine publicity. The concealed leaders (powerful but unrecognized except by key leaders) are predicted to come from Types C, E, and G. Symbolic leaders (believed more powerful than they really are) are of Type F. They receive attention because of their issue activity but lack other important bases of exerting influence.

The comparisons of leadership types that promise to be the most fruitful are those between reputational and positional and between reputational and issue. We repeat our earlier assertion that reputational leaders represent the best single base for any comparison, and new research is bringing additional validity to this claim.[5] These are leaders whom top influentials define as the most influential. This judgment cannot be taken lightly if one accepts the proposition that top leaders have the most knowledge of community decision-making processes and the people who participate in them. What is always problematic (although not very logical) is whether this judgment is based on actual behavior or merely on hearsay. To find that a reputational leader is also a positional leader gives additional confidence that he has an official base that carries important decision-making authority. That is to say, he has potential power and is reputed to use it in community decision making. Finding that a reputed leader is also an issue leader gives perhaps even greater confidence that the leader is actively involved in decision making and his "reputation" is deserved. Presumably a leader operating simultaneously as a reputed, issue, and positional leader should be accorded the highest confidence. It can be predicted that he will be named a key influential (i.e., in the top 10 or 15 in influence). In this study all three comparisons were made and the results will be reported.

The typology suggests that leadership that poses highly problematic questions is found in Types E, F, and G, where leaders achieve a simple identity as reputed, issue, or positional only. Who these people are and how they exercise influence is another challenging area of study. No research has been conducted on this problem.

In Cordoba four of the leadership types set forth in the typology were identified among the 37 top reputational leaders. The three (8 percent) who are Type A leaders are a newspaper publisher, a powerful political leader, and a holder of a major governmental position. Fifteen (41 percent) are Type B leaders who combine reputational and issue-decisional influence, and 14 (38 percent) are Type C leaders who combine reputational and positional influence. Five (13 percent) are Type E leaders who have reputational influence only. It is evident that reputational leaders generally build their influence on a multiple power base.

Assessment of Methodologies for Identification of Influential Leaders

LEADERS OPERATE WITH DIFFERENT KINDS OF POWER: positional, reputational, and issue. These kinds of power relate to different varieties of decision making that affect the community. We have seen that there is a wide difference in the scope of decision-making influence among leaders. This suggests that the community power researcher has a choice: he can focus on a given issue or area of decision making and eliminate other areas from his consideration as Rossi and Dentler have done in *The Politics of Urban Renewal;* or, he can elect to study community decision making—all decisions, programs, and projects that have a high impact on the life of the community. If he does the latter he must assess the various kinds of power as leaders generate influence by position, repute, or issue participation. He must make a composite judgment of this behavior and interpret the power phenomena which he observes as persons, groups, associations, and institutions function interrelatedly.

We have elected this latter approach. The system model of the community power structure is a framework designed to guide in this direction and will be used to test the hypotheses regarding Cordoba's power structure.

Analysis of the Test Hypothesis

THE COMMUNITY POWER STRUCTURE of Cordoba is composed of five interrelated parts with business, military, religious, and political leaders dominating as key influentials at the apex of the structure.

The reputational method was used to secure an approximation of the institutional power structure of Argentina. Top influentials were asked to rank each of the 13 institutional sectors for their relative strength and influence in getting things done and in influencing the nation when nationwide issues and projects are debated. The rankings in the first column of Table 30 show that the national power structure is believed to .

TABLE 30.   *Rank of Reputed National and Community Influence of Institutional Sectors in Argentina and in Cordoba.*

INSTITUTION	Overall rank in Argentina	Overall rank in Cordoba	Difference in ranks
Military	1	5	−4
Religion	2	1	+1
Business and finance	3	2	−1
Government	4	3	−1
Labor	5	4	+1
Society and wealth	6	9	−3
Political parties	7	8	−1
Independent professions of medicine and engineering	8	10	−2
Education	9	7	+2
Mass communication	10	6	+4
Social welfare	11	12	−1
Culture and art	12	11	+1
Recreation	13	13	0

* Rankings were made in June and July 1963, while Argentina was being governed by the military junta and prior to the national election of August 1963.

give the largest influence to military, religion, business, government, and labor in that order. Three additional expert panels confirmed these judgments with a high degree of agreement. One was composed of selected faculty members from the University, another was composed of the 22 Argentine graduate research associates, and the third was an Argentine organization composed of 30 Argentines who had received university training in the United States. A coefficient of agreement was calculated for the rankings of top influentials and for the three expert panels with a coefficient of .88.[6] This gives high confidence in the agreement among judges and on the relative rank of the institutional sectors in the nation.

The institutionalized power of the community was also assessed using the reputational method. The top influentials ranked each of the institutional sectors for its relative strength and influence in getting things done and in influencing the community when community-wide issues and projects are debated. The second column in Table 30 shows the rankings made for Cordoba. The coefficient of agreement for the top leaders and the three expert panels referred to above is .84. Note that that same five institutional sectors are given highest ranking but the order now is religion, government, business, labor, and military. The influence of the military was rated as lower because the local government at that time was in the hands of civilians and elections were soon to be held. Although democratic processes had been halted, the local administrators were making independent decisions about local problems. Military men were seen only at ceremonies in which they normally participate.

If the rankings are converted into influence units, the institutionalized power structure of the community appears as shown in Figure 10. Such a profile contrasts with Seattle, where business, government, labor, mass communication, and education are reputed to be of most influence in the order named. Military influence is nonexistent in Seattle except in a very indirect manner. Religion has never attained a ranking higher than fifth position in any American city reported in community power research.

The community power complex was ascertained by asking top influentials which of 15 selected organizations are the most important in getting things done and in exerting influence when issues and projects are debated in Cordoba. The organizations given highest rankings include a leading political party, a business organization, two newspapers, the two major associations for businessmen, a Catholic action organization, the regional confederation of labor, and the supreme council of the state university.

It appears that a high correspondence does exist between the community power complex and the institutionalized power structure of the community. The strength of business, religious, political, and labor organizations is predicted by the model. The strength of mass communication and education is also represented according to the model. Only a community organization to represent the military is lacking.

The extent to which all of these organizational influences may con-

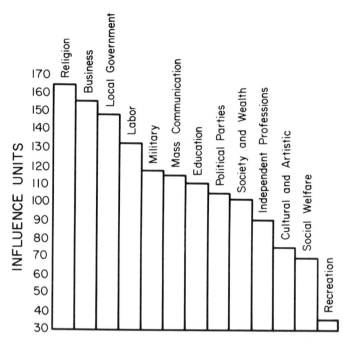

FIGURE 10.   *Institutionalized Power Structure of Cordoba in 1963 as Designated by Top Influentials*[*]

[*] These rankings are established by converting each ranking by a respondent into influence units. The conversion was made by giving a first rank rating a score of 13; a second rank rating of 12; and decreasing until a thirteenth rank rating received a score of one. Each rating given by all respondents in each group was cumulated for each sector according to the formula: Total Institutional Sector Influence Score = f(13) + f(12) + f(11) + f(10) + f(9) + f(8) + f(7) + f(6) + f(5) + f(4) + f(3) + f(2) + f(1).

dition the rise of leaders to represent their interests will be examined through the nominations of top and key influentials.

The 37 top influentials in this study represent the following institutional sectors of the city: business (9), government (6), education (4), political parties (4), independent professions (3), religion (3), mass communications (3), military (2), labor (1), cultural and artistic (1), recreation (1). The 22 who were interviewed were asked to describe their acquaintance pattern and their committee work with the entire group. They were then asked: "If you were responsible for a major project which was before the community that required decision by a group of leaders—leaders that nearly everyone would accept—which persons on the list would you choose, regardless of whether they are known personally to you or not? Add names if you wish."

Key influentials are the acknowledged leaders of the top influentials.

TABLE 31. *Key Influentials in Community Influence Leadership as Chosen by 22 Top Influentials*

Key influentials chosen	Percentage of votes
1. Wealthy owner of large real estate company	64
2. North American president of the largest private industry	64
3. Publisher-editor of newspaper (with large stock interest held by Catholic Church)	60
4. Merchant	55
5. Owner of large engineering firm (engineer)	55
6. Banker (and university professor)	50
7. President of a large university	46
8. Political party leader	46
9. Owner of a very large construction company	41
10. Wealthy society leader (and university professor)	41
11. President of a large university	36
12.1. High-ranking national government official (also a physician)	32
12.2. Political party leader	32
12.3. Vice president of a large university (and influential Catholic lay leader)	32

Fourteen nominees have been selected by a high consensus. They will be identified by their relative ranking and their occupations. Table 31 shows their rank by percentage of votes received. Six (43 percent) of the fourteen are business leaders, three are educators, and three are from politics and government. One society leader and one mass communication leader complete the list. No religious, military, labor, or public school leader or representative is included.

A number of validating tests have been made to ascertain if these nominations correspond to actual performance. These include the committee participation pattern, acquaintance pattern, and histories of issue participation. Newspaper accounts were used to verify the activities of influentials and organizations in relation to community issues and projects.

Identification of chief spokesmen in a large variety of areas was attempted in order to determine whether specialized leaders existed apart from general community leaders. Top influentials were asked: "If the members of the following groups wanted to send someone to defend their interests, whom would you regard as the best representative?"[7] The groups included merchants, military leaders, manufacturers, bankers, labor, university, society and wealth, social welfare, local government, religion, political party in power, opposition parties, cultural and artistic interests, local newspapers, doctors, lawyers, and public school teachers. They were also asked to indicate the best local man for contacting federal officials in Buenos Aires (besides legislators). To discover if situational leaders might exist apart from general community leaders, the top influentials were asked: "To what persons should the community turn for leadership when the economic welfare of the community is threatened? when a civic project needs to succeed? when political influence or power is needed?"

A summary assessment indicates that reputed leaders show high participation patterns in the associational life of the community. Key influentials show significantly more committee participation than do top influentials; their acquaintance scores are higher; 7 of the 14 key influentials were chosen as chief spokesmen of their occupational groups. However, leadership is often segmented. Government and political party leaders dominate when controversial issues are debated; many specialized leaders do not participate in general community projects. Situational or "crisis" leaders are commonly key leaders. Some leaders are not chosen to be key leaders because they are "too controversial," "want to go it alone," and "won't do anything for the community." However, a high proportion of reputational leaders were shown to be active in issues (60 percent of the 20 top influentials) and to hold high official positions (50 percent of the top 20).

APPLICABILITY OF THE SYSTEM MODEL OF THE COMMUNITY POWER STRUCTURE. Five component parts of the community power structure have been identified. An interrelationship is clearly indicated between the institutional power structure of society and the institutionalized power structure of the community, with a Spearman rank correlation of .84. However, the influence of the military drops from first rank in the nation to fifth rank in the community. Religion takes over first position in the community. Mass communication shows a marked rise in influence from tenth place in the nation to sixth place in the community. This shift will be examined more carefully as we look at the other component parts of the model. The community power complex reveals that the associational structure tends to parallel the institutionalized power structure of the community. Business, religious, and labor organizations do show high rankings. The newspapers play an important role in the estimate of top influentials. As is expected, the top influentials include a number of representatives from business, government, religion, education, and mass communication, but representation from military and labor is relatively weak.

The key influentials present a structure picture similar to that of the top influentials except we now find that no religious, military, or labor leader is included, although all of these institutional sectors have been ranked as having high influence. Informants give various reasons for the absence of key leaders in these three institutional areas. Religion is influential through lay leaders of the church and also through independent actions taken quietly by church leaders. Religious leaders of the Catholic clergy tend to work through their own welfare, labor, and political party channels rather than with other community groups. The resources of the church are relatively large and various. The supply of labor leaders was largely cut off for many years because Perón appointed only leaders he wanted to be in power. After the Perón revolution, democratic labor leaders of experience were not available and a gap still exists. The military is not integrated into the community life, but there is no doubt that it holds coercive power in reserve and that civilian officials always serve under the supervision of military authorities and must "stay in line." During the reign of the junta military commanders placed their power in the hands of civilian administrators in Cordoba and retired to bases located outside of the community. These commanders are frequently rotated and do not take an active part in community life except on ceremonial occasions. In general, there is an unfriendly feeling about the military in the civilian community. They are accepted and respected for their military function, but are regarded as intruders into governmental affairs. Many regard them as untrained and incompetent to administer governmental functions.

The five components of the system model show a positive interrelationship as one examines the impact of the national power structure of Argentina on the successive components of the community power structure in Cordoba. The national institutional structure predicts that the power sectors of the community will be the military, religion, business and finance, government, and labor in that order. This relationship can be seen in the successive community components, but the interrelationship is lowered by a number of significant exceptions. The first slippage occurs in the institutionalization of power in Cordoba. The ratings show that the five highest ranked national power sectors appear in highest influence in Cordoba but not in the same order. Religion becomes most important and military drops to fifth position. Then, the military is not represented in the community power complex, suggesting that the military is isolated from community life. A weakness in correspondence is further demonstrated when only two military leaders are among the 37 top influentials. Likewise, only three top religious leaders appear and one top labor leader. Education and political parties, each represented by four top leaders, appear to gain unexpected strength. When 14 key influentials are identified, business leaders, with six, emerge as most numerous. Politics and government is represented by three key influentials. These leadership representations verify the test hypothesis in part. A breakdown occurs when no religious, military, or labor leader is nominated as a key influential.

The value of the system model is that it identifies such discrepancies and forces explanation. It is becoming more clear that the power structure of a community must be viewed as having both a collective and a personal leadership base and that power is both potential and active. If it is so viewed, then the strong, emergency power of the military can be understood for what it is—a powerful latent sector with powerful positional leaders who occupy temporary assignments and are therefore almost "faceless" and unknown to the public generally. To understand collective power the researcher must now turn to social structural analysis, examining the resources of the collectivity, its means of wielding power,'its willingness and efficiency. These collectivities must be viewed within the distinctive social character of the city and nation. It is at this point that the researcher must come to grips with the larger social system in which the community power structure is embedded.

Social Characteristics of Cordoba and Argentina

CORDOBA HAS MANY DISTINCTIVE CHARACTERISTICS which make it different from the other cities in this study. Eight of these are discussed in the following pages.

Strong emergency power of the military. For 34 years, the military has been a powerful force either directly influencing the national government of Argentina or active behind the scenes. Four times the military has revolted and has overthrown the government. They have deposed both democratic and dictatorial leaders. They have sometimes won popular approval for their actions and sometimes severe disapproval. This use of military power to intervene in government is acceptable to the Argentine people only as an emergency measure. The popular demand is for constitutional government with elected representatives. In July 1963 Cordoba was administered by civilian representatives of the military junta and was without a city council or other democratic policy-making body. There was a great desire to return to representative democracy, and the military was regarded as unduly restrictive. However, the presence of Perón supporters had required strong policing in order to hold an election from which Peronista candidates had been excluded. It is this unilateral use of the military in policing and seizing power which gives it an isolated, conflicting, but pervasive place in the social structure.

Traditional importance of religion in the life and institutions of the city. Although it was frequently charged that the Catholic Church had lost great influence, especially among the industrial workers, top influentials of the community ranked it first in importance. An inventory of church roles shows that its ties are pervasive, based on its commanding position as the state religion. Important roles are played by the Catholic Church in business and property, politics and government, education, military, welfare, mass communication, and unions.

The Church has much property, both business and residential. The Church will act through the government to protect its property from taxation or confiscation and receives a subsidy for property it has consigned to the state. The Conservative party, which has a strong role in politics and government, is primarily a Catholic party. Catholics may be favored in certain appointments, and it is said that the President must be Catholic. In the legislature and in the council Catholics may follow the Church's wishes. The Catholic Church operates a parochial school system ranging from primary grades through university; there is also a national public school system from primary grades through university. Overcrowding in public schools is forcing more students into Catholic-operated schools, and the Catholic University is growing rapidly. Major military leaders are generally active Catholics, and military schools require that recruits be members of the Catholic Church. A fascist and nationalistic sector of the military and the Church is known to exist. Important civilian ceremonies are conducted jointly by Church and military authorities. The major part of private welfare is furnished through the Catholic Church and its agencies. Catholic Action and Fraternal Catholic Aid furnish clothes and food to the poor. The Church operates clinics for the needy and provides nuns as nurses in all state and private hospitals. The Church provides camping clubs for children and youth and a family service agency which helps with marital and parental problems. The newspaper regarded as most influential is Catholic-owned: 35 percent of the stock is owned by the Church, 35 percent by a few Catholic families, and the remaining 30 percent by the publisher, who is a Catholic. Teachers' unions are heavily Catholic; teachers will not oppose interests of the Church and are occasionally advised by the Church. Religion thus emerges as a most influential sector, but its clergy play quiet roles largely "behind the scenes." It is also alleged that the confessional gives the clergy a powerful communication network that encompasses every facet of institutional life.

Recent industrialization. The city is like a pre-industrial community which has only recently been overlaid by modern industrialization. Three large heavy industries have appeared since World War II: a large aircraft company, a major automotive company, and major tractor plant. The rise of industry has caused shifts in the institutionalized power profile of the community. Top influentials ranked the institutional sectors according to their influence in 1963 and what they judged their influence had been in 1940. The rankings were:

	1963	1940
Religion	1	1
Business	2	5
Local government	3	4
Labor	4	10
Military	5	7
Mass communication	6	9
Education	7	2
Political parties	8	8
Society and wealth	9	6
Independent professions	10	3
Culture and art	11	11
Social welfare	12	12
Recreation	13	13

A comparison shows the rise in influence of business, government, labor, and mass communication. Education, society and wealth, and independent professions have fallen in influence.

Foreign control of major industrial enterprises. The North American automobile company and the Italian tractor plant provide a major part of the manufacturing in the important metallurgical industry and are under challenge to demonstrate the need for foreign administrators. Attitudinal studies conducted simultaneously by Eva Chamorro and the author revealed desire for more foreign capital, but the presence of foreign executives brings mixed feelings. These findings are reported in detail in Chapter 10.

Limited activity of voluntary organizations and leaders. Committee structure is used much less frequently in Cordoba than in Seattle and Bristol where comparable data were gathered. Top influentials in all three cities were asked to check their acquaintanceship pattern with each of the other top influentials. They were also to indicate the top influentials with whom they had worked on committees during the last two years. The comparable scores for top influentials in the three cities are shown in Table 32. The scores for Cordoba on both acquaintanceship and committee participation are significantly lower. The reason for this is imbedded in traditional patterns of meeting needs through independent use of institutional sectors like government, religion, business, and society and wealth. Opportunities for committee activity are reduced by

TABLE **32.** *Acquaintance and Committee Participation Scores for Top Influentials in Seattle, Bristol, and Cordoba**

	Acquaintance score	Committee participation score
Seattle	106.8	11.6
Bristol	107.1	10.5
Cordoba	77.1	3.0

* Difference between mean of Cordoba and the means of both Seattle and Bristol significant at .01 level.

a daily time schedule which includes a siesta period at noon and an afternoon work period that stretches to 7:30 and 8:00 p.m., forcing public meetings to begin as late as 9:30 or 10:00 p.m. This social characteristic is further explained by the two which follow.

Multi-occupational roles of top influentials. Eighteen of the 37 top influentials draw their livelihood from two or more paid positions. University teaching is commonly combined with professional practice in law, engineering, architecture, or medicine. Lawyers combine private practice and government service. This heavy overlap provides dual identity, but the increased activity does not seem to lead to greater activity in common community projects.

Specialized professional training of the top influentials. The 37 top influentials are largely university trained, and all university training is devoted almost exclusively to professional training. As a result the occupational backgrounds of the top influentials show the following distribution: lawyers, 10; engineers, 5; priests, 2; physicians, 2; architects, 2; military officers, 2; professor, 1. The remaining ten have various non-university backgrounds. The former President of Argentina was a physician. Cordoba was governed before the national elections by a federal interventor who was an engineer. The mayor also was an engineer. It is possible that the specialized training does give the top influentials a particular view of community life that diminishes their support of voluntary community activity. There is evidence from research on the United States that physicians who have less training in the liberal arts are not as active in community life as those who have more.[8]

Multiparty system. There are nine parties active in Cordoba. This multiparty system, generated by recurring crises and supported by the habit of political partisanship among the people, increases the number of persons active in the leadership of parties and interested in politics generally. Heterogeneity (introduced by numerous immigrant and ethnic groups) and marked social stratification are also effective forces. Most observers cry that so many parties make democratic choice too difficult, but none will deny that multiple parties provide intense political activity.

These eight structured characteristics give Cordoba a distinctive ethos. The social setting is dynamic and there are educated leaders, but many community needs remain unmet. The social welfare sector is largely under the aegis of the Church. Community projects are not commonly carried out by voluntary organizations. Foreign enterprise is a central support of the economy but with a few exceptions does not provide community leadership. Government is asked to play a large role in responding to city needs, and the military is always in the background to compel stability. Over all is the traditional hand of the Church which provides a moral and secular thrust to a wide range of activity. Its power of legitimization and of sanction is not easily seen or heard, but is omnipresent.

Comparison of Cordoba With Seattle, Atlanta, and Bristol

IN THE COMPARISON OF KEY INFLUENTIALS shown in Table 33, Cordoba shows closest correspondence to Bristol, since each displays a wide representation of institutional sectors among the key influentials and the influence support that is shown by the sectors. Perhaps in Cordoba, as in Bristol, social class identities bring together coalitions which are hidden by the apparent diversity of institutional representation. Business contributes six of the fourteen leaders, but there is representation of five other sectors: education, political parties, government, mass communication, and society and wealth. Like Bristol, Cordoba is more than four hundred years old. Each has developed industrialized patterns on top of feudal institutions and fairly rigid class divisions.[9] However, Cordoba, like Bristol and Seattle, fits an institutional ring power model and is depicted in Figure 11. In such a model influence is shared with a wide number of institutional segments, but with considerable segmentation within the influence system. No one segment dominates although business is shown to have major influence because of the larger role played by its top influentials. Important systemic linkages may be identified at many points between business and finance, government, religion, mass communication, military, society and wealth, independent professions, education, and conservative political parties. Leaders in these sectors are well educated, tend to share a high social class identity, and have common stakes in maintaining the status quo. Labor, liberal and radical political parties, and certain segments of education and religion com-

TABLE 33. *Key Influentials as Selected by Top Influentials and Ranked by Their Standing as Community Leaders of Influence*

	ARGENTINA	UNITED STATES		ENGLAND
	Cordoba	Seattle	Atlanta (by Floyd Hunter)	Bristol
1	Owner, real estate company	Manufacturing executive	Utilities executive	Labor party leader
2	President of largest private	Wholesale owner and investor	Transport executive	University president
3	Publisher-editor	Mercantile executive	Lawyer	Manufacturing executive
4	Merchant	Real estate owner-executive	Mayor	Bishop, Church of England
5	Owner, large engineering firm	Business executive (woman)	Manufacturing executive	Manufacturing executive
6	Banker	University president	Utilities executive	Citizen party leader
7	University educator	Investment executive	Manufacturer-owner	University official
8	Political party leader	Investment executive	Mercantile executive	Manufacturer-owner
9	Owner, large construction company	Bank executive investor	Investment executive	Labor leader
10	Society leader	Episcopal bishop	Lawyer	Civic leader (woman)
11	University educator	Mayor (lawyer)	Mercantile executive	Lawyer
12	National government official	Lawyer	Mercantile owner	Society leader
13	Political party leader			
14	University educator			
	Business representation: 43 percent	Business representation: 67 percent	Business representation: 75 percent	Business representation: 25 percent

pose the major forces in opposition to the status quo. There is sufficient power in the opposition and its coalitions to contest with the dominant power sectors and to give Cordoba a high degree of pluralism. There is no hard evidence to assert that a landowning aristocracy dominates community decision making or that any other single institutional sector

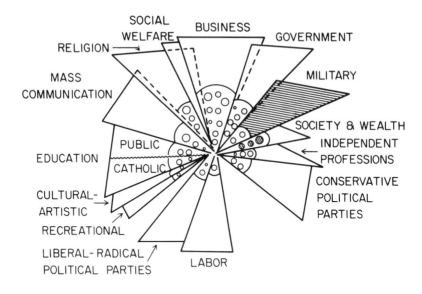

○ = represents a top influential in sector

◍ = top influential named in another sector

FIGURE 11. *Cordoba Depicted as an Institutional Ring Power Model.* Relative influence of sectors is based on influence of leaders and institutional influence. The military is shown as a segmented latent sector. Society and wealth leaders are subsumed under other sectors such as business, education, and independent professions where these leaders are also named. However, the society and wealth sector is identified as of independent influence in community decision making.

can enforce its will. Even the military with its coercive power has definite limitations.

It is clear that a modern industrial society is a society of power pyramids and segments. Intercommunication must be nurtured and interrelationships must be forged. The community power researcher tries to map these interconnections. This task is vital if the most important questions about power are to be answered. Do businessmen dominate government? Do the church and military work closely together? Is labor able to dominate a political party? Is there a coalition of forces strong enough to block all social reform? These questions became more demanding in Lima, and the following chapters will show increased efforts to find answers.

CHAPTER 10

COMMUNITY POWER PERSPECTIVES

AND ROLE DEFINITIONS OF NORTH

AMERICAN EXECUTIVES IN CORDOBA*

No STUDY IN COMMUNITY POWER has ever attempted to secure the community power perspectives of Americans in a foreign community compared with those of the top community leaders. I wanted to find out how closely the perspectives of North American businessmen agreed with the perspectives of the community leaders around them. It seemed to me that the degee of agreement would be a good indicator of the extent to which the North Americans accurately understood the social environment in which they lived and worked. The social environment is important because North Americans everywhere in South America are surrounded by an undercurrent of antagonism born of fears of the United States—fears of economic exploitation, of increased dependence on the American market, of political dependence, and of military intervention. It is true that the United States has also acquired the image of a kindly, rich uncle who aids industrial development and provides jobs for nationals, extends financial aid, provides help to schools and colleges, reinforces the country's military arms and defenses, sends technical assistance, and offers its Peace Corps with its dedicated young men and women.

An American-operated automobile company of 8,000 employees had been producing cars for the previous eight years in Cordoba.[1] Forty

* Adapted from the author's article of the same title published in *Administrative Science Quarterly*, X (December 1965), 364–80.

North American executives of this company had been living in the city during this period, many of them for the entire eight years. In the same firm a number of the responsible executives are South Americans. This structure of management made possible a comparative analysis of the perspectives of both North and South American executives toward the community power structure as defined by top influentials of the community. Moreover, it made possible the comparison of the role definitions of the North American executives with those prescribed for them by South American executives and Cordoba's top influentials.

In Cordoba attitudes toward foreign capitalists (especially North Americans) range from warm friendship to ambivalence to sharp hostility. Americans are both admired and envied, trusted and mistrusted, hailed and reviled. The reservoir of good will is high, but "Yankee Go Home" signs sometimes appear. The North American executive is a conspicuous model, with his fine home, his servant, and his car. How is he to conduct himself in his community role where he is as much judged as in his work role? The proposition that North American business executives can be isolated from the community power structure and that they hold role definitions divergent from community expectations becomes the major hypothesis for this study.

Hypotheses Regarding Cultural Marginality

A THEORY TO EMBRACE THE ROLE BEHAVIOR of North American executives must anticipate their possible isolation and alienation from the local community. An assessment of the social climate faced by the North American business executive is necessary. Against this background the aim is to account for the executive's own role definitions and for the role prescriptions made by the citizens of the host country.

The concept of cultural marginality appears to be especially appropriate for examining role adjustments of the executive and members of his family. The Americans in this population were not trained or prepared for foreign assignments. Few of the executives were able to speak Spanish on arrival and most still could not conduct professional conversations in Spanish; yet relatively few community leaders speak English. In this setting, Americans seek a way of life that is satisfying to their values and habits while adopting habits and attitudes of the host country that will provide harmonious living with their work associates and neighbors.

The marginal man is a person who has incorporated most of the ideas and belief patterns of one culture and some from a host culture and who lives on the margin of the host culture, never completely accepting it or being accepted by it. He finds it difficult to define a role that completely satisfies him and also satisfies the members of the host culture in which he moves. Misunderstanding and conflict result even when tolerance and accommodation are high. Intercultural irritation is a common and natural product of marginal social participation. Three hypotheses were formulated to test the hypothesis of cultural marginality.

Method

THE RESEARCH DESIGN involved the selection of samples from North and South American automotive executives, top influentials, and Cordoba's adult citizens. Sample populations from the executives included twelve North American and nine South American executives. These respondents were chosen to represent the full range of all departments found in the firm. All were part of the same management group, but the North Americans were on transients' visas and expected to return to the United States, whereas the South Americans were citizens of Argentina who expected to pursue permanent careers in the company at Cordoba.

The top influentials of Cordoba had been identified previously as described in the preceding chapter.[2] It was from this population that an approximation of the community power structure was drawn. A random sample of 108 Cordoba adults was drawn by area sampling techniques. It represented responses to the attitude items which were included in an industrialization study conducted simultaneously by Eva Chamorro and associates.

The interview form presented to the top influentials and to the North and South American executives was an eight-page schedule. English and Spanish versions were prepared and interviews were conducted in the language requested by the respondent. The interview schedule contained an attitude scale and two open-end questions to discover role definitions ascribed to American business executives. Respondents were asked to assess a carefully selected list of the most influential institutions, leaders, and organizations and to describe their roles in community projects and issues. Eva Chamorro and graduate students at the Institute of Sociology of the University of Cordoba interviewed all the Spanish-speaking respondents.[3] Each top influential was interviewed singly and usually at his place of work. Business executives, on the other hand, were brought together in groups of from four to six, with the help of the public relations department, and were interviewed at the firm. After the executives had filled in the interview schedule, open discussions were held for one half to two hours. These discussions centered around role problems which they and their family members faced in an international environment. Careful notes were taken at these oral interviews.

Efforts were made to ensure that important questions would be asked and also that interpretations were accurately made. A graduate seminar of 22 Argentines met three times a week to analyze the findings and to interpret them. Most of these students were citizens of Cordoba, holders of the Doctor of Laws degree, and active participants in the life of the city.

INFLUENCE OF NORTH AMERICAN EXECUTIVES. The first hypothesis states that North American executives will fail to reproduce the community power structure as defined by top influentials; South American executives will show close correspondence to the assessments of top influentials.

All the business executives and the South American top influentials were presented with 13 institutional sectors and asked to rank these for their relative strength and influence in getting things done and in influencing the community when issues and projects are debated. The rankings are shown in Table 34. In evaluating the rankings, the assumption is made that the top influentials are the most knowledgeable persons in

TABLE 34. *Ranking of Institutional Sectors in Cordoba According to Their Community Influence by Top Influentials and North and South American Executives*

Rank order*	Top influentials	North American executives	South American executives
1	Religion	Military	Business and finance
2	Business and finance	Business and finance	Local government
3	Local government	Labor	Religion
4	Labor	Political parties	Mass communication
5	Military	Mass communication	Military
6	Mass communication	Independent professions	Political parties
7	Education	Religion	Labor
8	Political parties	Local government	Society and wealth
9	Society and wealth	Society and wealth	Independent professions
10	Independent professions	Cultural and artistic	Education
11	Culture and art	Education	Social welfare
12	Social welfare	Social welfare	Cultural and artistic
13	Recreation	Recreation	Recreation

* These rankings are established by converting each ranking by a respondent into influence units. The conversion was made by giving a first-rank rating a score of 13, a second-rank rating a score of 12, and decreasing until a thirteenth-rank rating received a score of 1. Ratings given by respondents in each group were cumulated for each sector by summing the resulting scores over all respondents.

the community about the structure and processes of community decision making. They have participated in more of the important decisions than anyone else and have observed community decision making for a long period of time. Since the greatest care was taken to identify these leaders, the rankings by top influentials are used as the standard of comparison.

The most pronounced differences in all of the rankings are those given by North American executives for the military and religion. Note that North American executives rank the military as the most influential institution whereas both top influentials and South American executives place it in a fifth position. Also North American executives put religion in seventh position but top influentials put it in first position and South American executives rank it third.

These differences can be interpreted to mean that much of the value structure of Cordoba is not being observed or adequately interpreted by the North American executives. It may be that the face of the community revealed to members of a foreign industry struggling for contracts, facilities, and legal protection is quite different from that turned to a life-long resident, who participates in a wide range of community life. The hypothesis that North American executives are isolated from the wider community power structure is given partial support by this evidence.

The South American executives do show close agreement with the top influentials, and a Spearman rank correlation between the two sets of rankings is .90. The North American executives show a rank correlation with top influentials of .65. This is a lower correlation of congruence, and the differences in ranking would seem to be especially important in focusing upon significant differences in community power perspective between North American executives and the two Argentine groups.

Another test of ranking congruence is a comparison of rankings by North and South American executives who designated the top 12 most influential leaders of Cordoba. When their nominations are compared with the nominations by top influentials, North American executives show a 58-percent agreement and South American executives show a 50-percent agreement. This degree of agreement is low for the nomination of key influentials, where a very high consensus is usually obtained from knowledgeable leaders, and it indicates that neither North American nor South American executives have close contact with the key influentials.

The acquaintanceship scores reveal the extent to which each person knows the top influentials.[4] These scores are especially valuable in diagnosing community participation. Each respondent was asked to mark each one of the 37 listed influentials in one of five ways: don't know, heard of, know slightly, know well, know socially and exchange home visits. Weights 0–4 were assigned and a score was cumulated for each person; the highest possible score was 148. The actual mean scores were 77.1 for top influentials, 43.5 for South American executives, and 19.7 for North American executives. The differences between scores of top influentials and the two groups of executives are all statistically significant at the .01 level. They indicate a very low order of acquaintance between North American executives and the top influentials. A mean score of 19 could be attained simply by having heard about 19 of the 37 top influentials. The score clearly shows that many North American executives are not even reading any of the three daily Spanish-language newspapers in the city. The acquaintance scores of North American executives range from 7 to 42. These are all under the mean score of the South American executives, but even the latters' acquaintanceship with top influentials is not high. It was very evident in all interviews that most executives only heard of or knew only slightly key influentials whose names were most commonly mentioned in conversation.

It is not known how a group of corporate executives would score on a similar test of knowledge of leadership in the United States, but the evidence here does tend to support the hypothesis that the North American executives in Cordoba are isolated from the community power structure. One conspicuous exception is the North American president of the automobile company, a key influential who knows and is known among leaders in the community. South American executives have a better acquaintance and greater understanding of the community power structure, but their perspectives are not broad either. It is important to point out that this evidence indicates that North American executives are not manipulating the community power structure as some critics charge; on the contrary, they are not an active part of it. This hard fact contrasts with some of the opinions held by the general population of the city as shown in the test of the second hypothesis.

ATTITUDES TOWARD NORTH AMERICAN EXECUTIVES. The second hypothesis states that upper socio-economic groups will be favorably disposed toward North American executives and foreign capitalists generally. However, a random sample of Cordoba's adults (cutting across all social classes) will show diverse attitudes, ranging from friendly to hostile, toward foreign capitalists and American businessmen.

Attitude scales were constructed to reveal opinions of the four groups as they reacted to statements about foreign capitalists and North American businessmen.[5] Samples were drawn as described earlier. Table 35 shows three items to measure attitudes toward foreign enter-

TABLE 35. *Agreement of Top Influentials, Cordoba Adults, and North and South American Executives with Statements about Presence of Foreign Capitalists*

Group	Strongly agree	Agree	Uncertain	Disagree	Strongly disagree
1. We need to have foreign businesses in Cordoba					
Top influentials (22)	29%	47%	0%	6%	18%
Cordoba adults (108)	22	50	15	8	5
N. Amer. executives (12)	33	50	0	17	0
S. Amer. executives (9)	0	45	11	11	33
2. All foreign capitalists should be encouraged to build more factories and businesses in Cordoba					
Top influentials	65	36	0	0	0
Cordoba adults	36	40	7	15	3
N. Amer. executives	41	25	17	8	0
S. Amer. executives	67	33	0	0	0
3. All foreign capitalists should get out of Cordoba					
Top influentials	0	0	0	30	70
Cordoba adults	7	7	9	39	38
N. Amer. executives	0	0	0	33	67
S. Amer. executives	0	0	0	33	67

prise. The items were phrased in consultation with an Argentine sociologist, since they were presented in Spanish to all but the North American group. The use of "capitalist" is deliberate in order to describe the foreign investor as understood by the Argentine people. This term is the one used by many politicians when they refer to foreign enterprise.

The items are arranged in order of their acceptance. If a respondent marks Item 3 as strongly disagree, he will tend to mark Item 2 as strongly agree, and Item 1 as strongly agree. Any weakening of the strongly disagree on Item 3 weakens support of foreign enterprise in the scale patterns, because Item 3 states that "All foreign capitalists should get out of Cordoba." This is the strongest negative position. Item 2 states that "All foreign capitalists should be encouraged to build more factories and businesses in Cordoba." This is a strong positive position. But Item 1 is still more positive. It states that "We need to have foreign businesses in Cordoba." This suggests perpetuation, which to many is unacceptable. The desire is that foreign enterprise invest capital but turn the factories and other enterprises over to Argentines for operation. Moreover, many believe that there is sufficient local capital, if invested, to support the needed industrial expansion.

Note the pattern of responses to the third statement. The top influentials and Cordoba adults are community-wide samples; the two samples of business executives are from the American-controlled automobile company. It can be seen that 100 percent of the top influentials disagree but 23 percent of Cordoba adults either agree or are uncertain. It is to this minority that antiforeign spokesmen make their appeal. The two business executive groups respond with overwhelming disagreement. To both groups, foreign enterprise has meant greater opportunity.

Both the top influentials and the Cordoba adults favor the second statement, but the top influentials favor it more strongly. It can again be noted that 25 percent of Cordoba adults either disagree or are uncertain. They believe that foreign business is exploitive and commands influence over their government.

North and South American executives also show a favorable response to foreign capitalists, as expected. What is unexpected is that 25 percent of the North American executives disagree or are uncertain. A later probing of this response revealed that this minority fears unscrupulous foreign competitors who bribe and corrupt government officials. There was an Italian firm which some Americans believed was unfair in its dealings with government officials. The South American executives (many of Italian extraction) did not share this view; they saw greater opportunity for themselves and the community with the increase in foreign enterprise.

Opinions are scattered on the first statement. The underlying desire to free the city from the need to have foreign business is evidenced by some responses in each group. This desire reaches its peak in the South American executives, where 44 percent either disagree or strongly disagree with the statement. These executives believe that Argentines have the skills to run the businesses and that they are being denied opportunity for further advancement in the automobile company because North American executives occupy most of the better executive positions. Different interests explain the disagreement of respondents in the other samples. Note that a few North American executives also disagree. These are executives who were transferred to the South American plant, where doing business is entangled with many governmental and labor problems. The top influentials and the Cordoba adults, who agree, are both exposed to damage to their pride. Perhaps they are responding in a characteristic pattern when they resent the foreigner conducting a business in their community. Although it was well recognized that foreign enterprise had been the largest single element in raising the standard of living in the community during the past ten years, it is surprising that so many agree to the need. It is this recognition—and the belief that Argentine business needs a model of better business practice and efficiency—which has built a high degree of acceptance for the foreign entrepreneur.

Table 36 directs attention to two items relating to the roles of North American executives in the automobile company. Item 2 states: "The North American executives of the auto company are dominating the economic, political, and social life of Cordoba." All groups express a high degree of disagreement with this statement, but a large number of Cordoba adults (54 percent either agree or are uncertain) apparently believe this is so. Note that South American executives and the top influentials have the same belief pattern, and a small number are prepared to believe in North American domination. This is a most surprising result, since only 40 North American executives are involved in a city of more than 600,000 people, and the pattern of community participation of North American executives shows a very low involvement with the community. Although the president of the company is very active and the firm plays a large role in assisting philanthropic endeavors, an objective analysis fails to reveal the reason for the acceptance of the statement.

TABLE 36. *Agreement with Statements about Roles of North American Executives by Top Influentials, Cordoba Adults, and North and South American Executives*

Group	Strongly agree	Agree	Uncertain	Disagree	Strongly disagree
1. The North American executives of the auto company brought a leadership to the community that is needed.					
Top influentials (22)	18%	10%	24%	24%	24%
Cordoba adults (108)	12	37	23	22	6
N. Amer. executives (12)	17	58	0	8	17
S. Amer. executives (9)	11	33	12	11	33
2. The North American executives of the auto company are dominating the economic, political, and social life of Cordoba.					
Top influentials	0	6	13	44	38
Cordoba adults	12	23	19	37	9
N. Amer. executives	0	0	17	33	50
S. Amer. executives	0	6	13	44	38

The first item states: "The North American executives of the auto company brought a leadership that is needed." Opinions on this statement diverge widely within all four groups. Perhaps the most interesting response pattern is that of the South American executives, where an equal number agree and disagree. The group oral interviews revealed that the problem phrase was "that is needed." The objections indicated a fear that North American and other foreign enterprises would interpret their present acceptance as meaning that only they were qualified to operate or own the capital equipment. The American automobile company began its operations with a policy of replacing North Americans as fast as possible. The factory force is completely Argentine, with 350 Argentine supervisors and 8,000 Argentine workers. Only the plant superintendent is North American. In the management group, 15 South Americans were appointed to strategic positions such as personnel director, public relations director, medical director, and so on. Then abruptly the firm changed its policy and placed North Americans in most of the technical and higher administrative positions. Resentment was aroused because South Americans felt that they are being denied some of the better management positions. Some South American executives are very critical of their North American colleagues who live in the American colony, cannot speak Spanish, and do not understand or appreciate the Argentine way of life. The plant has abolished the siesta, denied the use of wine at mealtime (Coca Cola and milk are furnished), and put everyone on North American standards of efficiency. The South American executives respect the North American standards, but efficiency criteria often work at cross currents with all other business and community folkways.

COMPARISON OF ROLE DEFINITIONS. The third hypothesis states that the community role definition of North American business executives will compare closely with those prescribed for them by South American executives in the same firm; however, top influentials of the community will express strong disagreement in their role prescriptions for North American executives.

This hypothesis was formulated on the belief that there would be a high agreement between North and South American executives in the same firm about the appropriate role of the North American executives. It was believed that company policy would have set out clear guides and that the executives would agree upon similar role definitions. On the other hand, top influentials could be expected to have many differing conceptions since they included leaders from business, the church, government, the university, and many other institutional sectors.

To ascertain the role definitions, two open-end questions were asked: What is the role of the American businessman in Cordoba? How are they affecting the life of the city? These questions were answered by the top influentials and by the North and South American executives. Respondents were urged to discuss observed role behavior and what they thought it should be. They were asked to evaluate the effect of this behavior on the life of the city. Most respondents wrote a full page in response and many discussed the question orally after they had finished.

The North American executives expressed three different views of their appropriate role in Cordoba. Since most of the men were trained engineers, they emphasized that their primary role was to provide technical and administrative competence:

> We make our influence felt in the plant by showing how work is done competently and with increasing productivity. We were sent down here to do a technical job. A good businessman works to expand his market, make profit, increase pay rolls and standard of living, and thus improve the community.

The second role conception is one of combining the work role of technical respresentative with that of a neighborhood citizen. Such a citizen does not participate in the larger community, but he goes to church and helps the school. He invites Argentines to dinner or for bridge; his wife engages in charitable activity (usually with other Americans.) He says:

> Why don't you ask us how many Argentines we have in to dinner and play bridge with? This is the way we have Argentine contacts. We don't do so much in the way of community activity because we don't feel fully members of the community, but we do have many contacts with Argentines on a social basis.

The third role is one of more active participation in the life of Cordoba. A small group (about 10 percent) support the binational cultural center. A few serve on school boards, and a few belong to service clubs. This is definitely a minority role. The majority opinion is one of isolated detachment.

> We came down here on an assignment. We didn't expect to stay when we came and we don't now. None of us really volunteered to come here. We came because our company wanted us to come to take a technical assignment. We didn't expect to get into the community and try to do much. Of course, we know we dare not get into anything political.
>
> We are at a handicap in getting along with Argentines. We like to have a light lunch and work in the afternoon. They like a heavy lunch and to have a siesta. They like to eat dinner late and we like to have it earlier. The men go out together for social occasions. We take our wives to everything. Even arranging a golf date is difficult. We play in the morning and they want to play in the late afternoon when our families want to have dinner.
>
> Of course, most of us don't speak Spanish well. So we set up our own school, our own golf club, and our own social organizations. Most of us had a verbal agreement that we were coming for two years and then we would come back home. It didn't seem worth while to buy a home and act

like you were going to stay. If I knew when I came what I know now I would have bought a house and learned Spanish.

The whole American community in Cordoba is transient with no intention to influence directly the economic, political, or social life. We remain hermetic having very little intercourse with Cordoba. Whenever possible we organize our own institutions to preserve our patterns such as schools, church, Boy Scouts, etc. We don't want our children to stay here too long. Not beyond the second year of high school. We want them to be Americans and after the second year of high school they are going to be Argentines or at least have difficulty in American schools and colleges.

When asked how they affected the life of the city, they interpreted their role largely as executives working through the company. They listed such consequences as:
—increased the economic activity of the city.
—helped build many supporting industries.
—raised the standard of living for the workers. (However, this has also stratified society—automobile workers have increased their standards markedly, while others are paid much less.)
—increased cultural contacts between North and South Americans.
—helped modernize some hospitals.
—increased problems of the city as population growth stimulated need for many more urban facilities.

The South American executives are divided almost equally between those who accept the role of the North American businessman as one restricted primarily to the plant and those who believe that the North American businessman must play a wider community role. The second group stresses the importance of learning Spanish and Argentine customs and participation in Argentine life. A respondent of this second group writes as follows:

His individual role does not have any importance. They do not exert a direct influence in community life. His social action is limited to his own foreign group. He is interested in community life in an indirect way—through the enterprise, its action or activities. His relationship could be better. He could have more Argentine friends.

The top influentials' view of the North American executives is indicated by the following replies:

"His role is limited to the job in the plant. They do not play any role outside the work plant."

"Their influence is exerted by reason of the money they have and the way they spend it in the community."

"Their role is to teach Argentines how to organize the enterpise, but they must learn how to adapt to Argentine ways and mentality."

"American businessmen must exert their influence through their own enterprise. If they get money from the community they are obliged to give money back in some cultural and social work."

"Their influence has been favorable. They know how to work in accordance with their techniques."

"They have their influence through the enterprise which increases our industrial development."

"They do not have an immediate influence in the community. They are serving as a model for other enterprises on how to organize, but they do not exert an influence on community life generally."

"They have a democratic system which must be imitated."

These conceptions of the role of the North American businessman include prescriptions that are divided between a role as worker, which would isolate him, and a role as community leader, which would involve him. The same conflict over the role of the businessman can be observed within most North American communities. In a foreign setting, it is more important because not only the growth of the business but sometimes its survival is at stake. Moreover, the North American businessman molds opinions about all Americans in the host country.

Since the ideological struggle is a continuing one, the American businessman is caught within it and becomes a "quasi-official" representative of the United States government. What should his role be under these circumstances? Robert H. Scholl, director of public relations for the Standard Oil Company (New Jersey), made this statement on May 8, 1963 to the House Committee on Foreign Affairs in Washington, D.C.:

> Let me touch on a policy to which our affiliates adhere. It is to strive always to recognize and support cultural traditions and interests of the host country and the aspirations of its people. We believe that this is a very important area of concern and one that is perhaps too frequently neglected by business. It requires imagination and resourcefulness in a field outside business pursuits. Jersey Standard tries to select for foreign service people who will make an effort to learn the local language, people who will engage in community activity and not confine themselves to small American enclaves, and people who will be accepted and live by the citizens of their host countries. I'm sure our record is not perfect, but I think we have been generally successful in this. It is certainly a preoccupation with us.[6]

The Isolated North American Executives

THE ROLE BEHAVIOR of North American business executives of a major industrial firm in an Argentine city has been examined within the framework of a theory of cultural marginality. The tests of the three major hypotheses support the theory. The American businessmen are living on the margin of the host country. They are accepted in their limited roles as workers and as guests within the community; however, they are not accepted as people sharing the culture. The businessmen came on technical assignments by transfer from an American part of the firm. They did not expect to stay, they did not know Spanish when they came, nor did most of them learn the language. The firm did not encourage community activity on the part of the executives, although officially the president and the public relations department were very active. The firm has a good reputation in the community despite some very bitter labor trouble.

The North American business executives and their families have tended to live together in one residential district; they support their own school, country club, and recreational facilities. This pattern of segregation has isolated these Americans from the host culture. The consequences are twofold: they avoid problems by withdrawing from most areas of community life, but their affluent way of life invites envy, suspicion, and distortion, partly because top influentials and most Argentines do not get to know them personally. A planned policy of executive preparation and encouragement of community participation might provide a marked improvement in the knowledge of community leadership and organization.

The findings demonstrate that American businessmen are clearly not manipulating the power structure of the community, as is often charged by some critics; despite this a sizable proportion of the general adult population of Cordoba believes that they are. Role performance becomes interlocked with the political forces and ideologies within the host culture whether the pattern is isolation or participation. The dilemma here requires careful study, because it is very important in international relations.

CHAPTER 11

LIMA, PERU:

Center of Embattled Political Parties

THE STUDY OF CORDOBA revealed new institutional power distributions and different power allocations to organizations and leaders. The study of Lima* invited comparisons. The requirements of the comparative design fixed the central hypothesis, which states that the power structure of Lima is dominated by the business, military, religion, and political sectors of the community. A corollary hypothesis states that the domination of these sectors will be manifest in the institutional structure of society and community, in the community power complex, and in the top and key leaders.

In the light of the Cordoba study it seemed most important to prepare for the likely finding that the religion, labor, and military sectors would not be represented by many influential leaders but would be ranked, nonetheless, as important institutional sectors. This suggested that special attention should be given to these sectors as power collectivities and that new ways of appraising them should be undertaken.

I spent six months in Lima before making a final decision about other hypotheses. During this time I read histories of Lima, examined newspapers and magazines published during the preceding five years,

---

* Note: The Lima described here is the precarious democracy of 1963–68. The military rule now in force (1969) is almost an expected interval in the repeated efforts to achieve a democratic government in Peru. The power structure depicted in this study is the deep-seated base which is always latent, if not overt, in Peruvian life.

read about the current issues, talked with sociologists in Lima, discussed plans with my students at San Marcos University, and listened to Peruvian and American government officials. More than twenty hypotheses were formulated. During this period, I was told that the key to my study would be found in the interlinking of the old families. I was told that everything depends on the military. I was told there is a group that have the property and that they work together and always get what they want. I was told all government and political leaders are crooked and that any of them could be bought. I was told the big American monopolies held the country in their grip. I was told that one could not get three or more people to work together and should not expect much from voluntary organizations. I was told that the church and military work closely together. I was told the church and military do not have much in common except that both hate Communism.

Hypothesis of Institutional Linkage

THESE POSITIONS, so often contradictory, were the basis of a second test hypothesis. It states that principal business, religious, military, and political leaders function together in a group of high solidarity when the most important decision affecting the community are made. This hypothesis led to study of the interrelationship of the military, the church, and the old families. It directed me to a search for "economic dominants" and their political ties. It focused attention on old families, their marriage and inheritance patterns, and their role in community life. The mapping of institutional linkages between business, religious, military, and political leaders became a requirement.

It was apparent that the test of the design and the institutional linkage hypotheses would represent giant tasks. All other possible hypotheses were dismissed, but new additions to methodology were planned.

Additions to Methodology

Use of two different criteria for selecting leaders. During the Seattle, Bristol, and Cordoba studies, top leaders were asked to select the most influential leaders of the community according to Hunter's well-known criterion: "If you were responsible for a major project which was before the community that required decision by a group of leaders—leaders that nearly everyone would accept—which 10 on this list would you choose, regardless of whether they are known personally to you or not? Add other names if you wish." In the Lima study this was modified to read: "Please select 15 persons from this list that represent the most influential leaders to provide possible support for a civic project or issue in Lima where public approval is required. Think of those persons that (1) have high influence, (2) that work on community problems, and (3) that cooperate with other leaders. Add other names if you wish."

Judges said that this was a very difficult assignment. They said that few leaders would agree to work on community problems and that it was even more difficult to get people to work together; that tradition, prestige, and political conflict made it difficult to designate the civic leaders; and that many individuals would not sit down together at the same table. I persisted, and after a lengthy session, most judges selected from 10 to 15 names. One day a judge said, "Why don't you just ask us which leaders are most powerful? We all know who they are." My answer was, "Fine. Go back over the list and place the letter P (poderso) before each name that you regard as most powerful, regardless of how you feel about him and his ideas." This request brought many new names to the fore. Many were political leaders; some were men of finance and of property; a few were labor leaders. I then decided to collect two lists: one would list the most powerful leaders of Lima and the other, the civic leaders of Lima. The criterion for selection of the most powerful leaders of Lima was stated as follows: "Regardless of how you feel about the persons on the list and their ideas, please select 15 persons that are the most powerful in initiating, supporting, or vetoing acts that have influence upon the issues and events which affect the community in general."

Depicting leadership profiles of power. Using the ten types of mutually exclusive forms of power set out in Chapter 1, each of the respondents in Lima was asked to indicate the principal bases of the power which a given leader drew upon for his influence. The profiles of power which resulted made it possible to analyze the bases of power of the key influentials named among the most powerful leaders and those named among civic leaders. The role of individual leaders can be better understood when their bases of power are identified.

Measurement of cultural patterns and norms. It is well known that community decision making is confined within certain value boundaries. The process of issue conflict and resolution always takes place within normative patterns. It was my hope that an intercultural comparison of the norms of the United States and Peru could be made as an adjunct to the study. Fifteen normative patterns were established and rankings were made by carefully selected judges to determine possible differences between the United States and Peru. Measurements have also been made between the United States and Argentina, Spain, and England. The measurement instrument and the results are presented in Chapter 14.

Method

A NUMBER OF CONVENTIONAL RESEARCH STEPS had to be taken in order to test the central hypothesis that the community power structure of Lima (and Cordoba) is composed of five interrelated parts with business, military, religious, and political leaders dominating as key influentials. The first task was assembling lists of influential leaders, associations, and issues. Top influential nominees were assembled from the various institutional sectors of the city: religion, government, military, business and finance, labor, society and wealth, education, political parties (Alliance composed of APRA and Odrista parties and Coalition composed of Popular Action and Christian Democratic parties), independent professions, culture and art, mass communication, social welfare, and recreation. This was not an easy task in a capital city of more than two million which dominates all phases of national life. The list for business and finance was the most difficult to assemble. Originally it contained 273 names, including the principal officers, directors, and managers of 20 banks, 3 investment houses, 5 insurance companies,[1] 25 principal industries and mercantile establishments, and all the large landholders.[2] Judges added other names which they felt should be included. Then the task of cutting the list was begun. A panel of five men was selected and asked to examine the list, to add names of leaders not given, and then to select the most influential business leaders. This panel included two owner-managers of industries, a public relations officer for a large bank, a top manager for a large industry, and an executive secretary for an important association of businessmen. A relatively high consensus among them made it possible to cut the list of influential business leaders to 21 names, which were now included with the list of 365 other community leaders already gathered by interviewing a knowledgeable person in each of the listed institutional sectors.[3]

Fourteen expert panel raters were then selected on the basis of their thorough knowledge of the community leaders in one or more institutional sector, broad knowledge of the community, and many contacts with top influentials. Raters meeting these qualifications included the executive head of a top executive training institute, the head of an educational foundation, the executive secretary of a businessmen's association, a director of an art institute, a society leader, a lawyer and Popular Action political leader, an APRA political leader, a governmental official, a Catholic priest, a military officer, a labor leader, a college administrator, a social welfare director, and a newspaper reporter. Raters were asked to designate "persons who are most powerful in initiating, supporting, or vetoing policy decisions which have the most effect on the community." Those nominated most frequently were selected for interviewing. The final list included 120 persons who will be called the top influentials. The panel of raters also selected the most influential organizations from a list of 54 previously identified as leading organizations. Finally, the most salient issues of the community and of the nation were determined by votes of the same panel of raters. The panel was urged to add names, organizations, or issues that they felt should be included. It should be noted that this gives the researcher a second opportunity to check upon the validity of his list. A third check is made when the final interviews are conducted and influentials are asked to review the list and add names.

Personal interviews were now held with "approved" influentials— those whom officials of the United States Embassy felt would not embarrass the United States, the Fulbright Program, or the researcher. There was ample reason for this precaution.[4] It was decided that influential leaders who were friendly to the United States would constitute the best approach to safeguard the completion of the study. The final list of 120 top influential nominees included 25 leaders in the various institutional sectors who met this criterion, and 21 were subsequently interviewed. It is possible that this criterion introduced a bias, but every effort was made to secure a representation of persons who were thoroughly familiar with the community. These 21 approved influentials held positions representing institutional sectors as follows: business, 5; government and political parties, 4; military, 1; religion, 2; education, 2; independent professions, 2; culture and art, 1; labor, 2; society and wealth, 2.

Each of the 21 leaders in this sample of top influentials was asked to check a social acquaintance scale for each of the 120 top influential nominees by don't know, heard of, know slightly, know well, know socially. He was then asked to choose the 15 most powerful leaders regardless of how he felt about them and their ideas. He identified their bases of power among the ten types and indicated if they had participated in any of the major issues or projects. Similarly, he was asked to choose as civic leaders those with high influence who worked on problems of the community and cooperated with other leaders. Their bases of power were also judged. (See Appendix II.)

The interview included questions on current issues, ratings of most influential organizations, judging the relative influence of the 13 institutional sectors in the national power structure and in the community power structure. In order to get a validating measure of the influential organizations and key influentials, the question was asked: "In your opinion, what groups are most important for securing the support for a project or issue that affects the entire community?"

In addition to the interviewing, newspaper and magazine accounts were used to learn about activities of top influentials, debate on community issues, and interactions between institutions of the community. Special informants and documents were used to establish the most influential positions in the economic, religious, military, political, and society sectors. A positional analysis was made with the standardized schedule in order to ascertain the relationship between positional and reputational leaders.

Power Structures of Peru and Lima

TOP INFLUENTIALS were asked to rank the 13 institutional sectors for their relative strength and influence in getting things done and in influencing the nation when nationwide issues and projects are debated. The first column of Table 37 shows that the national power structure is be-

TABLE 37. *Rank of Reputed National and Community Influence of Institutional Sectors in Peru and in Lima*

INSTITUTION	Overall rank in Peru	Overall rank in Lima	Difference in ranks
Government	1	1	0
Political parties	2	2	0
Military	3	4	−1
Business and Finance	4	3	+1
Labor	5	5	0
Mass communication	6	6	0
Education	7	8	−1
Religion	8	7	+1
Society and wealth	9	9	0
Independent professions	10	10	0
Social welfare	11	11	0
Culture and art	12	12	0
Recreation	13	13	0

lieved to be strongly structured to give the largest influence to government, political parties, military, business and finance, and labor in that order.[5] In all studies the top influential agreed almost unanimously upon the sectors to be placed in the top five positions of influence. There was always high agreement on the institutions with the lowest influence, and these were invariably recreation, culture and art, and usually social welfare.

The institutionalized power structure of the community was also ascertained by the reputational method. The top influentials ranked the institutional sectors for their relative strength and influence in getting things done and in influencing the community when community-wide issues and projects are debated. The second column in Table 37 shows that the same five institutional sectors are again given highest ranking with only one change in order: the influence of the military was rated lower by one rank and business and finance higher by one rank.[6] The reason judges gave for these differences was that business and finance is concentrated very heavily in Lima and must be given greater weight. The military, on the other hand, is believed to play a larger role in the various provinces of the country than in the capital city. At the time, the military was actively engaged in fighting guerrillas in the mountains. It was also busy with many civilian construction projects, giving much attention to the marginal highway in the Selva region of the country.

All told, there is scarcely any variation between the rankings of institutional sectors for the nation and for Lima. This results from Lima's position as the capital city, dominating the economic, political, and social life of the country. The national government is highly centralized, making it extremely difficult to mark out special spheres of policy making for the city government. It is only since 1963 that mayors have been elected in Peru; during the forty preceding years they had been appointed by the national government.

If the rankings for the city are converted into influence units, the institutionalized power structure of the community appears as shown in Figure 12. The profile shows the high importance of government and political parties; because of their close interrelationship there is little difference in their influence ranking in Lima and in Peru. In 1963, President Belaúnde, seeking a solution to the demands for nationalization of oil fields owned and operated by the Standard Oil Company, called Víctor Haya de la Torre, leader of the APRA party, and Manuel Odría, leader of the Odrista party, to the presidential palace for a high-level conference. It was apparent that the political party leaders rather than governmental leaders would make the policy decisions. At the local level, the political party is the instrument of policy, and political party leaders are of highest influence. Neither Víctor Haya de la Torre nor Manuel Odría holds a government office; they give full time to the affairs of the party and "call the shots" in both national and local party policy.

The community power complex was ascertained by asking respondents which of twenty-four selected organizations support with most effort and influence a civic project or issue that arises within the community for public approval. The organizations given highest ranking included (in order of rank) the national federation of labor; a newspaper strongly backing the President; Popular Action, the political party of President Belaúnde; APRA, the largest political party; the lead-

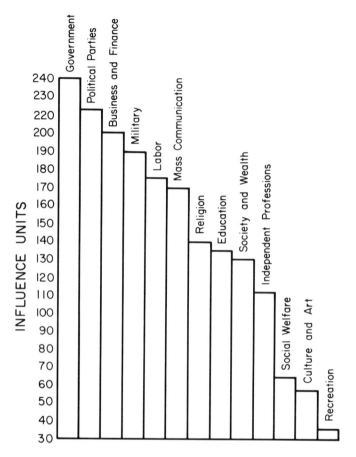

FIGURE 12. *Institutionalized Power Structure of Lima in 1965 As Designated by Top Influentials.* This profile is established by converting each ranking by a respondent into influence units. The conversion was made by giving a first rank rating a score of 13, a second rank rating a score of 12, and decreasing until a 13th rank rating received a score of one. Each rating given by all respondents in each group was cumulated for each sector according to the formula: Total Institutional Sector Influence Score $= f(13) + f(12) + f(11) + f(10) + f(9) + f(8) + f(7) + f(6) + f(5) + f(4) + f(3) + f(2) + f(1)$.

ing conservative newspaper; the Christian Democratic party, a political party with strong Catholic support; the national association of mercantile enterprises; the Odrista party, Peru's third largest political party, headed by a former President, General Odría; a private organization studying and supporting industrial development; a government institute engaged in national planning; the national federation of educators; the national association of manufacturers; and an association of North American businessmen.

In terms of institutional sectors, five of these organizations represent political parties and government and four represent business interests. Mass communication is represented by two leading newspapers, labor by the powerful national federation of labor, and education by its national association. The private organization for industrial development is composed largely of young engineers and can be considered as representative of independent professions.

It appears that a correspondence exists between the community power complex and the institutionalized power structures of the community. A slippage occurs in religion and military where no important civic organization exists. Catholic Action does function with an impressive program, but it is more an educational and social organization than one that develops support for community issues and projects. Such support will come from the chief officers of the Church itself. The military has social organizations but deliberately refrains from participation in community issues and projects. Again, if such support is deemed necessary, it will come from the chief officers of the military.

Top Reputational Leaders

THE TOP INFLUENTIAL NOMINEES in this study number 120. This is a large number, but the city is large (over 2,000,000) and the nominations indicated a wide dispersion of leadership. Twenty-one approved top influentials were asked in interviews to describe their acquaintance pattern with all of the 120 and then to determine the most influential leaders by the two different criteria described earlier for the civic and powerful leaders. The respondents were asked to select 15 civic leaders who had the highest influence, worked on community problems, and cooperated with other leaders. The respondents said it was difficult to identify persons who would work on community problems because there was little participation in voluntary organizations and community activities. Two responses were:

> Most men are interested in their own businesses only. They don't see that work in the community brings anything to them. Besides, in our firms we must do our own work and that of the "middle level" also—so few are capable at the "middle level." As a result, the major executives are overworked and don't have much time or energy for community affairs in the evening.
>
> Generally people want the status but they do not want to work.

153

Respondents said it is even more difficult to get people to work together.

People of opposite political parties will not work together. Put X on a committee and no Aprista will attend; put Y on a committee and no one from the Popular Action group will show up.

When a community leader really tries, people think he has another intention. They are always looking for the second intention. One of our leaders in our firm talked to a group of industrialists yesterday. He wanted to advise them to make an important change in their business methods. They all thought he wanted to hurt them and kill their businesses. They went out determined to do just the opposite of what he had advised. That hurts a community leader; pretty soon he is just operating quietly.

Many leaders work quietly—they don't put their names on memos. They use the telephone but will not make speeches or talk to the press. The reason why they work quietly is that whenever a man starts to get big, others start tramping on him.

One judge said he was deliberately omitting political leaders because they were so controversial that their usefulness in civic work was severely restricted. These controversial people were brought forward by the alternative criterion of leadership selection, which stressed the importance of selecting the most powerful leaders "regardless of what you think of them and their ideas." It is believed that the 33 individuals nominated on this criterion best represent the leaders in the power structure of Lima. These 33 top influentials represent the institutional sectors of the city as follows: business, 10; political parties, 6; government, 6; religion, 2; military, 1; education, 4; mass communication, 2; labor, 1; independent professions, 1. This distribution bears out the expectation that business, political, and government leaders would be numerous. Religion and military are represented—as was expected—but the sectors have few top leaders. Education and mass communication are better represented than expected, and labor is less well represented than expected.

A search was made to find out if these top influentials were positional leaders and if the standardized schedule would reveal a high correspondence. Positional analysis was carried out as in the earlier studies. Eight raters, each familiar with three or more institutional sectors, identified the most powerful positions of the city. Table 38 indicates the positions of highest power in Lima.[7]

The schedule is very similar to that which was first developed for Seattle and extended to Bristol and Cordoba. Because of the larger size of Lima, more positions were included in the business and finance sector. As was necessary in Cordoba, military positions were provided.

TABLE 38. *Formal Positions of Highest Potential Power in Lima*

BUSINESS AND FINANCE

Manufacturing
President, Fábrica Nacional de Tejidos Santa Catalina
President, Industrias Reunidas
President, Cia. Oleaginosa del Perú (copra)
President, Cia. Peruana de Cemento Portland

Investment Houses
President, Peruana Suiza de Fomento e Inversiones
President, Financiera Peruana, S.A.
President, Del Peru, Financiera y Comercial, S.A.

Largest Department Stores
President, Sears, Roebuck and Co.
President, Oeschle
President, Casa Welsh

Largest Real Estate Holders
3 largest holders

Largest Hotel Owner
Lima Country Club (local owner)

Presidents of Most Important Business Associations
President, Cámara de Comercio
President, Corporación Nacional de Comerciantes
President, Sociedad Nacional de Industrias

Largest Bank Presidents
President, Banco de Crédito
President, Banco Popular
President, Banco Internacional

Largest Real Estate Company
President, Empresa Inmobiliaria Nacional

Largest Insurance Company
President, El Pacífico

MASS COMMUNICATION

Owner, *El Comercio*
Owner, *La Prensa*
Director, Red Radioemisoras "La Victoria"
Director, Televisión Panamericana

GOVERNMENT

President of Peru
Mayor of Lima
Immediate past mayor

POLITICAL PARTIES
Popular Action party
Christian Democratic party

TABLE 38.—*Continued*

APRA party (Alianza Popular Revolucionaria Americana)
Odrista party

EDUCATION

Rector, University of San Marcos
Rector, Catholic University
Minister of Education
General Director of Education
President of teachers' association

LABOR

Minister of Labor
Secretary General, Confederation of Labor of Peru

RELIGION

Cardinal of Lima
Bishop Auxiliar
Bishop Auxiliar, Vicar
Rabbi, leading Jewish Temple
Bishop, major Protestant church

INDEPENDENT PROFESSIONS

President, Confederation of Professional Institutions, Inc.
Dean, School of Law
President, Medical Association

MILITARY

President of the Joint Command
Minister of War
Minister of Navy
Minister of Aeronautics
Commander of the Army in Lima
Commander General of the Navy
Commander General of the Air Force

SOCIAL CLUBS

President, Club Nacional
President, Club Unión
President, Club Regatas Lima

Experience now shows a fairly standard schedule is possible for comparative studies.

In the Lima schedule, 58 official positions of high potential power were identified: business, 22; mass communication, 4; government, 3; political parties, 4; education, 5; labor, 2; religion, 5; independent professions, 3; military, 7; society, 3.

A comparison of the 33 top reputed leaders with the holders of these important positions shows that 55 percent of the reputed leaders hold one or more of these identified positions. It is interesting to note that each of the ten key influentials holds one of the positions of highest potential. It must be observed carefully that most of the top reputed leaders do have some kind of important official position. In a city the size of Lima, such a man may not hold one of the major positions on the schedule but still hold a very important post—for example, he might be president of the fourth largest bank in the city. Lima is headquarters for 21 very large banks. It can be seen that the validity of our positional schedule tends to be markedly reduced in the very large city because of the abundance of official positions from which able leadership may function. An analysis shows that all reputed leaders operate from an important positional base. Most are associated also with projects or issues they have supported. Often they are identified with the support they gave to a proposal that has been written into law; sometimes, it is a new program or practice which affects the community that they have introduced in their organization. Only political leaders tend to be highly associated with issues, the major ones carrying the brunt of the leadership required.

Key Reputational Leaders

THE KEY INFLUENTIALS are those leaders who are the acknowledged choice of the top influentials. Table 39 shows the positions of the individuals who were selected by high consensus as the powerful leaders

TABLE **39.** *Key Influentials Chosen as Most Powerful in Community Influence by 21 Top Influentials*

Key influentials chosen	Percentage of votes
1. President of the Republic and political party leader	100
2. Political party leader	81
3. Publishers of the newspaper	76
4. Cardinal of the Catholic Church	62
5. Political party leader	62
6. Publisher of a newspaper	57
7. National government official and University educator	48
8. University educator and religious leader	43
9. Mayor and political party leader	40
10. Political party leader	40
11. Educator	40
12. Banker and large real estate holder	33
13. Political party leader and educator	33
14. Educator and independent professional	33

of Lima in initiating, supporting, or vetoing issues or projects that have the most effect on the community in general. It can be noted that 7 out of the 14 (50 percent) are political or government leaders. Three are educators, and two are newspaper publishers. One business and one religious leader complete the list.

Our test hypothesis has now been partially validated. The strong influence of political parties and government that was foreseen in each of the four successive components of the system model is clearly shown. In addition, business and religion are represented by very powerful persons, although only one leader represents each sector. Mass communication and education show greater strength than expected. But the military is without a single representative. Labor is regarded as a powerful institutional sector, yet it has no representative.

The question arises as to whether a listing of key civic leaders (have high influence, work on community problems, and cooperate with other leaders) would reveal a different pattern. Table 40 shows the nomina-

TABLE 40.   *Key Influentials Chosen as Civic Leaders in Community Influence by 21 Top Influentials*

Key influentials chosen	Percentage of votes	Also chosen as powerful leaders
1. Cardinal for the Catholic Church	52	Yes
2. Publisher of a newspaper	48	Yes
3. Government official, writer, educator, lay religious leader	43	Yes
4. Industrialist	38	No
5. Educator and Catholic leader	38	Yes
6. Financier	33	No
7. Civic and society leader	33	No
8. University educator	29	Yes
9. Political leader	29	Yes
10. Major government executive	29	Yes
11. Industrialist	24	No
12. Radio-TV personality	24	No
13. Mayor and political leader	24	Yes
14. Government official and educator	24	Yes
		Overlap 9/14 or 64%

tions for civic leadership made by the sample of top influentials. It should be noted that there is a wider dispersion in the votes for civic leaders than in those for powerful leaders, indicating more difficulty in making choices. More than 50 persons actually received two or more votes. Respondents were often in doubt about the ability of the persons they chose to work together. Table 40 reveals that civic leaders do overlap the most powerful leaders: 9 of the 14 civic leaders (or 64 percent) were also among the most powerful leaders. The institutional representation of key civic leaders is very similar to the representation of the most powerful leaders. Political and government leaders again have the largest representation (36 percent), but only one political party leader is included among the civic leaders. Business representation (21 percent) increases. Again no military or labor leader is chosen.

How shall this pattern be explained? In Cordoba, no military leaders and no labor leaders were included, although, as in Lima, the military and labor institutions were reputed to be powerful institutional sectors. The absence of leaders in these two sectors provides a problem for study. The acquaintance schedule was used to ascertain the acquaintance patterns with each of the 120 nominees in Lima for the 21 top influentials who selected these key influentials. The acquaintance scores were tallied, and Table 41 shows the scores for labor and military

TABLE 41. *Mean Acquaintance Scores of 21 Top Influentials for Political, Mass Communication, Labor, and Military Leaders*

Leaders	Mean acquaintance score*
5 Political party leaders	48
3 Mass communication leaders	38
4 Labor leaders	22
4 Military leaders	22

* Weights assigned: 0, don't know; 1, heard of; 2, know little; 3, know well; 4, know socially.

leaders compared with those for political and mass communication leaders. Note that on the average the top influentials do not know or have merely heard of the most powerful military and labor leaders in the city and nation. An analysis of individual responses shows that 11 of the 21 top influentials say they have never heard of the chief of staff of the Peruvian armed services. Likewise, 11 of the 21 have never heard of the secretary general of the Confederation of Labor of Peru—the organization they helped to rank as the most powerful organization in the city. In contrast, the same respondents know well the political party and mass communication leaders.

Informants were asked to interpret these results. A labor expert said that the labor leaders were not generally known for two major reasons: first, the key men are new and they need time to make themselves known; and second, labor leaders do not get publicity as leaders. Only *La Tribuna*, the newspaper sponsored by the APRA party, carries much labor news. The labor expert was then asked: "Why is labor ranked so powerful?" His reply was:

> Labor is well organized, every plant has a union. Labor makes extensive use of the strike. Even teachers and public employees use the strike, legal or not. [At the time hospital employees were on strike and the Army had taken over the duties of nurses!] Labor, moreover, has close ties with the APRA party, the largest party in Peru. They have six labor deputies and three senators in the Parliament. Labor provides APRA with its base of political strength and so plays a major role in legislative activity.

A military expert was asked to explain the lack of knowledge which top influentials have of the military leaders. His reply was:

> They don't get publicity and they don't seek it. They try to stay apolitical. All other cabinet members outside the military have party affiliation (there are 3 military men in the cabinet representing army, navy, and air) and they like publicity. Besides, there is also little opportunity for other leaders to get to know military leaders. They stick to themselves. The military has its own social organization.

Applicability of the System Model of Community Power Structure

FIVE COMPONENT PARTS of the community power structure have been identified. A summary of relevant data is shown in Table 42. An interrelationship is clearly indicated between the institutional power structure of society and the institutionalized power structure of the community with a Spearman rank correlation of .93. This almost perfect correspondence probably results from the fact that Lima is the capital city and is thus clearly tied into the national government and economy. Only two minor differences in rank are noted: business and finance rises from fourth rank nationally to third rank in Lima while the military drops from third rank nationally to fourth rank in Lima, and religion is given slightly more influence in Lima than nationally, moving from eighth to seventh position. From the institutionalized power structure of the community, the theory of successive influence in the parts would predict that the community power complex and the top and key influentials would be dominated by government, political parties, business and finance, and the military.

A correspondence was noted between the community power complex and the institutionalized power structure of the community. Five of the organizations ranked as most influential in getting things done

TABLE 42. *Summary of Data Showing Interrelationships Between Component Parts of the System Model of Community Power Structure for Lima*

Power ranking of institutional sectors	Power ranking of institutional sectors	Institutional identity of 14 most influential organizations	Institutional identity of 33 top influentials	Institutional identity of 14 key influentials
PERU	LIMA			
		N (%)	N (%)	N (%)
1. Government	Government	1 (7)	6 (18)	3 (21)
2. Political parties	Political parties	4 (29)	6 (18)	4 (29)
3. Military	Business and finance	4 (29)	10 (30)	1 (7)
4. Business and finance	Military	..	1 (3)	..
5. Labor	Labor	1 (7)	1 (3)	..
6. Mass communication	Mass communication	2 (14)	2 (6)	2 (14)
7. Education	Religion	..	2 (6)	1 (7)
8. Religion	Education	1 (7)	4 (12)	3 (21)
9. Society and wealth	Society and wealth	..	..	..
10. Independent professions	Independent professions	1 (7)	1 (3)	..
11. Social welfare	Social welfare	..	..	..
12. Culture and art	Culture and art	..	..	..
13. Recreation	Recreation	..	..	..

in community life represent political parties and government, and four represent business and finance. However, an important slippage occurs in religion and military, where no civic organization is ranked as influential. On the other hand, labor (with an organization ranked as most influential), religion, and mass communication show greater strength than predicted.

Top influentials bear out partially the predicted relationship. Business, political, and governmental leaders are numerous. As expected, the military and labor are also represented, but each of these sectors has only a single representative. Key influentials likewise reproduce partially the predicted patterning of the component parts. A high representation (50 percent) of political and government leaders is found. Business and religion are represented, but by only one key influential each. The military and labor have no representation, while education has three and mass communication two.

The hypothesis stating that the power structure will be dominated by business, military, religious, and political leaders is partially validated. It has been clearly shown that political, governmental, and business leaders are ranked as influential forces in the life of the community as predicted by the other parts of the model. Religious leaders are reported weaker than was believed when the operating hypothesis was formulated. Educators and mass communication leaders are more important than indicated by the institutional ranking of their sectors.

The system model has revealed a pattern of interrelationships among the five component parts. It breaks down in the case of the military and labor: both were ranked high in institutional influence but no military or labor leaders were revealed as active influentials in the community. It is now clear that the model can approximate a predictable pattern, but that it will break down when community power is exercised by a collective representation that does not rely on highly personalized leadership.

Labor, the military, and the Catholic Church revere their established institutions and consider the needs of the institution more important than individual leaders. In fact, leaders are often rotated. Labor uses election machinery for this purpose; the military and the Church employ planned policies of rotation. Instead of setting up civic organizations and working upon issues and projects in the community life, they use their own collective power—labor, the strike; the military, threat or use of coercive force; the Catholic Church, moral persuasion and sanctions—for their own interests. Or they work through established organizations and institutions—labor has chosen a political party (APRA) to wield political influence; the military supports and pressures governments to follow its dictates; the Church functions through government, its own schools, and other community agencies to establish its influence. Each of these institutional sectors must be studied carefully to understand how it generates collective influence without highly visible leaders. In Lima, the military is almost a faceless institution. Many top leaders do not know the men who would command a military junta if it should come into power. The military is isolated from community life. This does not mean that the military lacks communication. On the contrary, three high-ranking military officers sit in the President's cabinet, they have close ties with the joint chiefs of staff, and General José Benavides y Benavides, chief of the national intelligence, is attached to the President's personal staff. One expert told me that the military has high concern in three matters: the threat of increased Communist influence and social disorder, the size of the budget for the armed forces, and concern over rapid inflation.[8] Any of these matters can bring military pressure. These are mainly national matters and so the military interest focuses at the national, not the city level.

Understanding the Community Power Structure of Lima

THE STRUCTURAL FEATURES of the community power structure of Lima have been presented. The problem facing the researcher who wishes to answer the question "why?" is one that leads to the historical roots of the national society. There are many subtleties that arise from values and social structures that lie deep in the society. Among these values are a depreciation of manual work, the legitimization of exploitative relations, the appreciation of social rituals and formal patterns of courtesy and ceremony, and the seeking of title and of office conferring high formal status. A number of distinctive social characteristics can be identified which produce many of the results shown. Perhaps the most important is the class system.

Lima is characterized by a fairly rigid class system legitimizing wide disparity in wealth. The income distribution of various segments of the population of Peru shows that about two thirds of its economically active population have an average per capita income of $238 a year. At the other extreme are the 7,500 property holders, whose annual incomes average $50,705. Between these extremes one finds sellers, small farmers, and workers in personal services, who average $630 per year; patrons or landlords, who average $2,533; and managers and professionals, who receive an average of $5,204 annually. (See Table 43.)

TABLE 43. *Income Ladder Showing the Distribution of National Income in Peru in 1963**

	Number of persons	%	Income in thousands of Soles	%	Average of each group Soles	U.S. $
I. Property holders (dividends, interest, and rent)	7,500	0.3	10,211,957	19.8	1,361,594	50,705
II. Professionals, managers, administrators of high level	26,600	1.0	3,712,628	7.3	139,572	5,204
III. Landlords	64,700	1.8	4,401,312	8.5	68,026	2,533
IV. Sellers, small farmers, personal service	1,099,800	31.4	18,557,217	35.0	16,873	630
V. Manual and white collar workers, craftsmen	2,286,800	65.5	14,607,911	28.4	6,387	238
TOTALS AND AVERAGES	3,485,000	100.0	51,491,025	100.0	14,773	550

* From Edgardo Seoane, "The Just Distribution of the Wealth," *Oiga* (Lima), February 25, 1966, p. 8.

In such a society the term capitalist tends to mean a person of great wealth who lives without work, drawing his income from dividends, interests, or rents. It also means an old family with Spanish ancestry, for the income ladder is paralleled by a status ladder. This status ladder was established in the colonial period when the population was ranked as shown in Figure 13.

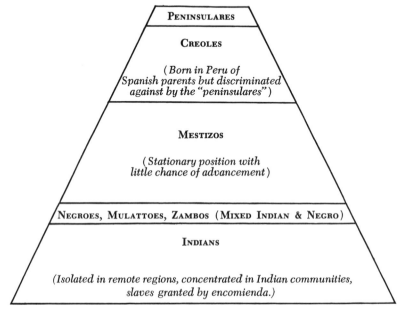

PENINSULARES

CREOLES

(*Born in Peru of Spanish parents but discriminated against by the "peninsulares"*)

MESTIZOS

(*Stationary position with little chance of advancement*)

NEGROES, MULATTOES, ZAMBOS (MIXED INDIAN & NEGRO)

INDIANS

(*Isolated in remote regions, concentrated in Indian communities, slaves granted by encomienda.*)

FIGURE 13. *Status Ladder of Peru in the Colonial Period.* The peninsular Spanish aristocracy included those Spanish nobles or adventurers who were rewarded by the Spanish crown with large land grants (encomienda) which included the Indians thereon as slaves of the holder. Other "peninsulares" were priests, soldiers, and adventurers.

The creoles, Peruvian-born Spanish regarded as inferior by the "peninsulares," subsequently produced the leaders who successfully led the revolt against imperial rule. The mestizos sprang from the union of Spanish men and Indian women. An Indian princess bore the children of the founder of Lima, Francisco Pizarro, and helped establish a respected pattern. The commingling of Spanish and Indian blood is ever increasing. Whites and mestizos now constitute roughly 55 percent of the total population. Negroes number fewer than 0.5 percent. The Indians comprise approximately 40 percent of the population.[9] Their traditional language is Quechua, their habitat the rural village community (ayllu), and their formal education low.

This status ladder has changed little since colonial times. Of course, the peninsular Spanish aristocracy is gone, but the creoles now think of themselves as the proud inheritors of pure Spanish blood and like to identify themselves with ancestors in Spain. They have the highest status position by virtue of wealth, education, social position, and power. Light skin color correlates with the European and Asiatic stock, which are represented in Peru by foreigners of many nationalities, notably Italians, Germans, Chinese, and Japanese. In addition North Americans, British, Swiss, Italians, and Germans form an important element in commercial and banking activities and in mining, petroleum, industrial, and other enterprises. Racial discrimination is almost universally denied, but there is a gulf between the whites and the mestizos, Negroes, and Indians. The low level of education of the darker skinned people is given as the reason for this gulf. Statistics are only partially reliable and estimates of illiteracy vary, but one source reports that 42 percent of the population 17 years of age and over is illiterate.[10] The International Institute of Leaders of Education and Social Service reports that 53 percent of the total population is illiterate, 42 percent semiliterate, and only 5 percent literate.

The stratification pattern shown in Table 43 reveals the great income gulf between the classes in Peru. The gulf is widened by differences in social status, education, and power. Democratic government does provide opportunities for political expression of social needs, and the many parties which arise can be interpreted as natural expressions of widely varying interest groups. In Lima, a growing white-collar class is a moderating influence between rich and poor. Increased educational opportunities in the state schools and universities are offering new hopes to lower middle-class youth. These youth seek rapid change and form an important pressure group that no government can ignore. The Indians and mestizos are increasing in number and are migrating to Lima at such a rate that the city has experienced a 400 percent growth, from 520,000 in 1945 to more than 2,100,000 in 1965. It is estimated that this population will double by 1980. The migrants pouring into the slums (barriadas) on the periphery of the city are desperately poor and are caught in the press of ever-rising prices. Boiling political pressures are bred in this climate. Democratic government is at present (1966) in a precarious position but is supported by the productivity of Peru's mines, oil fields, fish, cattle, and agriculture, by the rapid growth of foreign enterprise, and by foreign aid. It is in this context that government and political parties come to be viewed as the most influential institutional sectors of the society. Despite their internecine conflict, they stand between democratic government and chaos and military dictatorship.

Lima continues to exhibit the residual shell of the old Latin American power triumvirate of land, church, and army. It is well known that historical elites rise to leadership and power based upon tradition, family, land, and religion. The traditional elite in Peru included religious leaders, nobles, landowners, military leaders, and people who were given special privileges by the Spanish government. In the next chapter, the research findings on the elite structure are reported.

A landed aristocracy does exist in Peru. According to Carlos Malpica, the 45 families represented in the board of directors of the National Agrarian Society control 23 percent of the cultivated area of the coastal lands of Peru and more than 90 million square meters in the area surrounding Lima. Their investments outside the agricultural sector are also large. Of the 45 families, 56 percent are important stockholders of banks and financial companies; 53 percent are stockholders of insurance companies; 75 percent are owners of real estate developments; 56 percent hold investments in commercial enterprises; 65 percent are important stockholders in industrial enterprises; 20 percent possess stocks in mining companies; and 12 percent are stockholders in one or more oil companies. The directors of the Wool Growers Association own 10 percent of the grasslands in the Sierra; 36 proprietors hold 66.3 percent of the Selva (jungle). The great majority of the large landholders are known to support the Odrista party (many are directors), which has formed a coalition with APRA and holds the dominating majority in the Parliament.[11]

The Catholic Church is regarded as a source of influence that can never be discounted. Roman Catholicism is the state religion. The Church has maintained a strong hold upon family allegiance. It is closely linked to the state because of its various property and theological interests. "Good Catholic" lay members function at all levels and positions of government. The Church maintains a strong tie to the military, which serves as the shield against Communism and attacks on the Church. It operates a growing range of educational institutions at all levels and dominates private welfare services.

The military as the third member of the traditional triumvirate exerts a strong influence by its naked assumption of power when it chooses to topple democratic governments or dictators. This happens so frequently that the military can be regarded as a continuous government or shadow government. Interlinked with church and state it is constantly in being as an active or a latent force—governing or sanctioning governments.

There is not the slightest doubt that the old triumvirate of power still exists. What is indeterminate is the nature and degree of the power which these three institutions exert and the linkages which exist between them.

Lima has a highly centralized government in which the national government plays a primary role and the local government a secondary role. This pattern is paralleled by a government bureaucracy of favoritism and a politicized society. Both Colonial Spain and the Incas had highly centralized governments with relatively few powers vested in local governments. This heritage has persisted. The major part of the municipal budget of Lima is distributed by the national government and much of the budget for municipal work is controlled by various national ministries. It is almost impossible to trace the pattern of responsibility for many city functions.

The Institute of Public Administration located in Lima is preparing a handbook which attempts to trace relationships between the national and municipal governments in Lima. It is a complicated web and no one professes to know just exactly how everything works. It is common practice for critics to blame the President of Peru rather than the mayor for holes in the streets of Lima!

There are a number of forces which shape both the city and the national government in the image of the larger culture. These include the extended family system which encourages placement of family members in all sectors of government regardless of their proven capacity or training for a position. There is a political spoils system which encourages placement of party members. A strong religious bias favors Catholics. Moreover, among the worst elements inherited from the Spanish are such practices as bribery (mordida), kickbacks, lying, and deception. As a result, there is little concern for and trust of others. Some persons believe that the prevalence of corrupt practices has a very significant effect on political decision making. The nationalization of an industry such as oil or steel or the government operation of a city utility is often feared because of the possibility that the jobs within these organizations will go to favored rather than competent personnel and that corruption will replace honest and efficient management. A pattern of politicizing expresses itself in such intense political commitments of members and decision makers on every issue that compromise is exceedingly difficult. Albert O. Hirschman describes this behavior, saying that it can usually be traced to one or more of three underlying situations:

(a) The decision makers are a small upper-class group and every one of them is or has been actively involved in almost all phases of the country's political and economic life.

(b) Each issue that comes up is immediately connected with some overriding political schism and stands on it are taken strictly and strongly along party lines.

(c) The typical member of the society, even though he is far more

167

affected in his own immediate interests by one issue than by the other, feels honor-bound to acquire and propound strong opinions on both, either because it is macho (manly) to hold forth authoritatively on every subject or because a moral obligation is felt to ferret out and support the "right" answer to every question.[12]

Hirschman says the term "toderos," meaning specialists in everything, is often used in South America to express the idea that "we"—that is, the people who count—have a finger in every pie and absence of this particular infrastructure, we like to acquire and exhibit strong opinions on every issue. One result is that the compromise tactics so common in Western democracies are often replaced by unexpected and shifting alliances that bring the far right and far left together in common political positions on a given issue.[13] Just such a combination of political forces in Lima and Peru has brought the Odrista and APRA parties into a coalition that fights bitterly against President Belaúnde and the Alliance of Popular Action and Christian Democratic parties.

The large extended family kinship system concentrates wealth and power in Lima. A number of stratification forces—the inheritance of land, the propagation of large families, the system of extended families with reciprocation of favor, a high level of education, the ascription of status to old wealthy families, political influence, and finally the preservation and accumulation of wealth by intermarriage among upper-class "old" families—contribute to this concentration. The process started with the first large land grants made by Spain to favored persons. The large family system of the favored families and their tight intermarriage soon produced small empires. Anyone with the family name could call upon any other member of the family and expect consideration of his request for assistance. Even the kinship system of nomenclature spreads the honored names since a man adds his mother's family name to his, thus drawing status from the prestige of both families.

The number of persons carrying a given name may reach into the hundreds. This may be illustrated by the Pardo family. Don Manuel Pardo was President of Peru from 1872 to 1876. The state gave him the hacienda Tumán near the city of Chiclayo. His descendants are now the owners of 5,342 hectares, which are in sugar cultivation. The various branches of this family, Pardo Althaus, Pardo del Alcázar, Pardo Heeren, and González Pardo, are proprietors or large stockholders in 26 businesses. The family González Pardo is owner of the hacienda Chota, a holding of 20,000 hectares in the Sierra. Table 44 lists positions held by the more influential members of the family. Note that Juan Pardo Althaus is president of two companies, manager of five others, and director of four. This pattern of multiple direction of companies is not

TABLE 44. *Current Positions in Business Firms of Leading Members of the Pardo Family*

ING JUAN PARDO ALTHAUS

Manager, Agrícola San José Antonio, S.A.
Manager, Cia. de Inversiones Mobiliarias e Inmobiliarias, S.A.
Director, Cia. de Seguros la Fénix Peruana
Director-Manager, Cia. Inmobiliaria Huérfanos, S.A.
President, Fertilizantes Sintéticos, S.A.
Director, Industrias Reunidas, S.A.
Manager, Inversiones Até, S.A.
President, Inversiones Paralba, S.A.
Director, Metalúrgica Peruana, S.A.
Manager, Negociación Tumán, S.A.
Director, Petrolera Peruana, S.A.
Director, Sociedad Nacional Agratia

LUIS PARDO DEL ALCÁZAR

Director, Cosmos, S.A.
President, Consorcio Comercial Lanero, S.A.
Director, Inmobiliaria Santa Clara, S.A.

ENRIQUE PARDO HEEREN

Director, Backus & Johnstons Brewery del Perú, S.A.
Vice President, Banco Continental
Director-Manager, El Pacífico Cia. de Seguros & Reaseguros
Director, Empresa del Ferrocarril & Muelle de Etén
Vice President, Explosivos, S.A.
President, Inmobiliaria San Pedro, S.A.
President, Lima Rubber Company
Director, Negociación Tumán, S.A.
Director, Peruana Suiza de Fomento e Inversiones, S.A.
President, Petrolera del Pacífico, S.A.
President, Textil Algodonera, S.A.

JOSÉ PARDO HEEREN

Director, Agencia Philco
Director, El Pacífico Cia. de Seguros & Reaseguros
Director-Manager, Industrias Cerámicas, S.A.
Director, Industrias Eléctricas & Musicales Peruanas, S.A.
President, Inmobiliaria Urbana El Carmen, S.A.
President, Sociedad Inmobiliaria La Quinta, S.A.
Director, Sociedad Mercantil Exportación, S.A.
Director, Soc. Mercantil Internacional, S.A.
Director, Sociedad Nacional de Industrias
Director, Somerin Chiclayo, S.A.
President, Yutera Peruana, S.A.

JUAN PARDO HEEREN

Director, Agencia Philco, S.A.
Director, Colocaciones e Inversiones, S.A.
Director, Diarios Asociados, S.A.

169

TABLE **44.**—*Continued*

President, Gondela Trading Co., s.a.
Director, El Pacifico Cia. de Seguros y Reaseguros
Director, Hacienda "Chacrasana" de Juan Pardo Heeren
President, Industrias Tamet, s.a.
Director, Negociación Tumán, s.a.
Director, Soc. Mercantil Exportación, s.a.
President, Soc. Mercantil Internacional, s.a.
Director, Somerin Chiclayo, s.a.

ENRIQUE AYULO PARDO
President, Banco de Crédito del Perú
President, Cia. Agricola Punchauca, s.a.
President, Cia. de Seguros Rimac
Vice President, Empresas Eléctricas Asociadas
Director, Enrique Ferreyros & Cia., s.a.
President, Ferreyco, s.a.
President, Financiaciones e Inversiones, s.a.
President, Financiera Peruana, s.a.
President, Inmobiliaria Avenida Wilson 1282, s.a.
President, Inmobiliaria Camino Real, s.a.
President, Inversiones Angamos, s.a.
Director, Petrolera Peruana, s.a.
President, Sindicato de Inversiones Rústicas & Urbanas, s.a.

ERNESTO AYULO PARDO
Director-Manager, Cia. Agrícola Valle del Chillón, s.a.
President, Inversiones Pamplona, s.a.
President, Jockey Club de Lima
President, Lotizadora Sangrila, s.a.

FELIPE AYULO PARDO
President, Banco Internacional del Perú
Director, Caja de Depósitos y Consignaciones, s.a.
Director-Manager, Cia. Mobiliaria e Inmobiliaria "Santa María," s.a.
President, Inversiones Comerciales, s.a.
Director, Volcán Mines Company

VICENTE GONZÁLES PARDO
Manager, Negociación Chota-Motil, s.a.

atypical as can be seen by the managerial offices held by the other Pardos who are listed.

Family ties as well as economic ties proliferate. Table 45 shows how intermarriage has knit ties between the Pardos and the families of Canesco, Álvarez, Calderón, Olaechea, Pena, Piper, Velarde, Ayulo, Fellner, Gerenday, Aramburu, Pardo Althaus, Larrabure, Paredes, Escandón, Zela Sosa. These ties tend to give large dimension to a consciousness of a family system. In a tightly knit large family kinship sys-

TABLE 45.　*Major Family Ties of the Pardos*

PARDO ALCAZR

Enriqueta Pardo Alcázar married Bienvenido CANESCO.
Enrique Pardo Alcázar married Magdalena ÁLVAREZ CALDERÓN.
Luis Pardo Alcázar married Emilia OLAECHEA DU BOIS.

Through this family the Pardos acquire family ties with the CANESCO, ÁLVAREZ CALDERÓN, and OLAECHEA families.

GONZALES PARDO

Rosa Gonzáles Pardo married Richardo PEÑA ZAMBORAIN.
Vicente Gonzáles Pardo married Ruth PIPER.

Through this family the Pardos acquire family ties with the PEÑA and the PIPER families.

PARDO ALTHAUS

Manuel Pardo Althaus married Lauro VELARDE.
Cecilia Pardo Althaus married Enrique AYULO PARDO.
María Luisa Pardo Althaus married Federica FELLNER.
Rosa Pardo Althaus married Antonio GERENDAY.
Juan Pardo Althaus married Albina ARAMBURU.

Through this family the Pardos are associated with the following families: VELARDE, AYULO, FELLNER, GERENDAY, ARAMBURU.

AYULO PARDO

Enrique Ayulo Pardo married Cecilia PARDO ALTHAUS (see above).
María Ayulo Pardo married Carlos ÁLVAREZ CALDERÓN.
Felipe Ayulo Pardo married María LARRABURE.

Associations with the following families are made through this branch of the Pardos: PARDO ALTHAUS, ÁLVAREZ CALDERÓN, and LARRABURE.

PARDO HEEREN

José Pardo Heeren married Adriana PAREDES.
Carmen Pardo Heeren married Manual ESCANDÓN.
Juan Pardo Heeren married Guadalupe ESCANDÓN.
Enrique Pardo Heeren married Rosario PARDO de ZELA SOSA.

Gained ties with following families: PAREDES, ESCANDÓN, ZELA SOSA.

Previous contacts with other families are: BARREDA, RIVADENEIRA, SANTOS MENDIVIL, ALIAGA, BORDA, LAVALLE, CAVERO, LAOS, OSMA.

tem it is possible to think of one famous family as an "interest group" which seeks to preserve its identity, solidarity, wealth, status, and power. One technique of preservation is to prepare one or more sons to take over the family holdings. Brothers also commonly share in the responsibility. A famous old family, the Prados, are large landholders and investors in many enterprises. Mariano Ignacio Prado Heudebert, a large landholder best known as a banker, is also president of eight companies of various types and is a director of three others. He is now preparing his son for increased responsibility in some of these enterprises. Table 46

TABLE 46.   *The Positions of Father and Son: Mariano Ignacio Prado Heudebert Mariano Ignacio Prado Sosa**

FATHER:	SON:
Mariano Ignacio Prado Heudebert	*Mariano Ignacio Prado Sosa*
President, Banco Popular del Perú	Director, Banco Popular del Perú
President, Cia. Peruana de Cemento Portland, s.a.	Director, Cia. Peruano de Cemento Portland, s.a.
President, Almacenes Santa Catalina, s.a.	Director-Manager, Cia. Industrial de Alimentos, s.a.
President, Compañía A.B.C., s.a.	
President, Inmobiliaria de Teatros & Cinemas, s.a.	Director-Manager, Haras Michilin, s.a.
President, Popular y Porvenir Compañía de Seguros, s.a.	President of the Directorate, Inversiones e Inmobiliaria La Molina, s.a.
President, Refinería Conchan California, s.a.	
President, Tipografía Santa Rosa, s.a.	
Director, La Financiera Peruana, s.a.	
Director, Empresa Cinematográfica Libertad, s.a.	
Director, Fabricantes Técnicos Asociados, s.a.	

* *Who is Who in Peru*, Directory of Managers, Lima, Peru.

lists the positions held by Prado Heudebert and his son, Prado Sosa, and shows that the son has been placed in important positions in the extensive business holdings of the father in banking, cement, foods, tires, and real estate.

Other father and son chains which could be outlined would include those of Carlos Ferreyros Ribeyro, Augusto N. Wiese, Edward Dibos Dammert. They would show industrial holdings either transferred or in the process of transfer to the next generation.

The growth of the middle class is the single most important factor in altering political power and reshaping social structures. Peru is industrializing and becoming more urban. Manufacturing and mining have continued to expand and employment in agriculture has steadily declined. The number of manufacturing firms in Peru has increased from 3,255 in 1960 to 25,268 in 1964.[14]

The distribution of workers in the Lima-Callao district for 1962 is shown by Table 47. Note that approximately one fourth of the workers are in white-collar classifications. This segment continues to expand as government, banking, transport, and communications increase along with expansion of industry and commerce generally. The fish meal industry has grown dramatically to give Peru today its largest dollar volume export: 150 new factories for the processing of fish meal have

TABLE 47. *Distribution of Workers by Occupational Grouping in Lima-Callao District**

Occupational classification	Percent	
Administrators	2.2	
Professionals, technicians, and scientists	2.4	23.1
White-collar workers of office and sales	18.5	
Skilled and semiskilled workers	32.9	
Unskilled workers	36.7	76.9
Apprentices	7.3	
TOTAL	**100.0**	

* Based on a questionnaire sent to 604 establishments in the Lima-Callao District in 1962. Lawrence C. Lockley et al., *Guia Economica del Peru* (Lima, 1966), 103–04.

been developed, and a small group of new rich have appeared. By 1967 Louis Banchero Rossi, at 37 years of age, had built an industrial empire and a fortune, first from fish meal and then from interests in canned foods, boat construction, manufacture of agricultural tools and implements, and publication of a newspaper. A list of his offices indicates 21 positions from managing director to president of different enterprises in these categories. Son of Italian immigrants, Banchero was born at Tacna, Peru, where his father was a dealer in wines. He received a degree in chemical engineering and took a position as a salesman for an exporter. Later he formed his own business, first in lubricants, then in fish canning, and later with a fleet of fishing boats. This led to the processing of fish meal, and today his five plants process 6,000 tons daily. Many others have come to wealth through the fish meal and other industries that have undergone expansion in Peru. There are enough of these new enterprisers to create a "new rich" class.

Foreign enterprise also has brought rapid expansion. Perhaps most dramatic is the opening by Ford, General Motors, and Chrysler of new automobile assembly plants in the Lima-Callao district. In addition, Italians, Germans, Swiss, French, Japanese, and others have large commitments in Peru. All of these firms are adding thousands of workers in all categories and are helping to train skilled personnel in trades, offices, and administrative posts. These economic activities, domestic and foreign, are aided by loans and grants from national and international agencies. For example, the United States Embassy in Lima lists nearly 700 administrative and technical personnel attached to that office.

These indicators reveal that a middle class is present in Peru and it is increasing. Industry, banking, and foreign and domestic commerce continue to create opportunities for white-collar personnel, and universities, colleges, and training centers are actively supplying Peruvian professionals and administrators. This white-collar segment becomes an active leadership grouping. The popular mayor, Luis Bedoya Reyes, recently reelected for a second term, is a lawyer and former university professor. He heads a city council of 33 men and 6 women. The council consists of 18 members from the Alliance, 14 members from the Coalition, and 7 members who ran as Independents. Table 48 shows that most

TABLE 48. *Occupational Identity of Members of the City Council in Lima* (1966)

Alliance	(N = 18)	Coalition	(N = 14)	Independents	(N = 7)
Engineer	3	Lawyer	4	Engineer	2
Lawyer	2	Engineer	2	Lawyer	1
Librarian	2	Dentist	1	Chauffeur	1
Architect	2	Manager of factory	1		
Professor	1				
High school teacher	1	Fishing boat owner	1		
Economist	1	White-collar worker	1		
Manufacturing owner	1	Housewives	3		
Retailer	1				
White-collar worker	1				
Not able to classify	3	Not able to classify	1	Not able to classify	3

of these members are in the professions. Few, if any, are rich men. They are middle class, and an examination of the table shows no significant difference in the proportion of middle class in the three political categories.

A review of occupations of the senators and representatives in the national Parliament shows a very similar composition. A few rich landowners and industrialists are associated with the far right both as political party leaders and as members of Parliament, but the overwhelming majority of the legislators are professionals and businessmen. It is our contention that economic growth and political strength have brought the middle class to a new level of importance. The reshaping of society rests primarily in their hands.

Belief System of Lima

THE FOLLOWING is a tentative statement of beliefs widely shared in Lima which, it is felt, will provide a basis for understanding the community power structure of that city. The next chapter will reformulate some of the principal tenets of this belief system for empirical test.

Private ownership gives stability to the society by maintaining an established elite group of families who offer culture and leadership to the society. This is especially important in a nation composed of more than 40 percent Indians, most of whom are illiterate.

Private enterprise induces economic development which creates jobs and the rising standard of living that is so necessary for the maintenance of stability in a country with a rapidly expanding population. Economic development is absolutely necessary to the maintenance of private ownership and the preservation of the elite group. To this end inducements must be made to both domestic and foreign investors.

The Catholic Church and the military are two necessary supports for the preservation of the private property, anti-communist system. The Church provides moral force, the military offers physical force. Each has a special interest to protect: the Church is a large landowner, the military has prestigeful jobs at its command. Each shares opposition to Communism and this tie links them with landowners, large industry, small business, political parties, and government.

Government plays an arbiter role, serving as a buffer between entrenched interests and the have-nots. The welfare state with its social security system and some government ownership and control is a concession to persistent social needs and demands of low-income groups. The rapid growth of a middle class composed of professionals, managers, and white-collar workers provides a political balance. This class furnishes political leadership and reform of the society.

A large, extended family system holds elite groups together, expanding their number and influence through intermarriage, reciprocal bestowal of opportunities, and inheritance that is tightly held within the family structure.

Political influence is a necessary element in many transactions, so contacts are cultivated among political parties, government officials, businessmen, social leaders, military leaders, and church leaders.

The family, the school, and the social club become significant communication centers for exercising social and political control and for transmitting and maintaining the value system of the society.

The Catholic Church is given powers to transmit religious values to the total population through both Catholic-operated and state-operated schools.

Internal cohesion of the society is achieved by a consensus on common interests among business, government, religion, and military; an unyielding opposition toward all revolutionary Communist elements; reluctant cooperation with foreign businesses; and opposition to any so-called imperialist, interventionist acts of the United States or other foreign countries.

CHAPTER 12

DECISION-MAKING CLIQUES
AND POWER BLOCS IN LIMA

IN THE PRECEDING CHAPTER it was shown that political, governmental, and business leaders are ranked as the most influential in the life of the community. Military leaders were not nominated as active in community life. Educators and mass communication leaders are more important than believed, but religious leaders are less important than expected. Some of the questions left unanswered are: Do certain leaders and organizations work together to exert a unified influence? Does some group of men control the government and manipulate it to their interests? The hypothesis of institutional linkage states that principal business, religious, military, and political leaders function together in a group of high solidarity when the most important decisions affecting the community are made.

This hypothesis follows closely the often expressed statement that an oligarchy dominates Peru. Francisco Luis Quesada asserts that this oligarchy is a privileged group that dominates the political power.[1] He calls the group a plutocracy, but he is careful to point out that many of the businessmen of great wealth are not part of this group. Some observers place the number of families in the oligarchy at three hundred; others reduce this number to one hundred. Still another, former President José Luis Bustamante y Rivero, seems to set the number lower: "From the bank and industry a few dozen of men are the arbiters of the economy and impose their dictates on their own government and all the rest of the country."[2]

It is often said that this business-government nexus is joined by the military and the Church because they have conservative values at stake and are beholden to the oligarchy for many of their advantages.[3] Many observers see these groups working closely together. Roberto Maclean y Estenós writes that political affairs in Peru are not ventilated and so many times nominations of ambassadors and ministers, designation of senators and deputies, rise or transfer of magistrates, or promotion in the public administration are affected clandestinely.[4]

American observers make similar statements. Karl M. Schmitt and David D. Burks, writing in 1963, said:

> Peru today is one of the several countries in Latin America that has experienced little change from nineteenth-century political and social patterns. *A small upper class of landowners and wealthy urbanites dominates political life*, while the vast majority of the population—in large part Indian —plays no effective role. The small, fragmented middle class has little consciousness of unity. Many of the more ambitious among the latter strive to emulate the upper class rather than to develop a middle-class political program.
>
> In this pre-modern setting, pressure groups play a far more important role than parties (with a single exception) in national political life. Most of these groups promote the interests of the powerful oligarchy of closely interrelated families. In general, members of the elite have preferred not to hold political office, but rather to exercise their influence indirectly.[5]

Richard W. Patch, special observer of the American Universities Field Staff in Peru, described the country as one with an "archaic closed and rigidly stratified class structure." In 1963 he wrote:

> Fernando Belaúnde will have to make progress in all directions while under the watchful eye of the armed forces. There is every reason to believe that the military will move from the center of the stage of government and leave it to the new constitutionally elected president. They will, however, move no further than the wings, where any possible failings of Belaúnde and his party will be closely watched.[6]

All of these statements lead a disinterested observer to believe that there is high consensus that some kind of oligarchic power structure is present and that the government is subservient to it. But the evidence is weak, and some doubt that what observers believed was true ten years ago is true today.

Alberto Lleras, veteran observer of Latin American affairs, wrote recently that years ago some specialists in Latin American affairs classified all the societies of the region as traditional and feudal, composed of upper-class landowners, middle classes, and an immense mass of farmers and dispossessed urbanites. It was alleged that Latin America was governed by the landowners supported by the military and the clergy, and that together formed an invincible oligarchy. That summary description, he says, can neither be proved nor discredited altogether. So the term oligarchy, having gained an uncritical acceptance, continues to be repeated over and over. Lleras complains that few scholars observe that there are comparable stratifications in England, United States, and other countries. England has the establishment, and the United States has its power elites. He believes that for its size and power, the United States has a much more concentrated establishment. The establishment exists in Latin America as in Africa or in India, but in Latin America the idea is converted into the term oligarchy. He says observers go to Latin America prepared to find the oligarchy, assuming all the while that it exists there as a specific and unique group. He concludes that Latin America is moving toward a society less static and rigid, but that observers fail to see this.[7] David Rockefeller, an experienced American observer of Latin America, asks: "What are the chief impediments to achievement of the goals of the Alliance [for Progress]? In many quarters, the automatic answer to this is, 'The Oligarchs'."

This expression appears frequently, with little or no explanation, in news reporting out of Latin America. Yet surely this is a term that cries out for definition. If by "oligarchs" one refers to people who, with inherited or achieved wealth, are contributing to the over-all development, through efficient operation of productive enterprises, this would seem to be a socially useful—and, in fact, indispensable—class of men. If the word "oligarch" is used to suggest that political power rests in the hands of people of inherited wealth who are concerned solely with preserving their own privilege, who oppose and evade the equitable taxation of their wealth, and who make no contribution to the economic and social progress of the community, that admittedly would be a bad thing.

But in how many countries of Latin America is that, in fact, the case? My Latin American friends tell me—and my own observations confirm—that the stereotyped Latin American oligarch, the landed aristocrat who seeks to maintain a semi-feudal social order, is giving way to a new group of men in the politics of most Latin American nations.[8]

There is a paucity of data supporting any of these diverse points of view. Thus, the hypothesis that opens this area to study is important.

Method

OBVIOUSLY, the assembling of evidence to test the hypothesis that business, religious, military, and political leaders function together in oligarchic cliques is difficult. The ideal evidence would be tape recordings or eyewitness accounts of decision making obtained when the parties have actually been together. Such meetings would usually take place in privacy, but, it is not necessary for the parties to assemble physically. Decision making can take place by telephone, letter, or memo. Except in unusual instances, the social scientist cannot gain direct access to evidence of such activity and must therefore rely on indirect means. In this research study the test of the hypothesis relied on the following types of data secured from the interviews with top influentials and from documents: identification of decision-making groups and leaders; acquaintance pattern of top influential businessmen; power profiles of leaders; personal estimates by top influentials of clique behavior; identification of business, political, governmental and military, and religious dominants and a search for channels of communication; participation pattern of the most powerful leaders; identification of leading families and career aspirations for the sons; genealogical study (intermarriage patterns of leading families); economic interrelations (father-son patterns, interrelationship of landholding and industry); economic-political ties, military-political ties, church-political ties.

IDENTIFICATION OF DECISION-MAKING GROUPS AND LEADERS. The 21 top influentials were asked: "In your opinion what groups are most important for assuring support for a project or issue that affects the entire community?" and "Who are the key leaders in these groups?" There was high consensus on the groups and the key leaders. The following groups and leaders were named:

Groups	*Key Leaders*
Business community	Augusto Wiese, Carlos Ferreyros, Enrique Ayulo Prado, Mariano I. Prado, Fernando Berkemeyer
Politics and government	Fernando Belaúnde Terry, Víctor Haya de la Torre, Manuel Odría, Luis Bedoya Reyes
Newspapers	Pedro Beltrán, Luis M. Quesada
Catholic Church	Juan Landázuri Ricketts, Felipe McGregor, Víctor A. Belaúnde
Society and wealth	Juan Pardo H.
Education and culture	Luis Alberto Sánchez, Jorge Basadre
Labor	Julio Cruzado Zavala, Arturo Sabroso, Félix Loli Cepeda

It is interesting to observe that the military sector was not mentioned by any top influential. This corresponds to earlier results when it was noted that no civic organization representing military interests was active in the city and no military man received votes as a civic leader.

The identification of groups and leaders needed for wide community support of an issue or project provides a starting point for the search for an answer to the question: Do these leaders and groups work closely together in community decision making?

ACQUAINTANCE PATTERN OF TOP INFLUENTIAL BUSINESSMEN. From our data we have selected the interviews of five top businessmen and have computed their acquaintance pattern with individuals identified with the important supporting groups. Business leaders were selected since many observers allege political domination is exercised by business and that the property interests constitute the center of conservative interests. It is around this center that the church and military are supposed to give continuous support. Table 49 shows the rank of the business leader sample according to their degree of acquaintance with other leaders.

TABLE 49.   *Acquaintance Scores of Five*
Top Businessmen with the Leaders Named
as Needed for Community-wide Support
of Issues and Projects

Acquaintance with	Mean acquaintance score*
Business community leader	2.92
Political leaders	2.15
Newspaper leaders	2.90
Catholic Church leaders	2.50
Society and wealth leaders	2.80
Educational cultural leaders	2.70
Labor leaders	1.60
Military leaders	1.25

* Weights assigned: 0, don't know; 1, heard of;
2, know slightly; 3, know well; 4, know socially.

The acquaintance scores indicate that they know well all leaders with the exception of political, labor, and military leaders. They are especially isolated from labor and military leaders: the scores indicate that they have merely heard of them. Their acquaintance with political leaders is also slight: they say they know them but little. What does this mean? It must be deduced that they have infrequent contact; also there is some evidence that the tie between political, labor, and military leaders is very weak. Let us look at other kinds of evidence for a search for interrelationships.

POWER PROFILES OF LEADERS. All in the top influential sample were asked to indicate the principal bases of power for the 15 leaders they had selected as most powerful in initiating, supporting, or vetoing acts that have influence on the issues and events affecting the community in general. They indicated the bases of power by using the following list: political influence, economic power, governmental authority, military support, means of communication, superior qualities of leadership, well-liked, social prestige, special knowledge or skill, moral and religious persuasion. All respondents were able to make judgments quickly and without difficulty. Figure 14 shows the resulting profile of power for President Fernando Belaúnde Terry. It shows that he draws power mainly from institutional bases of influence and that this power is strongly reinforced by personal attributes.

The profile for the President shows an expected pattern in so far as

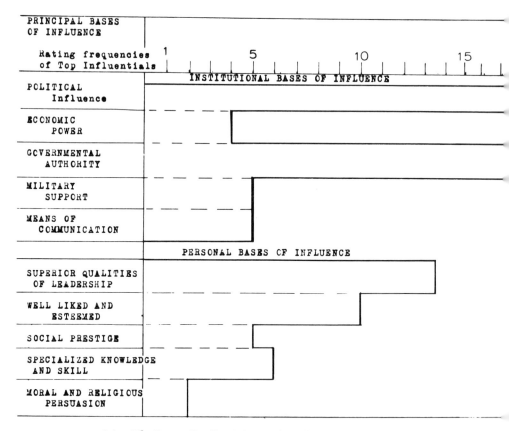

FIGURE 14. *The Power Profile of Fernando Belaúnde Terry, President of Peru*

political influence and governmental authority is concerned. He is the leader of his party, Popular Action, which he built and through which he achieved his presidential victory. His governmental authority rests upon his powers as President. Economic power, military support, and strong newspaper support (*El Comercio*) are important buttresses. His own personal qualities of leadership are well recognized. It is significant for our analysis to note that according to top influentials economic power is not a large base of his power. He is not a wealthy man and can command economic power only to the extent that his position enables him to exert influence over economic matters and over leaders of business and wealth.

Power profiles provide an instrument which appears useful in the search for patterns. What we would like to know, for example, is whether top political leaders demonstrate a high ranking of economic power and whether top bankers are shown to have high political influence. The power base of military and church leaders is also of interest because of the assertion that church and military are interlocked with economic and political interests.

The combined profiles of the major political leaders are shown in Figure 15. Note that a common pattern is revealed. All, of course, share the common trait that they draw their influence mainly from their political influence and, in contrast, a very minor part from their economic power. None are rich men. Since Fernando Belaúnde Terry occupies the presidency and Luis Bedoya Reyes holds the mayor's office, each draws mainly upon the powers of the office for influence. Military support is an important attribute since it gives stability to the President, and it has denied Haya de la Torre access to the presidency. In general, it can be seen that economic power and political power are not highly correlated as primary sources of power for political leaders. This does not mean, however, that economic support is not important. Our data does not permit us to conclude that the tie between economic interests and political influence is weak, but it does permit us to say that political leaders are not drawing their power from their own economic strength or influence over economic interests.

It is of interest to discover whether the reverse may be true of top bankers. Let us examine the power profiles of six top bankers as derived from the rankings of our top influential sample. Figure 16 shows that the power of bankers (and business leaders) rests upon a significant base of economic power but that their political influence is regarded as another strong base. Indeed, the bankers have a balanced base of power with relatively high rankings in economic power, political influence, and social prestige. The political leaders, on the other hand, rely heavily on

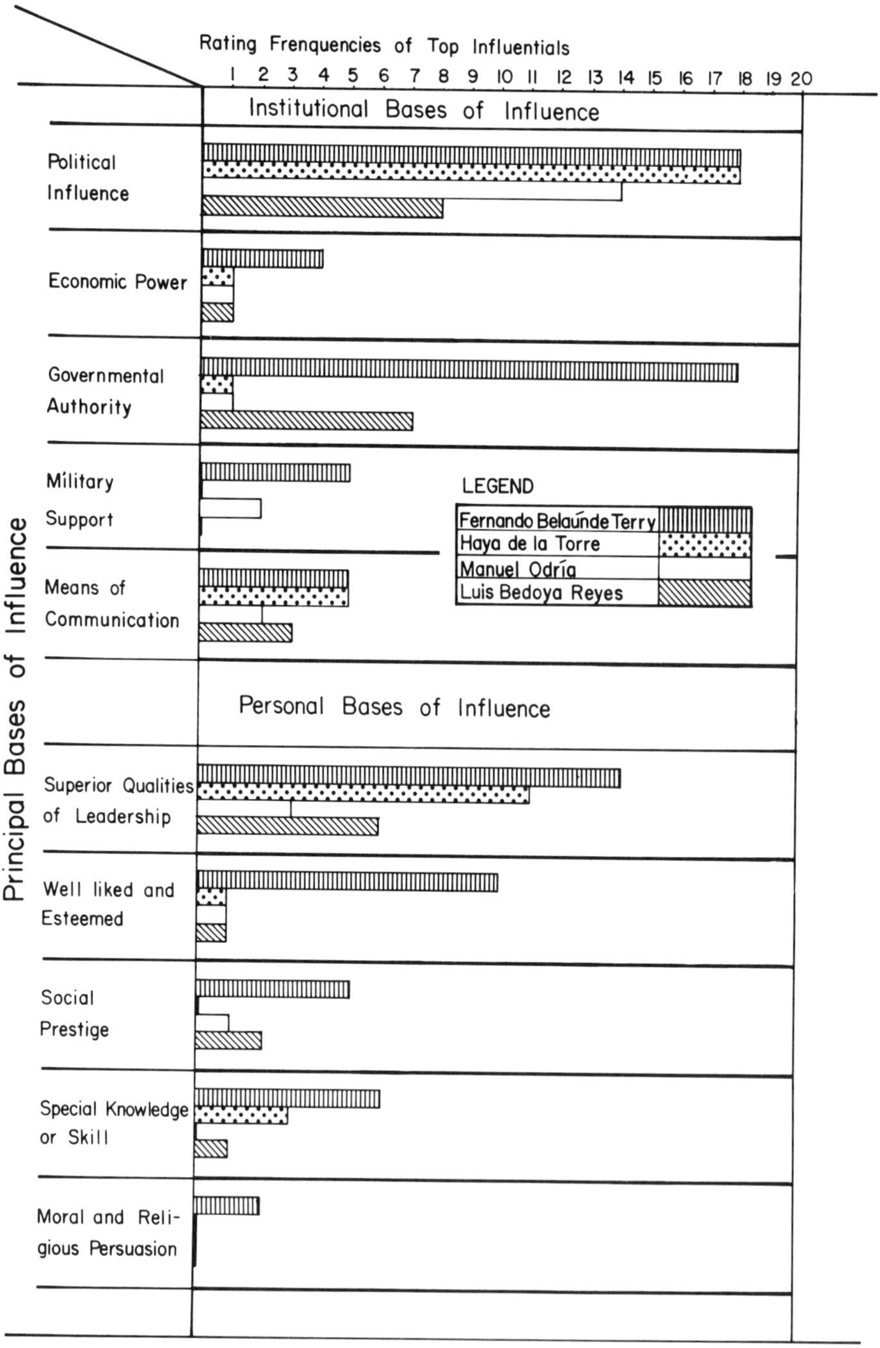

FIGURE 15. *The Power Profiles of the Four Major Political Leaders of Lima*

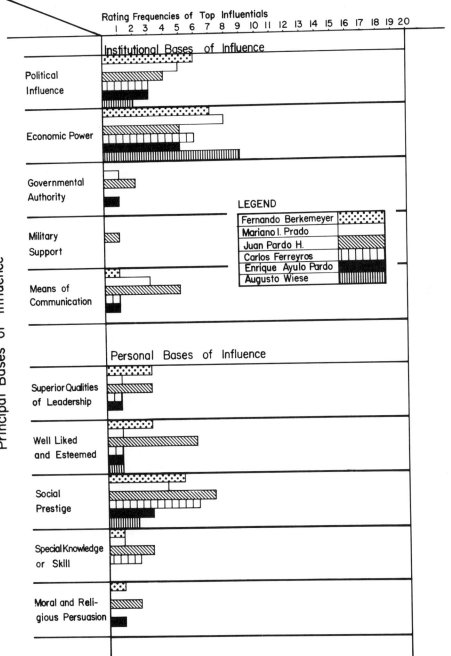

FIGURE 16. *The Power Profiles of Six Major Banking Leaders of Lima*

political influence, superior qualities of leadership, and—with the exception of two party leaders out of office—on governmental authority.

The key question of how the bankers wield their political influence is not answered by these data. We must rely upon what the top influentials will tell us in interviews. Extracts from the interviews will be presented with the discussion of cliques in a following section.

Power profiles of three religious leaders are shown in Figure 17. These men occupy quite different positions. Cardinal Juan Landázuri Ricketts is head of the Catholic Church in Peru; Felipe McGregor, a Catholic priest, is rector of Catholic University in Lima; Víctor Andrés Belaúnde, a university professor and distinguished writer, is Peru's representative to the United Nations and is regarded as the most important lay member of the Catholic Church. These men rank high in drawing their power from moral and religious persuasion and their influence is based heavily on their institutional roles as well as their personal qualities. It can be seen that they draw heavily upon the personal bases of influence, especially superior qualities of leadership, being well-liked, and possessing social prestige. Their political influence is respected, but the rankings do not indicate that this is an important base of their influence.

Communication leaders are represented by the publishers of the two leading newspapers. Pedro Beltrán was former Premier and minister of finance and is regarded as the voice of conservative interests. He is a large landowner and has many business interests. Luis Miró Quesada put his newspaper behind the candidacy of Fernando Belaúnde and has been a loyal supporter of the President and his party, Popular Action. Figure 18 shows the power profiles of these two communication leaders who occupy vital positions in the power struggles of the city and nation. Political influence and communications are ranked as principal bases of their power. Their personal qualities buttress their influence.

Labor leaders were seldom mentioned as important in getting support for community activities. Their attention is directed inward toward their unions. They work closely with the APRA party. Arturo Sabroso is best known as a labor writer and special counselor in the APRA party. Julio Cruzado Zavala is the chief of the National Confederation of Labor Unions representing most of the organized workers in Peru. However, he is new in the post and is not well known. A third labor leader, Félix Loli Cepeda was seldom mentioned by the respondents but he should not be ignored. He is a member of the APRA party, was elected to the national legislature, and does have a base in political influence. He is also a labor official with some visibility. Figure 19 shows the profiles for Arturo Sabroso and Julio Cruzado Zavala. Since few top influentials

186

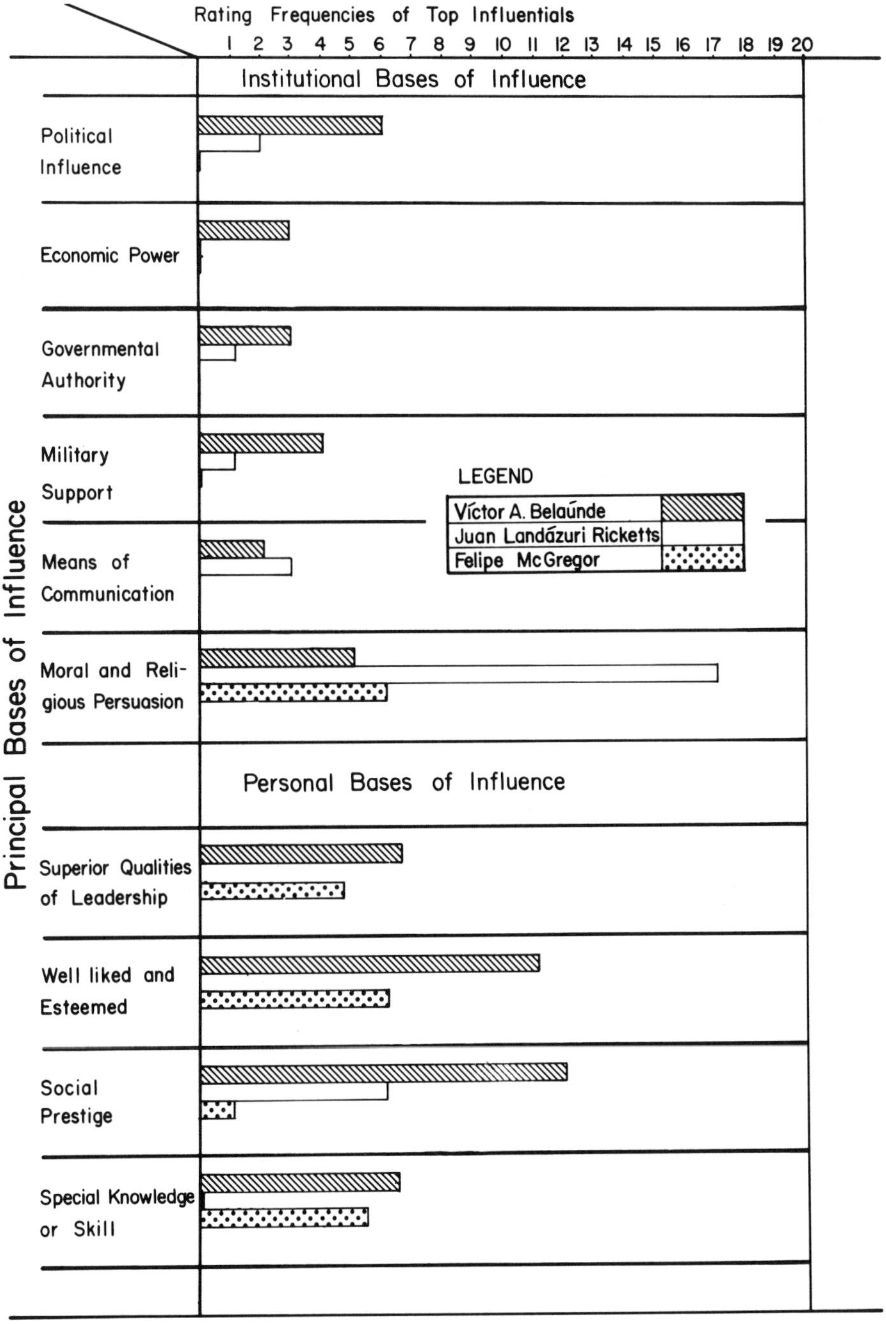

FIGURE 17. *The Power Profiles of Three Major Religious Leaders of Lima*

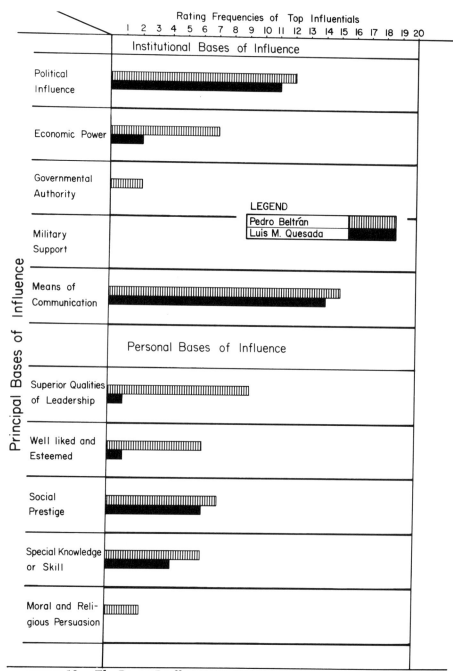

FIGURE 18. *The Power Profiles of Two Major Mass Communication Leaders of Lima*

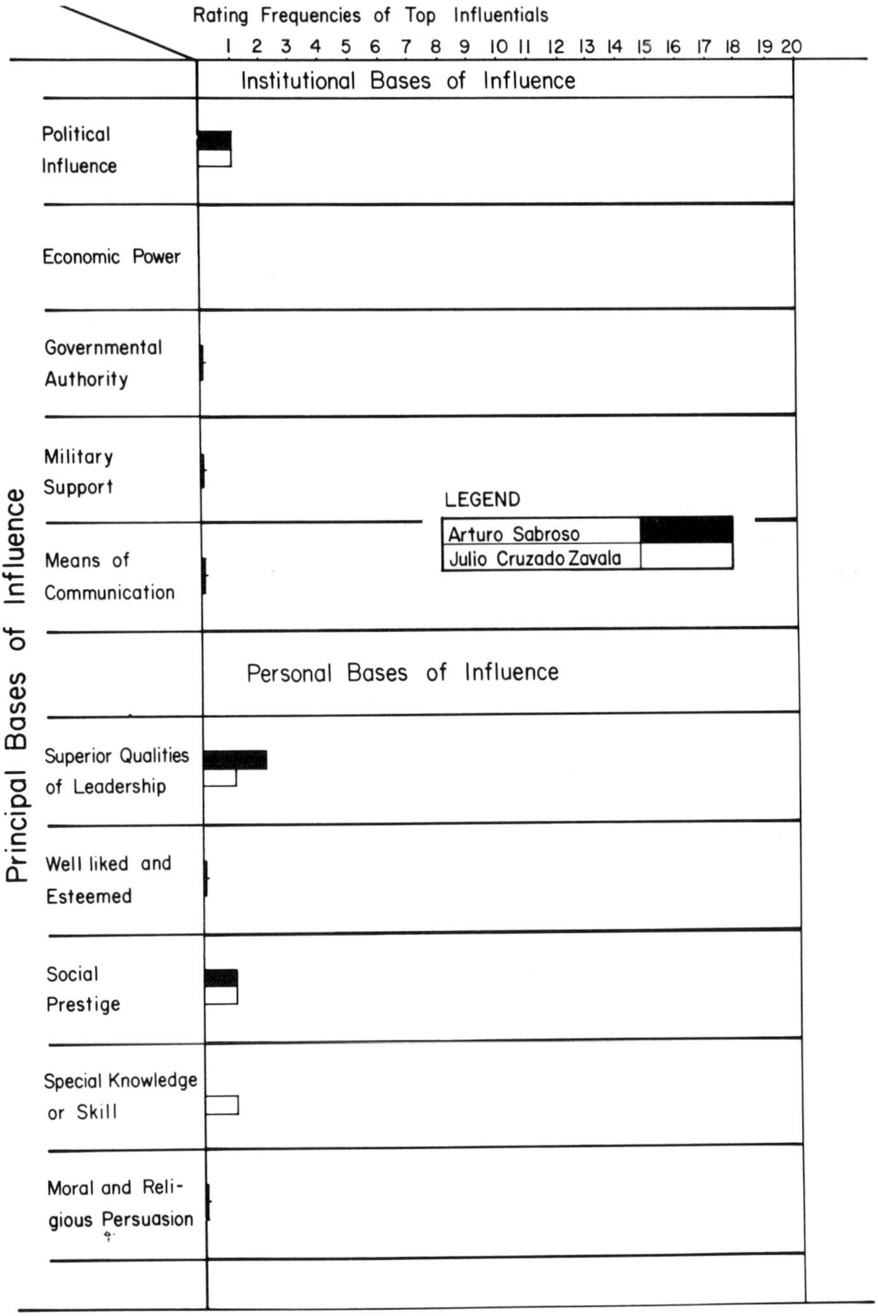

FIGURE 19. *The Power Profiles of Two Major Labor Leaders of Lima*

ranked them, for our purposes their political influence can be discounted.

No military leaders were chosen as important in getting support for community activities, and they must therefore be considered to have little effect in such matters.

In summary, power profiles suggest that the institutional power of leaders may be distributed primarily according to their principal offices. Political leaders draw their power from their political party leadership, bankers and businessmen from their economic position, religious leaders from their church position, and so on. Most careful examination is given here to the relationship of economic and political power. The rankings of the 15 leaders rated as highest in drawing their influence from economic power were compared with their rankings in political power among all top influentials and the resulting Spearman rank correlation of $-.40$ shows an inverse relationship!

It can be concluded that economic power and political influence are not necessarily in the same hands. At least it cannot be shown that such political influence leaders as Fernando Belaúnde, Víctor Haya de la Torre, Manuel Odría, Pedro Beltrán, Luis M. Quesada, Luis Bedoya Reyes, and Luis Alberto Sánchez are captives of economic power until such a case is made. This researcher does not rule out the possibility that some combination of economic, military, religious, and labor influence could bend political influence to its will. To explore this possibility, top influentials were asked directly about clique behavior. Their personal estimates will now be presented.

CLIQUE BEHAVIOR AMONG RELIGIOUS, POLITICAL, BUSINESS, AND MILITARY LEADERS: ESTIMATES BY TOP INFLUENTIALS. The sample top influentials were asked the following questions: "It is often said that religious, political, business, and military leaders work together to make the big decisions which affect the community of Lima. Is this true or false? Why?"

Twelve said "True," but most spoke with reservations; nine said "False," but also added reservations. In general those who said "True" wanted this to mean: leaders of the four groups do work together in a crisis; or the leaders keep in touch by informal checking; or communication takes place by an overlapping of leaders in the four groups, as, for example, religious with military, military with political, political with business. No top influential said that the members of the four groups got together in any one place to make a decision. As it turned out those who said "True" and those who said "False" really meant the same thing: it became obvious from their explanations that there was near consensus on how decisions were made and where communication takes place.

The following quotations reveal the consensus over how decisions are made:

Government and Business work together on some things—like the Montaro project (an electrification program). Military and government check with each other on some things. The Military have quarters right next to the President and keep him informed with advice. The church comes in once in a while on an important matter—say birth control. I don't think they all ever get together on an important matter.   MILITARY OFFICIAL

Every group acts independently to guard its interests. The only working together is one of specific interests—like a group of business persons seeking to influence a tax position of the government.   BANKER

Each group stays in touch through personal friends. The Archbishop and X (important financier) stay in close touch. These leaders do not meet together in one place but they see each other in friendships.   EDUCATOR

They do not meet together as a group. Usually if a group wants something—say business—it will put its request to some authority like government. They may try to get newspaper backing.
PUBLIC RELATIONS OFFICIAL OF A LARGE CORPORATION

These parties simply don't get together. It is always difficult to get anyone to work together in Peru. Now it is true that if business wants to get something done it may try to get support from the government, the military, or church. It just depends on what the proposal is. It is always easier to get the other party to help oppose something they don't want—take communism, etc.   UNITED STATES EMBASSY OFFICIAL

They don't work together but the President will check with each of the leaders in these four groups. I know the President has a consultative commission with representatives of Business, Government, Church, and Military. But they don't often meet together. The President calls them for advice. I know he calls the bank here.   BANKER

The following quotations express a common agreement on how communication takes place. The home predominates as the center of communication for these four groups of leaders, but communication can occur by telephone, in small groups, and by newspapers.

I don't think they ever get together in formal groups but there is a lot of fraternizing at parties. The men go off together and talk. Often parties are arranged to bring certain people together so the host can talk over an idea of interest to him.   SOCIETY LEADER

Decisions in Lima are made in the houses—in the homes. Not in hotels or clubs. Down at the National Club (most important social club for men) businessmen eat their lunch and talk but not to make decisions. Decisions are made in the house. There is a dinner party—the men get together and talk afterward and the women go off by themselves. When the men come out the party is over and everyone goes home.   INDUSTRIALIST

I think these persons check with one another—maybe not in any one place. I think two or three people talk and then one acts as an intermediary and gets in touch with another group.

I remember when the Cardinal took the lead in reducing the number of vacation days. He got the Chamber of Commerce to back it and the government came in. The Cardinal even checked right back to the Vatican. It went through and labor never did anything to oppose it.

RELIGIOUS LEADER

You know there is a lot in the ceremonial customs. You can tell from a list in the paper who is backing a man and you can get a good line on who is moving together. (A custom prevails of offering a banquet for a political candidate, candidate for an organization office, or for rector of the university. The names of supporting friends are then published in the newspaper.) It is very subtle but often you learn a lot about a man before you meet him.

CIVIC LEADER

The role played by groups and individuals is further illuminated by the following quotations from interviews with top influentials.

I have heard variously that 400, 100, or 40 families run Peru. How? The government officials are elected by the people and the government has power. No one can stand against the power today. The President has command of more than a billion of soles—that is more than any other person. If the President wishes to make land reform he can. The government ministers are not landowners. Government is mainly lawyers, some engineers, doctors and teachers. They have no stake. Of course, if the critics want to tear down the productive sugar plantations and turn them into non-productive sugar plantations, then I say, maybe it is well to resist change.

The military does not want power. They do not interfere until there is disorder. The church is constantly losing influence.

No, I say that if a person wishes to talk about those who resist change let him mention names of persons and not use words like minorities, oligarchies, old families, landowners, etc. What they are doing is making a charge that covers ignorance, are unwilling to seek facts, or are simply trying to make political capital.

BANKER

The military is not important except by keeping themselves behind the scenes and telling the politicians to behave themselves. I mean not to be soft on communists; not to let the country get caught up in runaway inflation.

INDUSTRIALIST

The army works behind the scenes. It simply wants a stable democratic government. It doesn't want to govern. When it steps in, it does so to fill a vacuum, to restore stability. And it does not act with other parties directly. . . . It is a military junta. But military men take an oath to support a democratic government and they don't want to run the country.

I see all four parties standing pretty independently drawing on one another for support when they need it. You can't even count on government and business being together on things. These people are pretty much different—there is lots of fighting between the ministries and business men.

INDUSTRIALIST

The closest tie is between government and business. The military just stands by. They have representatives in the cabinet (ministries of army, navy, and air) and they are satisfied with this government. They would be unhappy if they believed Communists were getting control or if they were unhappy with their budget.

BANKER

The government often takes positions opposing business. There are many taxes that have been imposed on business which it fought. I think the military stays out except for a crisis situation. I put labor as more important than business because they can put on a lot of pressure. For example, the government is always worried about what taxi drivers would do when a rise in gasoline prices was announced. They have worked out a deal now. The taxi drivers get their cars duty free and they are expected to be quiet when new prices of gasoline are announced. Labor gets its way.

ECONOMIST

Government, business, religion, and the military have different interests. Government rests on politicians who must win votes of a large group. Business covers many different interests who want low taxes and few rules. Religion has a few individual interests that other groups respect, like birth control. The Military just wants things to go along without trouble.

The only time they work together is when an interest is overwhelming in favor of public interest. Two examples are the polio campaign for immunization and civic action in road building.

NATIONAL GOVERNMENT OFFICIAL

When the Vice President of Peru says powerful minorities are blocking change he means economic groups—landholders blocking agrarian reform, banks which have very favorable conditions (15 percent interest on loans) and all those that get a cut on the development of projects, etc.

Then, too, big interests intervene in political campaigns—money is given to selected candidates. And then you have bribes to government officials. I think government is rotten to the core. I don't know what would happen to an honest man in government.

You know families have relatives in lots of positions where they can call for favors.

The Masonic Lodge is supposed to be important if a man wishes to get ahead in the Army. It's mainly a social organizaiton, not religious, and it gives backing politically to persons. Lots of members from the APRA party belong.

PUBLIC RELATIONS OFFICER

The role of the family was probed. Many families are large and it seemed feasible to believe that sons entering government, the church,

193

business, and the military could provide a wide base of common participation and influence. The top influentials agree that the sons of the old families are going into business and professional pursuits and almost never into the church and the military and seldom into government.

Old families are encouraging their sons to go into business administration or some branch of engineering. Of course, some enter the traditional professions—law, medicine, education. If a person can't find a profession or a way to education he goes into the army—if he can't make it in the army he goes into the clergy. Even government is not stable enough to attract the most able persons. Banker

There is no pattern among upper classes of urging sons to go into military, church, or government. Only middle-class groups support these three sectors. There are a few military men and church men who are from out of the old tradition—the Cardinal, Father McGregor, and Father Griffith. But upper-class young men are not coming in the church or military. The clergy must draw upon foreign priests to get good persons. The dictatorships in the 30's hurt government as a career. They were so corrupt that it blackened the reputation of government as an organization filled by corrupt men. Industrialist

The upper-class family does not have a tradition of urging their sons to go into the clergy or military. They want their sons to go into property and business developments. Many urge that their sons train as soil engineers, mining engineers, and other specialists for the future exploitation of the resources. A few sons go into the Navy but they are never encouraged to go into the Army. Educator

At this point a summary of all the evidence would lead to the conclusion that there is a minimum of collective decision making between these powerful groups. Economic and governmental power seem to operate in independent channels. Economic dominants control business operations; political leaders operate as professionals, small-town merchants, or labor representatives in a sphere in which their authority is legitimized by electoral or appointive processes. The church becomes involved in an issue only if it concerns a few specific interests (birth control, church property, etc.). The military remains inert except as it becomes concerned with a Communist threat, increasing inflation, or its own budget.

The haunting question remains: Is there a covert pattern, "an invisible government," that has not been revealed by the data? Too many observers keep insisting that a governing relationship exists between the political power group and the economic, military, and religious groups for us to abandon the problem.

IDENTIFICATION OF BUSINESS, POLITICAL, GOVERNMENTAL, AND RELI-
GIOUS DOMINANTS. How can an investigator penetrate into possible
covert networks? Our answer has been to seek data from selected informants. First, we asked these informants to help us identify those
positions most powerful in government, political parties, military, business and finance, and religion. We then asked them to rank the power
of these positions and indicate official channels of communication. Figure 20 lists the positions and the incumbent leaders the informants
considered most influential in the powerful institutional sectors of Lima.
All leaders are in some respects national as well as city leaders. They are
called "dominants" since they perform in important positions of authority, influence and communication.

There is every reason to believe, based on repeated ratings by top
influentials and informants, that if there is a pattern of power interrelationships in Lima it can be discovered among the dominant leaders of
these institutional sectors.

SEARCH FOR CHANNELS OF COMMUNICATION. The first step of significance in finding the channels of communication was to locate the
existing official channels in each sector and outline the lines of inter-
change. Figure 21 depicts a pattern of communication as it impinges
on the national and city governments. Since the national government
has jurisdiction over many matters that affect the city, it may be said
to dominate Lima. The city can claim few sources for its own financial
support other than the appropriations made by the national government.

Figure 21 shows communication of pressure groups through a mass
communication net and also directly to political parties and the executive branch of government at both the national and the city levels. Pressures are voiced through newspapers, magazines, radio and television
stations. The three most important newspapers, *La Prensa*, *El Comercio*,
and *La Tribuna*, represent the most influential "filter" power.

There is good evidence that the business and finance group exerts
pressure upon both major political groups—the alliance of the Popular
Action and Christian Democratic parties and the coalition of the APRA
and Odrista parties. The President sits in a precarious position between
these parties since the APRA and Odrista coalition, which opposes him,
has a majority of the membership in both houses of the legislature and
constantly harasses the cabinet members. One entire cabinet has re-
signed en masse and the second has been punctured by the numerous
resignations demanded by the opposition. All of the members of the
cabinet, with the possible exception of the military members, belong
to the Popular Action or the Christian Democratic party. As far as can

FIGURE 20. *Positions and Dominant Leaders of the Most Powerful Institutional Sectors of Lima (1965–66)*

Name of Official Dominant	Position
GOVERNMENT	
Fernando Belaúnde Terry	Leader of Popular Action
Daniel Becerra de la Flor	President of Cabinet and Minister of Public Health; Senator for Manague; Popular Action
Edgardo Seoane Corrales	First Vice President of nation
Mario Polar Ugarteche	Second Vice President of nation; Senator for Lima
Sandro Mariátegui	Minister of Interior; Deputy for Lima; Popular Action
Sixto Gutiérrez	Minister of Public Works; Senator for Madre de Dios; Popular Action
Javier Alva Orlandini	Minister of Government and Police; Deputy for Lima; Popular Action
Miguel Dammert Muelle	Minister of Labor and Indian Affairs; Senator for Lima
Rafael Cubas Vinatea	Minister of Agriculture and Deputy for Huanuco; Christian Democratic
Luis Bedoya Reyes	Mayor of Lima
Gen. Benavides y Benavides	Chief of Central Intelligence
José Novarro Grau	Minister of Education
Italo Arbulu	Minister of War
POLITICAL PARTIES	
Fernando Belaúnde Terry	Leader of Popular Action
Víctor Raúl Haya de la Torre	Leader of APRA
Manuel A. Odría	Leader of Odrista
Luis Bedoya Reyes	Mayor of Lima, important leader of Christian Democratic
Hector Cornejo Chávez	Leader of Christian Democratic; Secretary General; Senator for Lima
Armando Villanueva del Campo	Secretary General of APRA; Deputy for Lima
Oscar Trelles	Secretary General of Popular Action
Ramiro Priale	Senator for Junín; important majority leader for Senate
Julio de la Piedra	Secretary General for Odrista; Senator for Lima
Daniel Becerra de la Flor	President of Cabinet and Minister of Public Health; Senator for Managua; Popular Action
Luis Alberto Sánchez	Important Leader and Rector of San Marcos; APRA
MILITARY	
Italo Arbulu	Minister of War
Pablo Jhery Camino	President of the Joint Command of the Armed Forces
Julio Doig Sánchez	Commander General of the Army
José Heighes Paraz Albela	Minister of Aeronautics
Luis Ponce Vela	Minister of the Navy
Carlos Siles Barani	Commander General of the Peruvian Air Force

FIGURE 20   *(continued)*

Name of Official Dominant	Position
Julio Gianotti Landa	Commander General of the Navy
Juan Valasco Alvardo	Chief of State; Major in the Army
	BUSINESS
Mariano I. Prado	President, Compañía Peruana de Cemento Portland; President, Banco Popular
Enrique Ayulo Pardo	President, Financiera Peruana, S.A.; President, Banco de Crédito
Carlos Ferreyros	President, Industrias Reunidas; President, Del Perú, Financiera y Comercial, S.A.
Max Reiser	Peruano Suizo de Fomento e Inversiones
Luis Banchero Rossi	Owner of many industries with principal base in fishmeal
Juan Oeschle	President, Oeschle Department Store
Eulogio Fernandini	Large owner of residential and commercial property
Felipe Ayulo Pardo	President, Banco Internacional
A. F. Wiese	Owner, country club (banker)
Pedro Beltrán	Owner, *La Prensa* (large landholder)
Luis Miró Quesada	Owner, *El Comercio*
Ramón Aspillaga Anderson	Inmobiliaria Nacional
Juan Pardo Heeren	Owner of many export-import industries. (For list see Table 44.)
	RELIGION
Juan Landázuri Ricketts	Cardinal of Peru
Fidel Tubino	Auxiliary bishop
Rómulo Carboni	Nuncio of Lima (representative of Pope)
Mario Cornejo	Auxiliary bishop
José Dammert Bellido	Auxiliary bishop
Felipe McGregor	Director of Catholic University (Víctor Andrés Belaúnde, lay leader)
Hernando Vega Canteno	Dean of archbishopric of Lima
César Bellido	Deacon of the Church
Oscar Vidal	Deacon of the Church
Stanley Evans	Director of Movimiento Familiar Cristiano in Lima

be determined neither the President nor any cabinet member is a rich man. None can be identified as officers of banks or industries and none are large landholders. Most are professionals—lawyers, engineers, and doctors. The president of the cabinet is a small-town physician. The official communication is indicated as between the architect-educator, President Belaúnde, and the physician, cabinet president Daniel Becerra de la Flor. Strong communication ties exist between the other dominants and the President. As he surveys his cabinet of twelve members he sees

PRESSURE GROUPS

BUSINESS AND FINANCE

Powerful Economic Dominants	Powerful Economic Organizations

MILITARY

Powerful Official Positions & Leaders

LABOR

Powerful Official Positions & Leaders

Powerful Economic Dominants

Mariano I. Prado
Luis Banchero Rossi
Carlos Ferreyros
Fernando Berkemeyer
Augusto N. Wiese
Pedro Beltrán
Enrique Ayulo Pardo
Max Reiser
Felipe Ayulo Pardo
Eulogio Fernandini
Juan Oeschle
Ramón Aspíllaga Anderson
Juan Pardo Heeren
and many others

Powerful Economic Organizations

National Agrarian Society
National Society of Industries
National Mineral & Petroleum Society
National Fishing Society
Chambers of Commerce of Peru
Merchants Corporation of Lima
Chamber of Commerce of Lima

Powerful Official Positions & Leaders (Military)

Minister of War (Italo Arbulú)
President of Joint Command of Armed Forces (Pablo Jhery Camino)
General of Division Army (Julio Doig Sanchez)

Powerful Official Positions & Leaders (Labor)

Secretary General of Confederation of Labor of Peru (Julio Cruzado Zavala)
President of Central Union of Private Employees of Peru (Félix Loli Cepeda)
APRA Political Liaison Leader (Arturo Sabroso)

Foreign Enterprisers backed by their respective Government Embassy Groups

MASS COMMUNICATION AGENCIES

NEWSPAPERS

El Comercio

Strong defender of Pres. Belaúnde;
Vigorous opponent of APRA

(Luis Miró Quesada)

Catholic Organs
Actualidad

Provides support to Christian Democratic Party

(Victor A. Belaúnde)

POLITICAL PARTIES

OPERATE WITHIN
THE
CONGRESS

Coalition Parties in Executive Power
(Popular Action and Christian Democratic Parties)

Fernando Belaúnde Terry   Luis Bedoya Reyes
Héctor Chávez Cornejo

NATIONAL GOVERNMENT

PRESIDENT FERNANDO BELAÚNDE TERRY

Chief of National Intelligence   Consultative Commission & Consultants
(General José Benavides y Benavides)

Minister of Finance & Commerce	Minister of Public Works	Minister of Agriculture	Minister of War	Minister of Navy	Minister of Air
Deputy Sandro Mariátegui	Senator Sixto Gutiérrez	Deputy Rafael Cubas Vinatea	Gen. of Division Italo Arbulú	Admiral Luis Ponce Vela	Major Gen. José Heighes Pérez Albela

Minister of Labor	Minister of Government & Police	Minister of Justice	Minister of Foreign Relations	President of Cabinet & Minister of Public Health & Welfare	Minister of Public Education
Senator Miguel Dammert Muelle	Dr. Javier Alva Orlandini	Deputy Valentín Pariagua	Senator Jorge Vásquez	Senator Daniel Becerra de la Flor	Dr. Carlos Cueto

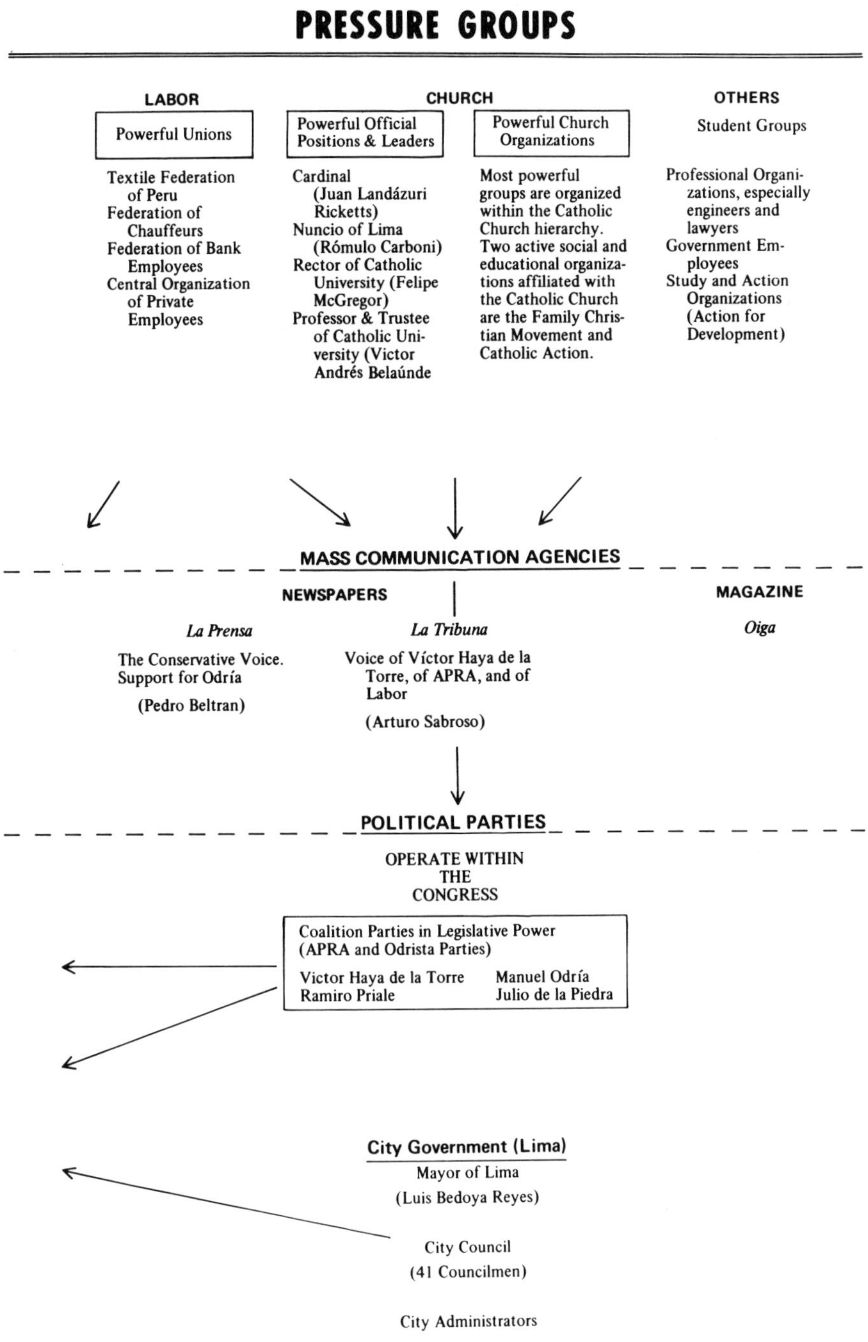

PRESSURE GROUPS

LABOR	CHURCH		OTHERS
Powerful Unions	Powerful Official Positions & Leaders	Powerful Church Organizations	Student Groups

LABOR	CHURCH	OTHERS
Textile Federation of Peru Federation of Chauffeurs Federation of Bank Employees Central Organization of Private Employees	Cardinal (Juan Landázuri Ricketts) Nuncio of Lima (Rómulo Carboni) Rector of Catholic University (Felipe McGregor) Professor & Trustee of Catholic University (Victor Andrés Belaúnde	Most powerful groups are organized within the Catholic Church hierarchy. Two active social and educational organizations affiliated with the Catholic Church are the Family Christian Movement and Catholic Action.	Professional Organizations, especially engineers and lawyers Government Employees Study and Action Organizations (Action for Development)

MASS COMMUNICATION AGENCIES

NEWSPAPERS   MAGAZINE

La Prensa   *La Tribuna*   *Oiga*

The Conservative Voice.   Voice of Víctor Haya de la
Support for Odría   Torre, of APRA, and of
                               Labor
(Pedro Beltran)
                               (Arturo Sabroso)

POLITICAL PARTIES

OPERATE WITHIN
THE
CONGRESS

Coalition Parties in Legislative Power
(APRA and Odrista Parties)

Victor Haya de la Torre   Manuel Odría
Ramiro Priale   Julio de la Piedra

City Government (Lima)

Mayor of Lima
(Luis Bedoya Reyes)

City Council
(41 Councilmen)

City Administrators

FIGURE 21. *Communication and Political Pressure Network
of the Community and National Power Structures*

three military men representing the Army, Navy, and Air Forces. These men report back to the president of the joint command of the armed forces. The President must watch his labor minister take strong pressure from the APRA party leaders and the strong labor organizations centered on the Confederation of Labor of Peru. His minister of agriculture and Indian affairs must deal with land reform and is constantly under the scrutiny of large landowners, cattle and wool growers, cotton and sugar owners. The minister of finance and the minister of public works are in key positions because they are responsible for the main bulk of the campaign promises. "Peru Builds" is the slogan of the Popular Action party. If better housing, more jobs, relatively stable prices, and a better standard of living are to be attained, these two cabinet officers must be effective.

The city government receives pressure to remedy such urban problems as bad streets, lack of running water, traffic congestion, garbage and sewage, and street vendors. However, labor problems in the city usually are referred directly to the national government, as are most other problems. When the appropriate national minister refuses to act the responsibility turns squarely upon the city government. But very often the mayor cannot act without funds and assistance from the national government. The President of the Republic and the Mayor of the city may be equally blamed on any given day for holes in the street, lack of adequate housing, crime and delinquency, traffic problems, or any other city problem.

The student groups and government employees use such weapons as demonstrations, strikes, work stoppages, and occasionally sabotage to bring pressure upon the authorities. Many of these groups are linked to the political parties and it is sometimes believed that their collective behavior is a planned action to fit a broader preconceived political maneuver.

Professional organizations vary in their effectiveness. One group of young professionals called Action for Development has been especially influential because it studies carefully capital needs of the country and examines proposals critically. It makes its findings known to the national and city governments.

Now the full play of influential pressures has been outlined. What does such an exposition reveal? It shows the sources of pressures and the nature of the communication channels and lines of pressure. It does not answer fully the question of whether a covert or solidary group of leaders work together. It is obvious that overlapping communication channels exist. It is possible for leaders to make formal and informal contacts in the course of their daily lives. A participation pattern of the most powerful leaders might shed more light on this possibility of social contact. The participation matrix of the top 33 leaders judged most powerful in the community life of Lima (Table 50) shows that these men might come into contact with one another through the 88 partially overlapping memberships they share as large landholders, bank presidents or directors, industry presidents or directors, political party leaders,

TABLE 50. *Participation Matrix of the 33 Leaders Nominated as Most Powerful in Lima*

LEADERS MOST POWERFUL IN ORDER OF RANK	Large landholder or property holder	Bank president or director	or director Industry president	Top official of political party — Very active	Active	Top official of formal organization (gov't, Lbr, Educ, Mil, etc.)	Old family society	Total social identifications
1. Fernando Belaúnde Terry					X	X	X	3
2. Víctor Raúl Haya de la Torre					X			1
3. Pedro Beltrán	X	X	X	X		X	X	6
4. Juan Landázuri Ricketts						X	X	2
5. Manuel Odría					X			1
6. Luis Miró Quesada				X		X	X	3
7. Víctor Andrés Belaúnde				X		X	X	3
8. Felipe McGregor						X	X	2
9. Luis Bedoya Reyes				X		X		2
10. Hector Cornejo Chávez				X				1
11. Honorio Delgado						X		1
12. Mariano I. Prado	X	X	X	X				4
13. Luis Alberto Sánchez					X	X		2
14. Rómulo Ferrero	X	X					X	3
15. Luis Banchuro Rossi	X	X	X					3
16. Carlos Ferreyros R.		X	X				X	3
17. José Benavides y Benavides			X			X	X	3
18. Augusto N. Wiese		X	X			X	X	4
19. Fernando Berkemeyer	X	X			X		X	4
20. Jorge Busadre							X	1
21. Fernando López Aldona Schwalb		X			X	X	X	4
22. Herless Buzzio			X			X		2
23. Julio de la Piedra	X	X	X	X			X	5
24. Arthuro Sabroso				X				1
25. J. Wesley Jones						X		1
26. Carlos Cueto Fernandini					X	X		2
27. Juan Pardo Heeren	X		X				X	3
28. Hernando Lavalle	X		X				X	3
29. Enrique Ayulo Pardo	X	X	X				X	4
30. Sandro Mariátegui				X		X		2
31. Eulogio Fernandini	X	X	X			X	X	5
32. Antonio Pinilla					X	X		2
33. Julio Cruzado Zavala					X	X		2
	10	11	12	9	9	19	18	88

top officials of formal organizations, and as members of the old family society. While there is wide diversity in the participation matrix, there is considerable overlapping of some groups. For example, the 10 large landowners or property holders share 40 possible overlapping social memberships. In contrast, the four major political leaders (Belaúnde, Haya de la Torre, Odría, and Cornejo Chávez) show only six total memberships, centered for the most part in political parties and government agencies. Labor leaders and military leaders continue to show an isolation from community contacts except those growing out of their own organizations.

To summarize, the leadership structure appears fragmented and not well enough connected to indicate support for the thesis that political, business, military, and religious leaders work together in cliques of high solidarity. However, the social stratification which gives persons of wealth so much prestige does suggest that further efforts should be made to discover possible interrelations. A number of additional studies are needed. These include the identification of leading families and a search for their interconnections in the power structure. Further study of father, son, and brother economic ties would be useful in understanding economic concentrations of power. A special effort should be made to search out economic-political ties, military-political ties, and church-political ties. These would take careful studies that perhaps can be undertaken successfully only by Latin American social scientists. Available knowledge shows a tightly knit upper class can be solidified through the growth of large, wealthy families who constantly intermarry. The great emphasis upon family kinship, nepotism in business and government, and favored educational preparation creates hereditary social groupings. However, industrialization has created a vigorous if not sizable middle class. This group is providing leaders in the professions, the political parties, the universities, the church, and the military. The working class has political parties and the trade unions to represent their interests. Together the middle class and the working class compose a significant amount of countervailing power. Because power relations in these groups are fragmented, power arrangements are indeterminate. Foreign enterprisers and the financial and political activities of foreign governments add to this indeterminacy. It is evident that conclusions regarding power arrangements should be extremely tentative. However, on the basis of this study it can be said that no monolithic power structure under tight oligarchic control is operating in Lima or in Peru today.

PART IV

The Community Power Structures of the World Cities of Seattle, Bristol, Cordoba & Lima: An Overview

THE POWER STRUCTURE STANDS *as a superstructure upon the economic, governmental, and social base of the community and of the larger society. Many similarities and differences of power structures can be foreseen through knowledge of the economic, political, and social factors. The central values around which issues are resolved constitute the immediate link to a given power structure because they reflect the dominant institutions of the institutional power structure of the community.*

We shall begin by comparing the institutional power structures of the four communities. We will examine the community power complex and evaluate the top and key influentials. A final test of the system model will be made by describing the extent to which the four communities exhibit successive associations among their component parts. Finally, the role of social values will be observed to determine how a power structure may be interpreted as a product of value systems.

CHAPTER 13

COMPARATIVE ANALYSIS
OF THE FOUR CITIES

Institutionalized Power Structures of the Four Communities

THE VARIETY OF THE INSTITUTIONALIZED POWER STRUCTURES of Seattle, Bristol, Cordoba, and Lima is apparent from the relative power rankings of major institutions shown in Table 51. There is much similarity

TABLE 51. *Relative Power Rankings of the Most Influential Institutions in Seattle, Bristol, Cordoba, and Lima**

SEATTLE	BRISTOL	CORDOBA	LIMA
Business and finance	Local government	Religion	Local government
Local government	Business and finance	Business and finance	Political parties
Labor	Political parties	Local government	Business and finance
Mass communication	Labor	Labor	Military
Education	Education	Military	Labor

 * Rankings were determined by the reputational methods with top influentials responding in Cordoba and Lima; judges were used in Seattle and Bristol.

in that business, labor, and government are among the top five most powerful institutions. The fact that all of the cities are industrialized communities accounts for this similarity. It is the rank order of the institutions which emphasizes the individuality of their community power structures.

Seattle is a community with its roots deeply set in a free enterprise tradition and power base. A strong business sector with high influence over the governmental structure is a distinctive characteristic of a city where economic progress has priority. Labor is well assimilated into the system. The strongest union accepts the basic tenets of the enterprise system and joins business in avoiding increasing governmental control over industrial relations. The newspapers and political parties fully support the basic values of the on-going system.

Bristol reveals strong governmental dominance, as has been shown in the discussion of its large council plan. In this power center, labor and its political arm, the Labour party, have wrested control from a strong business group. The city council has utilized a mild democratic socialist philosophy to provide social services, but it has not imposed urban socialism upon industry. There is much deference to the upper classes, education, and traditional institutions. Business remains strong because private enterprise is accepted as the dominant pattern of ownership; leaders of business rank high in education and general social status.

Cordoba is distinctive in the large role it assigns to religion. Top influentials may be exaggerating the dominance of the Catholic Church, but they insist that religion is their most influential institution. Leaders of business, government, and religion agree upon the importance of private property and the threat of both Communism and Peronism to the well-being of the country. As has been shown, the Catholic Church has direct ties to the property system and is active in political parties, welfare, education, and the general social life of the people. Indeed, it has influential connections in all institutions, especially business, society, mass communication, and government. The military institution is important; this sector is unrepresented in almost all Western cities but is omnipresent in Latin American cities.

Lima shares the Spanish tradition and the social and governmental instability of Cordoba. But, unlike Cordoba, Lima is functioning as a democracy and is relying on representative government and strong political parties (or coalitions) for its decision making. There is every reason to believe that the government has a relatively independent role. The political parties have real power and use the executive and legislative branches of the national and municipal governments as operating bases. Political party leaders are acknowledged as key influentials. Business and military groups ask primarily that Communism and inflation be contained and that private enterprise be respected and given encouragement. Labor has power primarily because the strike is a potent weapon both economically and politically. Moreover, labor has political power by its sponsorship of the APRA party, which has the largest representation in the national legislature and is a major party in Lima. The military in both Lima and Cordoba is recognized as capable of seizing power and as ready to do so if economic or political disorder threatens the country. The military is regarded as a legitimate but transitory governmental force. When it is in power, it relies heavily upon civilians for operation of the government, and it is sensitive to the popular demand for a return to a representative government. When it retires from governmental operation, it plays a watchdog role. It can safely be said that a democratic administration must maintain general military approval, but the government may enjoy independence as long as it functions within the relatively broad limits which the military sets for its intervention.

Perhaps the most significant similarity in these four cities is their common reliance on private business enterprise. In the midst of great political pressure to nationalize industrial operations, private enterprise has generally survived and flourished. Through the growth of enterprise, each city has grown, has offered more jobs at better rates of pay, and has watched a middle class constantly expand. While most of these cities own and operate many of their own utilities and some house nationalized industries, these public enterprises remain in small minority, not only because of economic or political pressure from the propertied interests, but also because nationalized industry can fall heir to a series of troubles: corruption; lack of efficiency; political appointments to jobs; technical stagnation; lack of worker motivation; waste; tax burdens for investment, maintenance, and expansion; and lack of capable leadership. Each city has experienced these problems in developing city- or nationally-owned industries and services. People in all social classes are aware of these dangers and so resist or are indifferent to political pressure and threats to throw private enterprise out. For more than ten years all major political parties in Peru have been calling with constant clamor for the nationalization of the oil fields and refineries of Standard Oil. Only naked military coercion finally prevailed in 1968.

A relatively stable power position is also held by labor and the political party it supports. In all four cities, these two elements represent the major countervailing force to economic power. When the labor-supported party is in power, the influence of labor is augmented. Usually, this results in a demand for and a provision of increased social services. Whether local governments are weak or strong in these four cities depends partly on the governmental structure (recall the contrast between Seattle's nine-man, elected-at-large council and Bristol's ward system of 112 members) and partly on the achievement of consensus within the party and between parties. Failure of consensus in Cordoba and Lima constantly threatens to lower the influence of the government by throwing it into deadlocks and impotence.

The most significant difference in these four cities is the presence of the military that intervene frequently in Lima and Cordoba as their countries fall under military dictatorships. This is so common in the recent history of these cities that each is constantly aware of military pressure and influence. When problems mount, disorder and political deadlocks appear and the temporary intervention of the military is expected. In contrast, Seattle and Bristol do not regard a military government as a possibility. It is interesting to note that under all kinds of government, "city hall" must continue to handle city business very much as usual. Even in the absence of a mayor and council, policy decisions must be made to meet the demands of urban life and experienced civilians are needed.

Other differences among the cities occur because they have different resource and stratification patterns. As a result, different political pressures are filtered through traditional patterns and values. These differences will be elaborated and interpreted as we proceed.

Community Power Complex

A FIRST STEP in discovering the community power complex is to ascertain the most influential organizations and the most salient issues that have arisen in the community. Table 52 is an exhibit of the associations ranked as most important in the four world cities.

TABLE 52. *The Most Important Associations in the Four World Cities*°

SEATTLE	BRISTOL	CORDOBA	LIMA
Chamber of Commerce	Bristol Labor party	Radical Party of the People	National Federation of Labor
Municipal League	Bristol Citizen's party	Industrias Kaiser Argentina	El Comercio
Central Labor Council	Bristol Trades (Labor) Council	Los Principios	Popular Action Party
Boeing Airplane Co.	Council of the University	La Voz del Interior	APRA Party
University of Washington	Society of Merchant Venturers	Commercial and Industrial Center	La Prensa
Teamsters Labor Council	Rotary Club	Fiat Concord Co.	Christian Democratic Party
Parent-Teachers Association	Bristol Cooperative Society	Catholic Action	National Mercantile Association
Seattle Times	Muncipal charities	Chamber of Commerce	Odrista Party
Seattle Post-Intelligencer	Transport Workers	Confederation of Workers	Action for Development
Seattle First National Bank	Chamber of Commerce	Superior Council of the National University	National Institute for Planning

° Associations were rated by top influentials in the four cities.

208

Seattle has a complex of business and mass communication organizations that are active in influencing community decision making. Members of the Chamber of Commerce and the Municipal League come almost entirely from business and the independent professions. The two newspapers, the Boeing Airplane Company, and the Seattle First National Bank support many community projects with funds and leadership and by general legitimization of what is good for the community. The University of Washington and the Parent-Teachers Association generally support community projects. The Parent-Teachers Association is an aggressive political force for public education.

The right-to-work issue showed that business owners and managers and certain professionals and white-collar groups who sought limitations on the union shop were opposed by organized labor, the Democratic party, and the Catholic Church. Education, welfare, local government, and the protestant churches remained neutral.

The equilibrium theory of the community power complex states that certain stabilities may be expected to appear in succeeding community power complexes according to the type of issue and the degree of community involvement.[1] Issues that involve tax fights, zoning, annexation, and strikes often give the community power complex a predictable stability. In Seattle, the Democratic party and organized labor often form coalitions, and sometimes the church joins. This was shown on the Sunday-selling issue in the same manner as in the right-to-work issue, except the protestant churches joined with the Catholic Church in the former case.

Bristol, in contrast to Seattle, has a strong Labor party and labor organization. These organizations receive support from the Cooperative Society. Labor dominance in Bristol is as strong as—if not stronger than—business dominance in Seattle. Opposition to labor arises from the Bristol Citizen's party, the Chamber of Commerce, and such groups as the Society of Merchant Venturers and the Bristol Club, and sometimes from the Council of the University. However, voluntary organizations play a lesser role in mobilizing public opinion than in Seattle because the city council is recognized as the central focus of community power. The political parties are represented on the council by influential community leaders, and each party forms caucuses and employs the "whip" to demand bloc voting. Parties thus assume power and responsibility. The large council uses an effective committee system to forge positions on issues.[2]

Cordoba relies even less on voluntary groups for formation of public opinion than does Bristol. In 1963, the city was governed by a civilian federal intervenor appointed by the ruling military junta. The city to all appearances seemed to be in civilian control even though no mayor or city council was operative. However, city hall went about its administrative business as usual. Political parties, girding for forthcoming elections, were setting out their platforms. Newspapers provided news and a forum for opinions. There was no tradition of looking to voluntary groups or leaders for the initiation of community projects. The Catholic Church through its Catholic Action and institutional efforts was expected to take care of social welfare and "good works for the needy." Solution of city problems such as housing, transit, roads, strikes, and zoning were regarded as being the exclusive responsibility of the city or provincial government. The low social participation in organizations and in committees, reported earlier, shows the striking difference between the United States and the Argentinian community. The American-operated Kaiser plant appeared in striking contrast to other community organizations. Its official policy of supporting art and cultural institutions and recreational and philanthropic activities made it an outstanding community agency. Its public relations department was more active in community life than were those of the Commercial and Industrial Center and the Chamber of Commerce, the two central business associations.

Regularities in the community power complex could not be observed as they would appear under a democratic government. Informants said political parties and government provided the central focus, with the church and business playing major roles. The military does not normally intervene in city affairs during democratic regimes.

Lima was functioning under a democratic government. It had a strong mayor and a large, vigorous council in which the two opposing political groups—Alliance and Coalition—were very evenly divided and politics was turbulent. The political parties and newspapers raised issues and mobilized for struggles in the council, the national legislature, and the national administrative departments. The lines of responsibility and authority are blurred between city and national officials. Often it is necessary to test which agency will act by applying pressure on it. The political party now serves as the most important focus of community decision making. The Alliance, which drew its strength from the backing of some business groups and the Catholic Church with the silent support of the military, could command a majority in the council only by the slimmest of margins. The Coalition gained its strength from organized labor, strongly supporting the APRA party of Haya de la Torre, and from its right element, the Odrista party. These two political blocs faced off in the council and the national legislature. All other organizations counted only in so far as they could generate political influence through the parties and government officials.

Table 53 demonstrates the issues with which each city was struggling. Seattle was concerned with traffic, water pollution, and civic facilities. Bristol had problems administering the 30,000 homes the city (corporation) had built to relieve the housing shortage. Problems of assignment and rental assessment were central. The extensive bomb damage of World War II also created problems of redevelopment and of rehousing of industry and commerce. Cordoba was wrestling with problems resulting from the Perón regime and the intervention of the military. Problems of transit, traffic, and roads stemmed from the growth of the city and its increasing industrialization. The coming of Kaiser and Fiat brought new problems such as the bitter labor strike at Kaiser. Lima, a

TABLE 53. *The Most Important Issues in the Four World Cities during the Years Shown*

SEATTLE (1953–56)	BRISTOL (1954–55)	CORDOBA (1961–63)	LIMA (1965–66)
Location of Lake Washington bridge	Rent issue in housing estates	Transfer of bus company from city ownership to workers' cooperatives	Improvement or elimination of slums
Pollution of lake and sewer issue	Inequitable tax rates	Transfer of train company from city ownership to workers' cooperatives	Problems of sanitation and water
Proposed Tacoma-Everett freeway	Bus fares	Federal military intervention in city and province	Improvement of transport
New public library	Comprehensive schools	Kaiser automobile plant strike	Control of crime and delinquency
University of Washington football issue (subsidization scandal)	National health issues	Acceptance of new city zoning plan	Abolition of proportional representation for municipal councilmen
Right-to-work petition	Rehousing of business in bomb-damaged areas	Traffic and street illumination problems	Containment of corrupt practices among city officials
Development of a civic center	Traffic	Provincial road improvement	Improvement of streets
Seattle as World Fair city	Redevelopment of city	Bringing television to Cordoba	Planning and zoning
Attracting new industry	Increasing industrial productivity	Bringing eucharistic congress to Cordoba	Improvement of public markets
Selling on Sunday	Local-national public health coordination		Control of ambulatory vendors

city with a very large growth of rural migrants, had a far greater slum problem than any of the other three cities. Housing, sanitation, water, traffic, transport, public markets, telephones, and other facilities were of poor quality or in short supply. Of all the problems facing the city, leaders agreed that the slums were the worst and urged that priority be given to this issue. The social problems in all the cities grow out of the presence of low income groups and rapid growth of population. These problems increase like a gradient across the four cities studied.

Top Influentials

THE INSTITUTIONAL IDENTITY of top influentials in the four cities is shown in Table 54. In each of the cities business and finance has a

TABLE 54. *Institutional Identity of Top Influentials in the Four World Cities**

INSTITUTIONS	Seattle (N = 44)	Bristol (N = 32)	Cordoba (N = 37)	Lima (N = 33)
Business and finance	33%	34%	24%	30%
Labor	14	19	3	3
Education	10	9	11	12
Government	17	9	16	18
Political parties	0	0	11	18
Independent professions	12	13	8	3
Military	0	0	0	3
Religion	7	9	8	6
Society and wealth	0	7	5	0
Mass communication	0	0	8	6
Social welfare	5	0	0	0
Culture and art	2	0	3	0
Recreation	0	0	3	0
TOTAL	100%	100%	100%	99%

* Top influentials were selected by panels of judges and evaluated by top influentials themselves. Where identity overlaps two or more institutions, the occupational identity which is used for classification is that which best reflects the institutional base of power of that individual.

greater proportion of top leaders than any other sector. There is very little or no representation from the recreation, military, social welfare, and culture and art sectors. Figure 22 shows the gradations in representation for the four cities.

The four cities show similarities in the proportion of top influentials from certain sectors. The highest proportion in all four cities comes from the business sector. Education, government, and religion also show high similarity in the proportion of top influentials they contribute. Each of these sectors develops leaders of high education and with wide-ranging interests in the community. The leaders often hold jobs that compel them to participate. Time is legitimately free and allocated to community life,

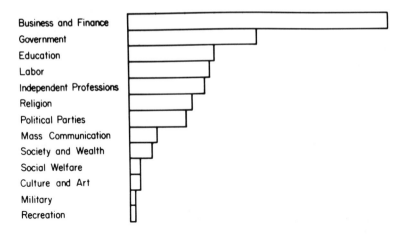

Business and Finance
Government
Education
Labor
Independent Professions
Religion
Political Parties
Mass Communication
Society and Wealth
Social Welfare
Culture and Art
Military
Recreation

FIGURE 22.   *Relative Representation of Institutional Sectors by Number of Top Influentials in the Four World Cities*

and the leaders are expected to provide service to the community. The small proportion of influentials in recreation, military, social welfare, and culture and art is shared by all four cities.

The most significant variation among the cities is the greater number of labor leaders who are top influentials in the Western cities and the greater number of political party leaders who are top influentials in the Latin American cities. The reliance on free and voluntary associations in American and British communities is reflected here. On the other hand, the reliance on government and political power is shown by the political party pattern in the Latin American cities, where many of the political parties have full-time leaders who devote themselves to the party and retain high influence without a government post of any kind. Haya de la Torre has given an entire lifetime to the leadership of the APRA party in Peru and has never held a government position. Instead, he has been repeatedly jailed and exiled.

The independent professional man can achieve influence in the Western cities through voluntary activity. The pattern in Latin American cities is for the lawyer and the engineer to associate with political parties or government to achieve influence. Physicians and dentists in all of the cities seem to avoid extensive community participation. The university professor or administrator rivals the lawyer in a movement toward politics and government, particularly in Latin American countries where dual careers in university and government are commonly observed and encouraged.

Key Influentials

THE OCCUPATIONS of all the key influentials selected in the four cities are listed in Table 55. It can be seen that all hold major positions in the

TABLE 55. *Key Influentials as Selected and Ranked by Top Influentials in the Four World Cities*

SEATTLE
1. °Manufacturing executive
2. °Wholesale owner and investor
3. °Mercantile executive
4. °Real estate owner—executive
5. °Business executive
6. University president
7. °Investment executive
8. °Investment executive
9. °Bank executive—investor
10. Episcopal Bishop
11. Mayor (lawyer)
12. Lawyer

BRISTOL
1. Labor party leader and councilman
2. University president
3. °Manufacturing executive
4. Bishop, Church of England
5. °Manufacturing executive
6. Citizen party leader and councilman
7. University official
8. °Manufacturer-owner
9. Labor leader
10. Civic leader (woman)
11. Lawyer
12. Society leader

CORDOBA
1. °Wealthy owner of large real estate company
2. °North American president of largest private industry
3. Publisher-editor of newspaper (with large stock interest held by Catholic Church)
4. °Merchant
5. Owner of large engineering firm (engineer)
6. Banker and university professor
7. President of Catholic University
8. Political party leader
9. °Owner of a very large construction company
10. Wealthy society leader and university professor
11. President of state university
12. High-ranking national government official and a physician
13. Political party leader
14. Vice president of Catholic University (influential Catholic lay leader)

LIMA
1. President of the republic and political party leader
2. Political party leader
3. Publisher of a newspaper
4. Cardinal of the Catholic Church
5. Political party leader
6. Publisher of a newspaper
7. National government official and university educator
8. University educator and religious leader
9. Mayor and political party leader
10. Political party leader
11. Educator
12. °Banker and large real estate holder
13. Political party leader and educator
14. Educator and independent professional

° Identified with Business and finance.

institutions of their cities. Owners or presidents of industry, banking, investment, and real estate lead the list. Political party and government leaders appear frequently. The mayor is almost always named, but his tenure as a key influential is often related only to his term of office. University presidents and their chief business officers are frequently mentioned.

The composition of key influentials by institutional affiliation is shown for the four cities in Table 56. It can be seen that the business

TABLE 56. *Institutional Identity of Key Influentials in the Four World Cities**

INSTITUTIONS	Seattle (N = 12)	Bristol (N = 12)	Cordoba (N = 14)	Lima (N = 14)
Business and finance	67%	25%	43%	7%
Labor	0	8	0	0
Education	8	17	22	21
Government	8	17	7	21
Political parties	0	0	14	29
Independent professions	8	8	0	0
Military	0	0	0	0
Religion	8	8	0	7
Society and wealth	0	8	7	0
Mass communication	0	0	7	14
Social welfare	0	8	0	0
Culture and art	0	0	0	0
Recreation	0	0	0	0
TOTAL	99%	99%	100%	100%

* Where institutional identity overlaps two or more institutions, the occupational identity which best reflects the insitutional base of power is used for classification.

and finance sector continues to furnish the largest percentage. Education, government, and political parties follow in that order. Figure 23 gives the relative representation of institutional sectors by number of key influentials in all four cities.

This figure reveals that labor's ability to produce key influentials is far below its ability to produce top influentials (see Figure 22); it drops from fourth position to ninth position. Actually, only Bristol has a key labor leader. In Seattle, where powerful labor leaders existed, top influentials often said that these men were too controversial for inclusion in committee structures. In Cordoba informants said that the Perón era denied opportunities for labor leadership to emerge. In Lima informants said that top labor leaders were newly elected to their posts and were unable to make their voices heard because of inexperience in community life. The most pronounced rise is in representation from political parties, which move from seventh position as contributors of top influentials to fourth position as contributors of key influentials. All these key influentials, however, are in political parties in the Latin American cities.

As producers of key influential leadership, the society and wealth, social welfare, military, culture and art, and recreation sectors can be

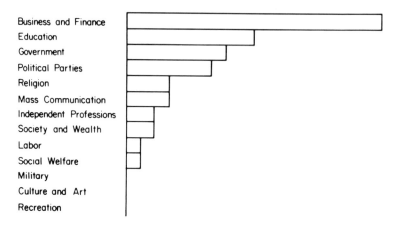

Business and Finance
Education
Government
Political Parties
Religion
Mass Communication
Independent Professions
Society and Wealth
Labor
Social Welfare
Military
Culture and Art
Recreation

FIGURE 23. *Relative Representation of Institutional Sectors by Number of Key Influentials in the Four World Cities*

written off. This is not to say that these sectors are without power and influence. It is to say that key influentials seldom come from these sectors. Their positional leaders may lead their organizational units effectively, but they do not win repute 'for their participation in community-wide issues and projects. Some of these findings are unexpected since the military junta was in power in Cordoba and the military power was very much in the awareness of Lima citizens. However, the role of the military was that of watchful caretaker, either awaiting general elections, as in Cordoba, or standing firm for democratic order in Lima.

The most significant institutional sources of key influentials are business and finance, education, government, and political parties. The education sector is something of an anomaly, however, because it provides many leaders but receives relatively low .ranking as an institutional influence. The high ranking of education leaders is often due to their roles as mediators or compromisers between competing groups. They can represent many sectors such as religion, social welfare, government, and culture and art. It has been noted that many leaders in education are also often identified with a political party or government office. This gives them high political influence, especially in Latin America where education conveys added status and recognition. In Lima the rector of the largest university in Peru (San Marcos) is also president of the national senate. The President of Peru is a former dean of the school of architecture at San Marcos.

Test and Evaluation of the System Model of Community
Power Structure

A BASIC PROPOSITION of sociological science is that social structure largely influences the functioning of a social system. The fundamental question is not why men act as they do but how men are compelled to act as they do. For the first time, sufficient comparative data have been assembled to make a good test of the system model of community power structure and to examine more intensively the influence of structural elements on community power processes. The data developed from the studies of the four world cities provide a good basis for a test of the model and its theoretical assumptions.

Relationship between the institutional power structure of society and the institutionalized power structure of the community. Spearman rank order correlation coefficients have been calculated for each of the cities comparing the relative power and influence of the 13 institutional sectors in the nation with their relative power and influence in community. The rankings have been derived in each case by expert judges or top influentials. The rank coefficients for the four cities are: Seattle, .87; Bristol, .90; Cordoba, .84; and Lima, .93. These coefficients indicate a high relationship and affirm the postulate of the interrelationship of the institutional structures in the nation and the community.

Interrelationship of the institutionalized power structure of the community and the community power complex. Table 57 compares the ranking of the five most powerful institutions of each city with the ten organizations ranked as most important in each city. A correlation can be seen but there are discrepancies in rank order. However, it can be noted that in Seattle 100 percent of the most influential organizations fall within the top five most powerful institutions. In Bristol it is 80 percent; in Cordoba, 60 percent; and in Lima, 90 percent. This is good evidence that institutions and organizations show a high correspondence.

There are good explanations for the discrepancies observed in rank ordering. Many meanings are attached to the word "organization," and organizations function in various ways in community life. Ordinarily sociologists wish to restrict the use of this word to voluntary associations. However, people in a community often see business firms and newspapers functioning like "voluntary organizations" when they provide community leadership, initiate community projects, and offer special financial support for community-wide activities. Even a city council is often viewed as an organ of popular expression in contrast to city hall, which

TABLE 57. *Relative Power Ranking of the Most Powerful Local Institutions in the Four World Cities Compared with the Number of Organizations Representing These Institutions*[*]

SEATTLE (N = 10)		BRISTOL (N = 8)		CORDOBA (N = 6)		LIMA (N = 9)	
Most important local institutions	Number from 10 most important organizations	Most important local institutions	Number from 10 most important organizations	Most important local institutions	Number from 10 most important organizations	Most important local institutions	Number from 10 most important organizations
Business	3	Local government	0	Religion	1	Local government	2
Local government	1	Business	3	Business	4	Political parties	4
Labor	2	Political parties	2	Local government	0	Business	2
Mass communication	2	Labor	2	Labor	1	Military	0
Education	2	Education	1	Military	0	Labor	1

[*] Rankings were determined by the reputational methods with top influentials responding in Cordoba and Lima and judges used in Seattle and Bristol.

seems more like the "government." All of these agents are recognized as having "associational" roles because of their involvement in community projects. In fact, in Cordoba the Kaiser automobile company with its policy of active community participation and its highly qualified Argentine-staffed public relations department was one of the most effective "organizations" in the city. A business firm or a newspaper may restrict itself primarily to its business interests, but it can also be very important as a social force if it so chooses. In addition, a newspaper can be a voice of business, labor, church, or political party and play a role that represents another institution rather than restricting its role to communication. These differences in role make it difficult to fit "organization" into a neat classification scheme.

In some institutional sectors no organizations as such exist. The local government is not ordinarily represented by any organization outside of its formal structure. Occasionally, some interested group organizes to play a quasi-governmental role. Examples are the Municipal League in Seattle and the Action for Development group of young professionals in Lima. A similar situation is often found in the religious sector. Also, the military often has no voluntary organizations except social clubs. Other institutions such as welfare may draw representation from many institutional sectors, as business, labor, and professional groups join activities of welfare organizations. One general characteristic of voluntary organizations is that they are open to all members of the community. This makes it difficult to identify many such organizations with specific institutional sectors.

In spite of these discrepancies some contours are clear. It is no surprise, for example, that in most communities of the United States, where business and finance is generally ranked as the most influential institutional sector, the Chamber of Commerce is just as often ranked as the most influential organization. Labor, which is ranked high in three of the four cities, is just as often recognized for its powerful central labor organization. Breakdowns in these correlations occur most commonly for military, mass communication, religion, and local government where voluntary organizations do not appear. It is now possible to anticipate these gaps and evalute their roles inside their own institutional structure. Certainly any list of important associations should carry important firms, churches, newspapers, etc. as "associations" if they play appropriate roles.

Relationship between the institutionalized power structure of the community and top influentials. The test of an association between the five most influential institutional sectors and the institutional identity of top influentials is exhibited in Table 58. An examination shows that an

TABLE 58. *Institutional Identity of Top Influentials in the Relative Power Ranking of the Five Most Influential Local Institutions*

PERCENTAGES OF TOP INFLUENTIALS

POWER RANKING OF LOCAL INSTITUTIONS	SEATTLE (N = 44)		BRISTOL (N = 32)		CORDOBA (N = 37)		LIMA (N = 33)	
1	Business	33%	Local government	9%	Religion	8%	Local government	18%
2	Local government	17	Business	34	Business	24	Political parties	18
3	Labor	14	Political parties	0	Local government	16	Business	30
4	Mass communication	0	Labor	19	Labor	3	Military	3
5	Education	10	Education	9	Military	0	Labor	3
TOTALS		74%		71%		51%		72%

association does exist. Only in Seattle, however, is there a truly close fit. In all cities a high proportion of related top individuals is found in the top five institutions of the 13 institutional sectors. In Seattle, it is 74 percent; in Bristol, 71 percent; in Cordoba, 51 percent; and in Lima, 72 percent. Discrepancies often occur because of problems in classifying the institutional identity of individuals. For example, in Seattle two newspaper publishers were placed in the business sector because it was believed their influence was best expressed there. In Bristol no political party influentials are shown because two powerful party leaders are classified as business and labor influentials. Many of the business leaders play a role in government, as do many education leaders. This problem of dual role is troublesome. As now classified, each influential is placed where it is believed he draws his major base of power. This tends to underestimate the identity of influentials in such institutional sectors as political parties, government, religion, welfare, culture and art, and recreation. Perhaps a double entry of influentials in their major and secondary roles, if they exist, would portray a more accurate picture. It must be remembered that there are also sectors such as labor, religion, and the military whose influence is accorded to their collective strength even when top influentials are lacking. Despite these difficulties, the model appears to do fairly well: with the single exception of Bristol, a majority of top influentials are found in the top three institutional sectors.

Relationship between the institutionalized power structure of the community and the key influentials. Our assumption has been that selection of key leaders by top leaders was a very rigorous test and that it would identify the foremost movers and decision makers of the community. The institutional identity of key leaders held high interest because if certain institutional sectors gave leaders a special opportunity to appear, the number of key leaders would provide a more accurate index of the power of such sectors. Table 59 shows that, in general, leaders tend to be concentrated in certain sectors: in Seattle 75 percent are concentrated in business and government; in Bristol 42 percent and in Cordoba 50 percent are from these same sectors. Lima has a concentration of 50 percent in political parties and government. On the other hand, certain powerful institutional sectors have almost no key leaders; the most striking case is in Cordoba where religion is regarded as most influential but has no key influential representing it. Other cases—labor in Seattle, Cordoba, and Lima and the military in Cordoba and Lima—reveal the commonly demonstrated fact that powerful sectors may exert influence without possessing a "key" leader as operationally defined here. Obviously, the presence or absence of key or top leaders cannot be a definitive test for the power of institutional sectors. Their absence, however, sug-

TABLE 59. *Institutional Identity of Key Influentials in the Relative Power Ranking of the Five Most Influential Local Institutions*

PERCENTAGES OF KEY INFLUENTIALS

POWER RANKING OF LOCAL INSTITUTIONS	SEATTLE (N = 12)		BRISTOL (N = 12)		CORDOBA (N = 14)		LIMA (N = 14)	
1	Business	67%	Local government	17%	Religion	0%	Local government	21%
2	Local government	8	Business	25	Business	43	Political parties	29
3	Labor	0	Political parties	0	Local government	7	Business	7
4	Mass communication	0	Labor	8	Labor	0	Military	0
5	Education	8	Education	17	Military	0	Labor	0
TOTALS		83%		67%		50%		57%

gests that other power mechanisms must be sought for explanation of sector influence.

The model can now be evaluated on the basis of all the tests of relationship that have been set out. A high correlation between the institutional power structure of the nation and that of the community has been clearly shown. Organizational and leadership structures do show relationships, but they are often not linear. When the model breaks down, it does so primarily because collective structures sometimes exert influence in their institutional form without the aid of associations and recognized community leaders. It breaks down secondarily because of dual or multiple participation and identification of leaders with more than one institutional sector.

A model is not expected to mirror a complex reality with complete validity. The system model of community power structure has proved useful as a guide pointing out the importance and relationship of institutions, associations, and leaders. It focuses attention constantly upon the *structure* of community power. It pinpoints the areas requiring special study and special techniques.

Power Models in the Four Cities

THE FIVE TYPES of power models presented in Chapter 1 could be placed on a continuum ranging in degree from monolithic to polylithic. A ring or cone structure model is a product of the social forces generated in most industrial cities especially by increasing heterogeneity of interests in the economic sector; the rise of new power structures, particularly labor, political parties, and government; and a growing autonomy and heterogeneity of interests in all institutional sectors which are experiencing growing specialization and professionalization.

These characteristics introduce diversity in power structures. In the four cities that is *no single solidary elite structure and no hierarchical dominance based on one institutional structure.* This statement can be made for cities both with and without highly stratified social structures and high class consciousness since all of these cities have democratic traditions which have allowed strong labor organizations to emerge. Also, suffrage has been sufficiently extended to create strong opposition parties and independent governments.

The economic sector is of course powerful in all the cities, and businessmen have a constant stake in most of the political contests in their cities, but no single hereditary economic structure exists in any city. In Bristol and Lima there are father-to-son or other family ties in some important business establishments, but in neither of these cities do we find this hereditary pattern in the bulk of industry. In fact, it is constantly diminishing, since modern technology, world market competition, and corporate enterprise all combine to break up hereditary consolidations.

We have noted that in all the cities business, government, and labor are among the five most powerful institutions. As was pointed out, independent political and labor organizations can act as strong countervailing forces to any oligarchy. In spite of the stereotype which pictures the military organization as a handmaiden of oligarchies, military rule has often imposed repressive measures on business. The military in both Peru and Argentina no longer follow the aristocratic model in which sons of the upper classes moved into the command positions and forged a monolithic power structure that was socially and functionally integrated with the civilian elite.[3] The military in Peru and Argentina may at times deem it necessary to capture civilian power, but this does not mean that they are subservient to some particular elite. They recruit their officers from the middle classes. Their social contacts with other institutional groups are decreasing. They develop separate social organizations and an independent power structure. Very often they act like an organization that enters national life only to protect its own investment in military gear and perquisite. They are as budget conscious as any business or government agency. The influence of religion also shows segmented character. In Cordoba, where religion was ranked of high influence, examples given of the influence of the Church related more to specific issues such as birth control, religious holidays, and Sunday closing than to a range of issues.

It may be concluded then that *the cone or ring structure predominates in all four cities.* A pool of top and key influentials, organizations, and institutions interact to produce various patterns of influence in community decision making. In all the cities, however, there are key influentials to whom all leaders look when the city is confronted with certain salient issues. One key influential in Seattle put it this way: "There are no 'crowds' as such. There are perhaps ten main leaders and the majority of them must be behind any controversial issue in Seattle to make it successful." Another top influential said:

> There are several recognizable blocs that usually present the same front. The Chamber of Commerce is probably the most important bloc both in initiating and in influencing. Labor is generally well organized. Educational groups are usually united on issues such as passage of bond levies, but are too divided to present any solid influential body. Welfare (and religious) agencies usually shy away from expressions of opinion and are not opinion molders. Newspaper and radio are not influential in local issues.

In the three other cities a similar pattern is observed. Its elements are: a small group of key influentials to whom the community turns for support when a project or issue of great importance appears; a complex of recognizable blocs of organized influence; and a large group of top and second-level leaders who have both the approval of top men and the youth and time to spend their energy in civic work. The leaders' institutional affiliations and the blocs change only as the institutionalized power structure of the city becomes different. Since there is generally a high correlation between the institutional power structure of the nation and that of its communities, a regularity is introduced in all intranational community power structures.

The Role of the Social Base

IN THE FOUR CITIES the social stratification pattern perhaps has more important influence on the community power structure than any other social factor. If the per capita gross national product is taken as an index to the nature of potential stratification differences, then the four nations may be ranked as follows: United States, 100 percent; United Kingdom, 43 percent; Argentina, 15 percent; and Peru, 7 percent.[4] Of course, the four cities would probably show higher per capita figures than those of the nation, but the relative rankings of the cities might remain the same. It is true that the per capita figure does not reveal social strata. It tells us nothing about the degree of inequality. Unhappily, this index is not available for the four cities.[5]

A heuristic diagram can be constructed to provide a suggested view of the social strata. Figure 24 depicts the upper class as small in all cities. The significance of the upper class is relative to the total stratification structure. The middle class is largest in Seattle and diminishes to successfully smaller proportions in Bristol, Cordoba, and Lima. The lower class shows a reverse relationship, with Lima possessing the largest proportion. In the power struggles between classes, generally the middle classes represent the bulk of support for center or left-of-center policies that will at the same time respect democratic institutions. The pressure from the left builds up in the lower classes. This may result in demands for land and tax reform, nationalization of various private enterprises, unionization, increased social security, or revolution. Voltaire wrote: "History is only the pattern of silken slippers descending the stairs to the thunder of hobnailed boots climbing upward from below." The stratification pattern provides a guide to many political and economic movements and to the nature of social controls exercised to maintain law and order.

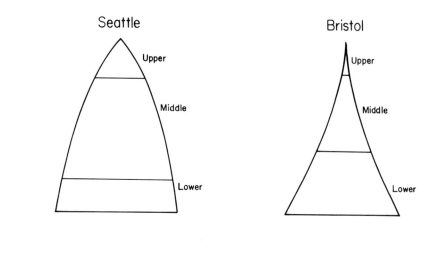

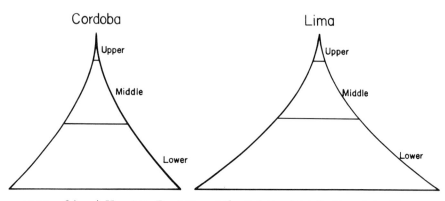

FIGURE 24.　*A Heuristic Depiction of the Relative Distribution of the Upper, Middle, and Lower Classes in the Four World Cities**

> * Many writers object to the use of class when referring to Latin America. They point out that the middle sectors are anything but a compact social layer. They do not fulfill the central condition of a class: their members have no common background of experience. Members of old Spanish and Portuguese families co-exist with mestizos, mulattoes, Negroes, and newcomers from Europe. Some members of these groups are strongly committed to the defense of personal initiative and private property; others may be little concerned with property rights or infringements upon what are often considered the domains of private enterprise.

In Seattle, a business civilization exists. Each member has a good chance to acquire a job and property. More than 50 percent work at white-collar jobs. Most persons believe strongly in individual initiative and private property. In Bristol, all but the very rich are poorer than their counterparts in Seattle. The growth of the democratic socialist philosophy, the rise of the Labour party, the nationalization of many utilities all result from the stratification pressures. Especially significant is the Labour party, which draws heavily from the larger lower class and the poorer middle class. In Cordoba, the squeeze from the bottom and the middle is even more pronounced. The desire for a "strong man" has dominated many workers who have sought Perón's return. Numerous political parties have risen and splintered into still more parties. Marxism as a political philosophy has many adherents. Democracy rises and falls and the military fills the void. Political contests are starkly revealed as efforts to exert more controls over propertied groups. In Lima, the pressures of proverty grind harder against the state with each passing year. Political parties and government are firmly entrenched at the center of power as long as they can maintain order. If they fail to do so the military intervenes. Nationalization of industry, increase of government services, the rising strength of unionization, and leftist terrorism all represent outcomes of the social forces boiling up from the stratification inequalities.

CHAPTER 14

THE ROLE OF VALUES

IN INTERNATIONAL DECISION MAKING:

Anglo-American vs. Latin American Differences

Value Systems in the United States

THE IMPORTANCE OF IDEOLOGIES, VALUES, AND BELIEF SYSTEMS in community decision making has been demonstrated directly or indirectly in almost all studies of community power. Robert A. Dahl, discussing the prevailing system of beliefs in New Haven, Connecticut, describes "the steady pressure of the [Economic] Notables against the expansion of public services and taxes" as a "familiar aspect of American politics: to gain services and benefits from government and as far as possible to displace the costs from themselves to others." He sees no conflict with any other significant groups in the community on this policy of keeping taxes and expenditures low. Even wage earners share it. Democrats and Republicans alike seek to outdo one another in their reputations for economy.[1]

Hunter and Dahl are in complete agreement about this political fact. Hunter reports for Atlanta: "In the realm of policy the top leaders are in substantial agreement most of the time on the big issues related to the basic ideologies of the culture. There is no serious threat to the basic value systems at this time from any of the understructure personnel, and many of the fears of the top leaders on this point appear groundless."[2] "The principle of keeping the taxes low, at the moment outweighs the principle of raising taxes to meet the real demand for better conditions. . . ."[3] Robert Presthus, reporting on his New York state communities, sees in Riverview an old guard of financial and mercantile leaders who remain imbued with the Protestant ethic and its somewhat anachronistic values of hard work, thrift, and saving.[4] "In Edgewood economic leaders can use their particular normative preferences for self-reliance and 'private' initiative over against governmental solutions to local problems."[5]

Robert C. Stone found in the small Arizona community of "Service City" that the chamber of commerce, the city government, and the school board were of greatest importance because they effectively monopolized the position of public spokesman. He claims that "a re-examination of the data shows how beliefs arising from the businessman's role control the pattern of action of all three leadership organizations."[6] He acknowledges the presence of a business creed that emphasizes the restriction of the authority of public institutions and the limitation of public services and recognizes the emphasis on individualism, freedom, materialism, productivity, competition, and progress as basic elements. He says

it is not difficult to see how this ideology has worked in Service City—but it is more difficult to explain how on various occasions, the Chamber of Commerce, speaking in the name of free enterprise, has acted in the community's name to achieve collective ends. To understand the public role occupied by the chamber and its ability to act collectively for the community, we need to comprehend the changes involved in transforming the free enterprise doctrine from that of private profit-making to the social realm of community action.—Historically, the free enterprise doctrine emphasizes private initiative, freedom to pursue self-interest without restraint by government, the self-reliance of the individual in seeking his own welfare, and the primacy of economic motives.[7]

Stone claims the free enterprise doctrine has been transformed from the realm of private profit-making to the social realm of community action by three elements: 1. Private enterprise now involves the need for collective action paralleled with the determination to maintain control in private hands. 2. Public matters are only a logical extension of the economic interests of businessmen. 3. Business leaders have a social responsibility to the community apart from matters of profit or the need to check the power of government.

In Service City this doctrine of social free enterprise does not go unchallenged by other groups who hold to different values and who seek different programs of community action. However, these groups have not succeeded in achieving the public spokesman role, not only because "they are at the periphery of economic control, but also because the values they espouse characteristically do not derive from the individualism and acquisitiveness of the business ethic."[8]

Gabriel A. Almond and Sidney Verba have made a five-nation comparative study seeking similarities and differences between political behavior and beliefs characteristic of Mexico, Italy, Germany, Great Britain, and the United States. They find the United States is a country in which civic participation is well developed, with persons frequently active members of voluntary organizations. Respondents in the United States, compared with those in the other four nations, are very frequently exposed to politics. They report political discussions and involvement in political affairs, a sense of obligation to take active part in the community, and a sense of competence to influence the government.[9] The large role of civic participation in community activity generally is well treated by Peter Rossi, who describes the many functions that community participation fulfills. He claims:

> The voluntary associations, ranging from the more permanent varieties—the Community Chest, Chamber of Commerce, and service clubs—to the ad hoc Citizens' Committees, have taken over many of the functions of initiating social change and marshaling community support for changes that are formally allocated to local government and to political parties. Although it is often true that voluntary associations eventually must move local authorities, the initial spark and a great part of the task of mobilizing public opinion have been performed for these authorities in advance.[10]

Value Systems in Great Britain

VALUE SYSTEMS IN GREAT BRITAIN are similar to those of the United States except in a few particulars. The first is the difference in occupational prestige values. It has been pointed out that "the social status of industry in England, and so of its captains, is low by comparison with law, medicine, and the universities."[11] This difference has the effect of permitting a greater entry of other institutional leaders into community decision making, as was shown in the community leadership structure of Bristol. A second difference is the strong entrenchment of democratic socialism in the Labor party, which results in greater respect for and acceptance of left-of-center attitudes. Labor leaders having both economic and political party power give decision making a different cast. An atmosphere of compromise rather than tension characterizes the political climate.

Value Systems in Peru and Argentina

ARGENTINA AND PERU, in contrast to the United States, are marked—in the view of well-informed judges—by a relative absence of consensus over philosophy and objectives of the society. Conflicting and splinter parties represent the divergent ideologies and cleavages. A belief in the wide mixture of private ownership and public ownership in all industries and services is prevalent, with groups ranging from advocates of extensive private ownership to advocates of extensive public ownership. Norms of secrecy, graft, and self-interest are strongly interlaced with other institutional values. Many view the social scene as a great political arena in which a privileged minority is entrenched and against which all other citizens must battle if they wish to achieve democracy and justice.[12] The climate in which community decision making takes place is almost continuously tense.

The free enterprise values described for the United States, and which persist less strongly in Great Britain, prevail in Peru and Argentina, but in different forms. It is true in all four cities that private enterprise sees the need for collective action paralleled with the determination to maintain control in private hands. It is understood that public matters are only logical extensions of the economic interests of businessmen.

There is not, however, in Cordoba and Lima a belief that business leaders have a social responsibility to the community apart from matters of profit or the need to check the power of the government. Voluntary activity in civic organizations is minimal. Government and political parties are regarded as the bodies responsible for civic life. Pressures from the right and the left are exerted with growing intensity and government is forced to make decisions under heavy pressure. Power is wielded in coalitions that make even party positions unpredictable and unstable.

Fundamental Assumptions Relative to Structural Properties of the Underdeveloped Countries in General and to Latin American Countries in Particular

A BELIEF SYSTEM FOR LIMA was set forth earlier, and it now seems feasible to make a final formulation of assumptions; some relate to underdeveloped societies in general and others to Latin America in particular. Taken together they represent the contours of the larger social system in which these community power structures are encompassed.

GENERAL ASSUMPTIONS FOR UNDERDEVELOPED SOCIETIES. Underdeveloped societies by definition possess limitations in various kinds of socially defined offerings: manufactured goods and varieties of foods, clothing, and housing, certain varieties and number of specific jobs, education, income, transport, and communication.

With large disparities in wealth and education, rigid stratification systems develop with low opportunity chances for members of the society who are outside of the privileged classes.

Under these conditions, value consensus is lacking and ideological diversity dominates political orientations.

The above factors combine to produce among the members of society lack of confidence in their institutions and in the motives of others. Common end products include inability to work together in groups, lowered efficiency in all aspects of community life, corruption in government, and high level of crime and delinquency.

CONTINUING ASSUMPTIONS FOR LATIN AMERICAN SOCIETIES. A South American country with a Spanish feudal heritage has a social structure that is characteristic by the presence of three influential institutions: the Roman Catholic Church, a landed aristocracy, and the military.

The growth of industrialization adds an overlay of new business and white-collar groups, both native and foreign, to the existing economic and social order. These groups are providing economic, political, and educational leaders who seek progressive, orderly social changes within a democratic government. New power structures are appearing, with political parties, labor organizations, newspapers, and universities providing forces for change. Radical parties, while not dominant, exert strong pressures. Much strength is drawn from student groups.

Normally, all power groups are splintered and tend to be non-cooperative.

In a crisis, the threat of Communism, or of any substantial change in the existing structure brings the Church, military, landed aristocracy, business, and much of the middle class into loose, consensual agreements and coalitions. Numerous informal contacts enable vested interest groups to maintain linkages.

Foreign governments and foreign economic interests are important levers in pressing for liberal or conservative reactions to political and social movements. (Latin America sells 35 percent of its exports to the United States; the United States controls 40 percent of the production in Latin America.)

The threat of Communism, economic chaos, or political stalemate and stagnation often evokes the entry of the military, which claims sovereignty by default and legitimizes its intervention as "caretaker."

The large extended family, the school, and the Church are major agencies of socialization inculcating beliefs and values. Values affecting significant community processes of decision making center around motives and integrity of others, role of work and career aspiration, belief in democracy, political ideology and role of labor union, belief in civic participation in voluntary organizations, role of government in the property system, and integrity of government.

These assumptions are set forth as a frame of reference for understanding organizational behavior in Latin America. It is not contended that they have been proved "true," but they may be accepted as approximations. Certainly the degree of their validity and the conditions under which they hold seem to be a basic foundation to any understanding of community power structures in Latin America.

THE MEASUREMENT OF INTERNATIONAL PATTERNS AND NORMS*

THE IMPORTANCE OF VALUES AND BELIEFS in community decision making has been recognized. However, the measurement of values and beliefs remains a difficult research task and the literature shows relatively few efforts to make cross-cultural measurements using scaling methods.[13]

History of the Scaling Instrument

THERE IS A GREAT NEED in comparative community power structure research for a scaling instrument that will reveal cultural differences across national cultures. Ideally, such an instrument should show those important variations in cultural patterns that make significant differences when problems and issues are being debated or resolved in the decision-making process within the community. Efforts to find such a measure were fruitless, so plans were made to construct one. A first assumption was that the scale ought to reveal the norms which impede economic and social goals such as industrial development, political stability, and more equitable distribution of wealth and income. It became apparent that the search for such norms should lead to measures of attitudes toward work, toward belief in democracy, class consciousness, labor's orientation to society, consensus over general objectives, and the role of private and public ownership of property. Later, it seemed feasible that relatively "minor" values might be important, such as those residing in prevailing customs of social acceptance. In Latin America the foreigner is frequently told of the importance of ceremony, of the differing conceptions of time and punctuality, and of the most serious need to avoid injuring personal or national dignity. It is known that foreign business or government men might be impeded or facilitated in their efforts to establish and maintain enterprises abroad by such subtle

* Adapted from the author's article of the same title, *Southwestern Social Science Quarterly*, XLVIII (March 1968), 531–47.

values as social acceptance and trust in others. Thus, the goal was broadened to provide a highly universal instrument capable of detecting a wide range of international patterns and norms in or between any countries of the world. The strategy was to develop six-point rating scales on which expert judges might be able to make reliable and valid judgments. The first items selected were those regarded as the norms that a stranger to another culture confronts almost immediately and to which he must make an adjustment. These include social acceptance, standards of personal and community health, personal security and protection of property, and concern for and trust of others. Other areas of economic, social, and political patterning were then considered. Items such as consensus on general philosophy and objectives of the society were regarded as the type that require intimate knowledge of the society, and expert judges would be needed to rate such patterns.

Rating scales were developed one by one and submitted to judges for pretesting. A number of well-trained social scientists were in Lima during 1965–66 and they gave me their counsel.[14] Each was consulted about wording of the scales in order that the statements might convey exact meanings and proper gradations from the two poles of each value. And each was asked if there was any other value that should be measured. William F. Whyte pointed out the importance of a scale to measure concern for and trust of others, and James Morris pointed out the importance of securing a measure for the item, "Consensus over general philosophy and objectives of the society."

It soon became apparent that the concept "value" was too limiting. Value is usually defined as objects or activities of human desire or appreciation. Scales measuring family solidarity and belief in democracy might be designed to elicit judgments in this "desired" sense. But when the researcher is seeking an accurate judgment of what exists in the structure he does not want a judgment of "value" but a statement about the prevailing norms. The judgment should not be clouded by "desired" conditions. An attempt to measure desired conditions would show that everyone was in favor of the good life, however defined. Such an effort would collapse in meaningless ambiguity. The rating scales were therefore broadened to include what may better be described as fifteen pertinent norms or cultural patterns believed to be representative of the most important differences that separate national cultures. No attempt was ever made to prepare a single or all-embracing scale of national norms. The fifteen scale items have been developed as single rating scales. They provide a profile of the national culture. Their significance as a configuration or system of norms rests upon social and historical analysis.

The fifteen scales, after a pretest with ten judges, were ready for final tests of validity and reliability. It now began to appear that the scales might be used as a tool for a wide range of purposes such as measuring the impact of a culture on a foreigner. Foreigners experience important attitude changes as they begin to make more intense comparisons with their native country. Such behavior often results in "cultural shock." This, in turn, may have a psychological component that can be called "souring." These sociological and psychological phenomena seem capable of being measured. Moreover, I speculated as to whether national stereotypes might be measured by asking respondents to give their imagined judgments of other countries. A number of studies have been made by the writer using the scales to ascertain the influence of travel and educational training and the nature of national stereotypes. However, I have continued to be mainly concerned with what I might discover about the parameters of community decision making. The possibilities suggested many hypotheses and studies, but the immediate task involved a determination of the validity and reliability of the items.

DETERMINATION OF VALIDITY AND RELIABILITY. The test of validity set forth may be stated as follows: significant variations will occur as qualified judges rate the cultural norms of two or more nations. The criteria established for selection of a qualified judge include as a minimum that he be a college graduate, preferably a social science major; have six months or more consecutive experience in the countries to be rated; be able to read and speak the languages of the countries to be rated. Twenty-one Americans living in Lima met these criteria. Their occupation, sex, and time lived in Peru are shown.

Judges	*Sex*	*Months in Peru*
University professor (sociologist)	M	12
University professor (economist)	M	6
High school teacher	F	6
Professor, sociologist	M	6
Government official (transportation officer)	M	18
Government official (finance officer)	M	18
University professor (sociologist)	M	24
Research sociologist, anthropologist	M	12
High school teacher	F	24
Professor of psychology	M	6
High school teacher	F	6
Professor of arts and crafts	F	12
Government official	M	18
Economist	F	8

Judges	Sex	Months in Peru
Professor of economics	M	8
Professor, historian	F	12
Professor of economics	M	12
University administration official	M	12
High school teacher	F	12
Professor of sociology	M	12
High school teacher	M	60

Each of the judges was given a copy of the battery of scales of International Patterns and Norms which is reproduced on pages 238–42. The mean ratings given to the United States and Peru by American judges are reproduced on the scales. These ratings will be described in the tests of validity and reliability which follow.

The following instructions were explained to each judge:

You will find fifteen (15) social characteristics that apply to any national culture.

Each characteristic has been placed on a scale of six (6) points.

The descriptions defining the scale are shown at 1 and 2, 3 and 4, 5 and 6. Thus, the first characteristic, social acceptance, attributes highest social acceptance to number 1 position and lowest social acceptance to the number 6 position. The range between represents a continuum of different degrees of the characteristic.

Task 1. Establish anchor points for each scale by selecting countries from anywhere in the world that reflect the extreme positions of the scale for social acceptance. These countries may or not be known to you personally.

In making a selection *think of the way the pattern appears on the average throughout the country and as it is experienced by a person in the middle sector of society*—i.e. omitting the very rich and the very poor. When the selection has been made, write the names of the countries on the answer sheets. Proceed to select countries representing the extremes of all 14 remaining characteristics—i.e. standards of health, standards of personal and community health, etc. Write the names on the answer sheets.

Task 2. Now place the U.S. and Peru in their proper positions on all 15 characteristics. Again, think of the pattern as it appears on the average throughout the country and as it is experienced by a person in the middle sector of society—i.e. omitting the very rich and the very poor. Write answers on answer sheet.

Task 3. Place a third country on the scale if you have lived six (6) months or more within it. Write answers on answer sheet.

ESTABLISHING CRITERIA OF VALIDITY. The criteria for validity included the following requirements: (1) The mean difference on each rating scale must show an item value difference of 2.00 or more when the United States and Peru are rated and compared. (The assumption is made that the scales have a continuity ranging in intensity from 1 to 6. No assumption of randomness is made.) (2) The average deviation of each scale must not show a dispersion greater than 1.00 when either the United States or Peru is rated. (3) The judges' rankings will permit a structuring of the significant variations in the social patterning of the two countries.

The mean differences on each rating scale. Mean differences are found by utilizing the weights of 1 to 6 assigned by respondents to each corresponding point on the scale. Then the frequencies of response at each point are multiplied by the assigned weights and divided by the total number of responses ($f \times w/N$ = mean). Means are computed for the United States and Peru on all 15 scales and the differences established. For the first scale—social acceptance—the mean rating for the United States is 1.66; for Peru, it is 4.48; the difference between means is 2.82. Thus Scale 1 meets the criterion calling for a difference between means of 2.00 or more. Such a difference establishes confidence that the scale is measuring a real (not a chance) difference in social acceptance. All scales meet this test of difference with results as shown in Table 60.

TABLE 60. *Mean Differences in Scale Ratings between United States and Peru as Ranked by 21 Judges*

SCALE ITEMS Arranged by ranks in size of each difference	MEAN DIFFERENCE	RANK IN SIZE
Class structure and class consciousness	3.62	1.5
Civic participation and voluntary activity	3.62	1.5
Family solidarity	3.57	3
Standards of personal and community health	3.28	4
Definition of work and individual achievement	3.24	5
Independence of the child	3.10	6
Concern for and trust of others	3.00	7.5
Consensus over general philosophy and objectives of the society	3.00	7.5
Moral code and role definitions of men and women	2.90	9
Social acceptance	2.82	10
Confidence in personal security and protection of property	2.62	11
Definitions of religion and moral conduct	2.52	12
Belief in democratic political system	2.24	13
Labor's orientation to the prevailing economic and social system	2.23	14
Definition of role of private and public ownership of property	2.10	15

SCALE OF INTERNATIONAL PATTERNS AND NORMS

_____ Male _____ Female (Optional)

Native Country _____ Years lived _____ Name: _____

Other Countries _____ _____ Address: _____
_____ _____ _____

RESPONDENT: Kindly check if you are male or female and indicate years lived in native country and in other countries. Sign your name and give your address if you wish a final report. Read the accompanying directions carefully before you begin. Thank you.

1. SOCIAL ACCEPTANCE

U.S. 1.66 →
PERU 4.48 →

1	2	3	4	5	6

1 2: High social acceptance. Social contacts open and non-restrictive. Introductions not needed for social contacts. Short acquaintance provides entry into the home and social organizations.

3 4: Medium social acceptance. Ready acceptance in neighborhood and in community organizations but not in family and social life. Friendly in business and other public contacts.

5 6: Low social acceptance. Acceptance in specifically designated groups in which membership has been validated. Sponsored introduction is needed for social contacts in all parts of community life.

2. STANDARDS OF PERSONAL AND COMMUNITY HEALTH

U.S. 1.38 →
PERU 4.66 →

1	2	3	4	5	6

1 2: High standards of personal and community hygiene. Hygienic habits highly valued in all parts of society.

3 4: Varied. High community standards for water and sewage. Personal habits and community standards of cleanliness and hygiene vary widely across the community.

5 6: Personal and community standards of hygiene are not valued highly.

3. CONCERN FOR AND TRUST OF OTHERS

U.S. 1.75 →
PERU 4.86 →

1	2	3	4	5	6

1 2: High concern for others. Respect for the motives and integrity of others. Mutual trust prevails.

3 4: Moderate or uneven pattern of concern for and trust of others.

5 6: Lack of concern for others and lack of trust.

4. Confidence in Personal Security and Protection of Property

U.S. 2.33 → (between 2 and 3)
PERU 4.95 → 5

1	3	6
High confidence in personal security. Free movement, night and day, for both sexes. High sense of security of property. Locking of homes is optional.	Moderate confidence in personal security. Confidence of men is high in personal security but women are warned to take precautions. Movements of women restricted to daytime. Simple property precautions essential.	Low confidence in both personal security and protection of property. Men and women restrict all movements at night to predetermined precautions. Many property precautions obligatory. Extensive use of locks, dogs, and guards.

5. Family Solidarity

PERU 1.85 → 2
U.S. 5.42 →

1	3	6
High solidarity with many obligations of kinship relations within large, extended family system.	Relations of solidarity within a limited kinship circle with specified obligations only.	Small, loosely integrated, independent family with highly specific individual relations.

6. Independence of the Child

U.S. 1.33 →
PERU 4.43 →

1	3	6
Child is raised to be self-reliant and independent in both thought and action.	Child is given specified areas of independence only.	Child is raised to be highly dependent and docile.

7. Moral Code and Role Definitions

U.S. 2.00 → 2
PERU 4.90 → 5

1	3	6
Single code of morality prevails for men and women. Separate occupational and social roles are not defined for men and women. Similar amounts and standards of education prevail.	Variations between moral definitions for men and women exist for certain specified behaviors. Occupational and social role definitions vary in degree. Varying educational provisions for the sexes.	Double code of morality prevails. Separate occupational and social roles for men and women exist and are sharply defined. Amount and standards of education vary widely between the sexes.

SCALE OF INTERNATIONAL PATTERNS AND NORMS—*Continued*

8. Definition of Religion and Moral Conduct

	PERU 2.05 ↓			U.S. 4.57 ↓	
1	2	3	4	5	6

1	3	5
Belief in the sacred interpretation of life as primary explanation of purpose of life and role of death. Emphasis is placed on importance of worshiper role in fulfilling spiritual obligations and duties.	Belief in Supreme Being and a sacred purpose for life. Emphasis is placed on secular interpretation of moral values and importance of applying them to daily conduct.	Belief in secular interpretation of life. Emphasis on importance of achieving the good society for achieving the good life. Moral values prescribed by social and scientific definitions of human well-being in the society. Emphasis on social conduct as moral conduct.

9. Class Structure and Class Consciousness

	PERU 1.38 →			U.S. 5.00 5↓	
1	2	3	4	5	6

1	3	5
Highly conscious of class differences. Extensive use of status symbols. Social classes and social circles rigidly defined. Very small upward class movement. Contacts between classes limited by social distinctions. Private schools predominate for upper social groups.	Class consciousness prevails moderately. Upward class movement occurs but defining characteristics mark off and limit contact between classes.	Class consciousness low. Class differences devalued. Minimal use of status symbols. Considerable upward class movement. Relatively free social contacts between social classes. Public schools dominate for all social classes.

10. Consensus Over General Philosophy and Objectives of the Society

	U.S. 1.57 →			PERU 4.57 →	
1	2	3	4	5	6

1	3	5
High consensus over philosophy and objectives of the society as achieved through evolution. Competition and conflict between parties takes place within generally accepted goals of the society. Stable governments usually prevail.	Consensus is partial. Differing ideological system conflict. Stable government may be maintained but under threat of overthrow.	Absence of consensus (or very low) over philosophy and objectives of the society. Conflicting and splinter parties may represent the divergent ideologies and cleavages. Unstable governments prevail.

11. Labor's Orientation to the Prevailing Economic and Social System

1	2	3 PERU 3.10 →	4	5 US 5.33 →	6
	Highly alienated. Ideologically opposed to the prevailing economic and social system. Revolutionary in orientation.		Antagonistic. Party alienated with some unions ideologically in support and some in opposition to prevailing economic and social system.		Highly assimilated. Ideologically in agreement with prevailing economic and social system. Labor disputes over distribution shares of goods and services to working people but accepts on-going system.

12. Belief in Democratic Political System

1 US 1.42 →	2	3 PERU 3.66 →	4	5	6
Strongly committed. Deep and persistent belief in the democratic process regardless of problem or crisis.		Reserved commitment. Belief in democracy as process requiring careful control against mass abuse. Accept necessity of dictatorial intervention in crisis situations or special safeguards such as one party systems, relinquishing freedoms in internal crises, etc.			Lack of belief in democracy as political system. Regarded as weak and ineffectual in solving problems and improving the lot of the average man. Generally regarded as dangerous because it exposes government to mob psychology.

13. Definition of Work and Individual Achievement

1 US 1.52 →	2	3	4	5 PERU 4.76 →	6
A belief in hard work as obligation to self, employer, and God. Efficiency values accepted. Individual is expected to progress in his work life.		Work is important to the advancement of self and family. Efficiency values accepted. Achievement expectations vary.			Lack of belief in hard work. Work is regarded as necessary, but involves no obligation beyond delivery of minimum services. Efficiency values rejected. Individual is expected only to maintain family status at his inherited level.

SCALE OF INTERNATIONAL PATTERNS AND NORMS—*Continued*

14. CIVIC PARTICIPATION AND VOLUNTARY ACTIVITY

U.S. 1.19 → (at 1) PERU 4.81 → (at 5)

1 2	3 4	5 6
High civic activity. People work together to get things done for the community. High identity with volunteer groups. Civic participation and volunteer activity in groups is an important source of social prestige. Moral and altruistic motives are important sources of motivation.	Moderate activity in special area. Organized participation exists for economic or political self-interest but often is lacking for a general community need.	Low civic activity. Often deliberately avoided with no social sanctions. Low identity with volunteer groups. Civic participation is not an important source of prestige. Mistrust of motives is common since self-interest is generally assumed as the principal motivation for all persons.

15. DEFINITION OF THE ROLE OF PRIVATE AND PUBLIC OWNERSHIP OF PROPERTY

U.S. 1.19 → (at 1) PERU 3.29 → (at 3)

1 2	3 4	5 6
Strong belief in the right of private property for all persons in all types of goods. Private ownership and control of means of production is accepted for all industries and services except for a few natural monopolies (i.e., water, post office, etc.).	Belief in the wide mixture of private ownership and public ownership in all industries and services. Public ownership of large basic industries (steel, coal, electricity, etc.) and services (transport and communication) is especially common.	Strong belief in public ownership and governmental control of all industries and services except small enterprises. Private ownership accepted in the ownership of personal goods.

Average deviations of each scale. The average deviation was selected as a simple test of the degree of dispersion. The need here is to find whether an acceptable range of agreement is occuring among the judges. According to the criterion a dispersion greater than ±1.00 was unacceptable. Table 61 shows the mean and average deviation of the 21 judges as

TABLE **61.** *Mean and Average Deviation of Each Scale as United States and Peru Were Rated by 21 Americans Living in Peru*

SCALE	COUNTRY	MEAN	AVERAGE DEVIATION
15. Property	(U.S.)	1.19	±0.32
14. Civic activity	(U.S.)	1.19	±0.32
13. Work	(U.S.)	1.52	±0.35
8. Religion	(Peru)	2.05	±0.43
3. Trust	(U.S.)	1.75	±0.45
2. Health	(U.S.)	1.38	±0.47
6. Child	(U.S.)	1.33	±0.47
5. Family	(Peru)	1.85	±0.48
9. Class	(Peru)	1.38	±0.50
12. Democracy	(U.S.)	1.42	±0.53
10. Consensus	(U.S.)	1.57	±0.54
4. Security	(Peru)	4.95	±0.55
7. Moral code	(U.S.)	2.00	±0.57
8. Religion	(U.S.)	4.57	±0.57
9. Class	(U.S.)	5.00	±0.57
12. Democracy	(Peru)	3.66	±0.57
10. Consensus	(Peru)	4.57	±0.58
13. Work	(Peru)	4.76	±0.62
7. Moral code	(Peru)	4.90	±0.63
4. Security	(U.S.)	2.33	±0.66
14. Civic activity	(Peru)	4.81	±0.67
2. Health	(Peru)	4.66	±0.70
1. Social acceptance	(U.S.)	1.66	±0.72
1. Social acceptance	(Peru)	4.48	±0.74
6. Child	(Peru)	4.43	±0.78
15. Property	(Peru)	3.29	±0.79
11. Labor	(U.S.)	5.33	±0.82
11. Labor	(Peru)	3.10	±0.86
5. Family	(U.S.)	5.42	±0.87
3. Trust	(Peru)	4.86	±0.95

they rated the United States and Peru on each scale. The statistics have been arranged in rank order according to the size of average deviation. The smaller the deviation is, the better the consensus shown on each scale rating.

It can be seen that the average deviation is contained within the criterion (less than 1.00) for all ratings, providing further evidence for the validity of all items. It can be seen that the American judges have more difficulty rating Peru than rating their own country. In the first 15 scale ratings with the lowest dispersion, 11 are ratings of the United States and 4 of Peru. In the ratings of largest dispersion the situation reverses, 11 are of Peru and 4 of the United States. Note that very little deviation is recorded for the United States on the role of private and public ownership of property, civic participation and voluntary activity, and definition of work and individual achievement. At the opposite end of the rankings by average deviation we find that raters exhibit their widest dispersion on labor's orientation to the prevailing economic and social system, in both the United States and Peru; family solidarity, in the United States; and concern for and trust of others, in Peru. These wide deviations may result from ambiguity in the rating scale, real variations within a culture, or lack of adequate knowledge on the part of the judges. It is at the moment not possible to assign a given cause. It is known that many judges show lack of knowledge about labor's orientation, and that there are many variations within a culture on items like family solidarity, independence of the child, and concern and trust for others.

What is the meaning of these ratings? If the scales are valid, then they should provide a profile or system view of the national cultures— that is, the interrelationship of the norms that compose a national culture should reveal its ethos or general societal character. There is evidence that the scales exhibit such an overall view.

Significant variations in the social patterning of the two countries. Table 62 shows the items with the widest mean differences in rankings

TABLE 62. *Mean Difference between the Rankings of Peru and the United States on Class Structure, Family Solidarity, and Definition of Religion and Moral Conduct*

	MEAN PERU	MEAN U.S.	MEAN DIFFERENCE
Class structure and class consciousness	1.38	5.00	3.62
Civic participation and voluntary activity	4.81	1.19	3.62
Family solidarity	1.85	5.42	3.57
Definition of religion and moral conduct	2.05	4.57	2.52

between Peru and the United States. The scales reveal four major differences in social structure. Judges specify that Peru has a rigid class structure and high class consciousness; low civic participation and voluntary activity; high family solidarity within a large, extended kinship system; and sacred and ceremonial definitions of religion and moral conduct.

These four cultural patterns explain a large part of the differences between the two countries. There is not an equalitarian tradition in Peru, and the division between rich and poor is very great. Although racial prejudice is constantly denied by all levels of society (an extraordinary myth to the outside observer), economic and social discrimination is strongly practiced against Negroes and darker mestizos. It is alleged that this is due to their "backwardness" in education, manners, and work motivations, and not to their race. Family solidarity is affirmed in all segments of Peruvian society. It is a social cement which binds members to primary group identities in the midst of limited neighborhood interaction and associational life in voluntary groups. The extended family holds firm against the vicissitudes of death, ill health, marital difficulty, and governmental instability. Religious worship is a supplemental support that is viewed as an act of ceremonial obligation.

The United States with its equalitarian ideals, its small, independent, highly mobile families, and the more secular and social concerns of its religious practices stands out in contrast to Peru. One pattern that is especially significant in the dynamic functioning of the society is the low civic participation and voluntary activity of persons in the community life of Peru.

There is far more reliance in Peru on government and the Church for welfare, educational, and cultural efforts than in the United States. This difference has a fundamental consequence for the understanding of democratic processes. Wide popular participation gives way to formal representation of offices and officials usually possessing political "influence."

A number of belief systems also act like syndromes to cause clusters of traits to act in a concerted manner. Table 63 shows three major cul-

TABLE 63. *Cultural Syndromes of Peru and the United States in Character of Interpersonal Interaction, Work and Achievement, and Moral Code and Role Definitions of Men and Women*

		MEAN PERU	MEAN U.S.	MEAN DIFFERENCE
A. Character of interpersonal interaction	Concern and trust for others	4.86	1.86	3.00
	Confidence in personal security and protection of property	2.33	4.95	2.62
	Social acceptance	4.48	1.66	2.82
B. Work and achievement	Definition of work and individual achievement	4.76	1.52	3.24
C. Moral and role definitions of men, women	Moral code, role definitions of men and women	4.90	2.00	2.90

tural syndromes that involve the character of interpersonal interaction, work and achievement, and moral and role definitions of men and women. Peru is shown to have a pattern expressing a lack of concern for and trust of others, low confidence in personal security and protection of property, and low social acceptance of the person. Likewise, there is a lack of belief in hard work and a rejection of efficiency values. A dual code of morality exists for men and woman, and their separate occupational and social roles are sharply defined.

Independent observers attest to many kinds of behavior which validate these findings.

> To excel is a crime in Peru. No one can elevate himself with impunity above the given level of the prevailing mediocrity. . . . Peru is sick. It suffers from a collapse of citizenship. It is not mature. It does not achieve a rational equilibrium between desires and realizations. The struggle of those impatient persons is interminable seeking to achieve hoped for situations to which they would never arrive by their own merits.[15]

> Let me conclude with a barrier to Peruvian development which seems to me the most serious of all and which is as yet given little recognition: the Peruvian lack of faith in people. When people do not have much faith in each other, it is difficult for them to get together to build the organizations that progress and development require. In the United States, we find a much higher level of faith in people, and we find many Americans from different disciplines able to get together and work together.[16]

> Perhaps the most important Latin American characteristic is the habit of *not cooperating*. This is the continent of personalism, and since the early days of independence the various sectors of the population in most of the republics have had an aversion for cooperation: caudillo has been against caudillo, the capital city against those of the provinces, the inhabitants of the mountains against those of the lowlands.[17]

A REPLICATION TEST OF VALIDITY. Six months after their return to the United States, ten American students who had lived in Peru for one year (1965–66) were asked to rate the United States and Peru on the scaling instrument.[18] Table 64 shows the results of their ratings on each of the 15 scales. Criteria for validity are met fairly well. First, the differences in means (Column 5) for these student ratings are greater than 2.00 with the exception of three cases which approximate this difference (1.89, 1.85, 1.59). Second, the average deviations are under 1.00 with the exception of five out of the 30 ratings. These over-deviations are not excessive (1.00, 1.07, 1.12, 1.18, 1.50). Third, all mean differences on the 15 scales are in the same direction.

The greatest differences in means are found on three items: social acceptance, 3.55; class structure and class consciousness, 3.20; moral

TABLE **64.** *Mean Differences and Average Deviations for Scale Ratings of North American Students with One Year of Peruvian Experience as Compared with American Adult Judges Living in Peru*

	NORTH AMERICAN STUDENTS					AMERICAN ADULT JUDGES
	U.S. mean (col. 1)	Average deviation (col. 2)	Peru mean (col. 3)	Average deviation (col. 4)	Difference between means (col. 5)	Difference between means (col. 6)
1. Social acceptance	1.20	±0.33	4.75	±0.87	3.55*	2.82
2. Health standards	1.11	±0.22	4.00	±1.12	2.89	3.28
3. Concern and trust	2.30	±0.70	5.00	±0.66	2.70	3.00
4. Personal security	2.00	±0.83	4.55	±0.71	2.55	2.62
5. Family solidarity	4.81	±1.50	1.81	±0.74	3.00	3.57†
6. Child	1.50	±0.58	3.87	±0.65	2.37	3.10
7. Moral code	1.83	±0.83	5.00	±1.00	3.17‡	2.90
8. Religion	5.00	±0.80	3.11	±0.83	1.89	2.52
9. Class structure	5.00	±1.07	1.80	±0.97	3.20†	3.62*
10. Societal consensus	1.27	±0.39	3.87	±0.87	2.60	3.00
11. Labor	5.20	±0.64	2.10	±0.72	3.10	2.23
12. Democracy	1.41	±0.48	3.00	±0.25	1.59	2.24
13. Work	1.80	±0.80	4.33	±0.80	2.53	3.24
14. Civic activity	1.70	±0.56	4.77	±1.18	3.07	3.62*
15. Property	1.15	±0.25	1.15	±0.85	1.85	2.10

* Item ranks first in similarity.
† Item ranks second in similarity.
‡ Item ranks third in similarity.

code and role definitions of men and women, 3.17. These differences may be compared with the major differences expressed by the American adults: class structure and class consciousness, 3.62; civic participation and voluntary activity, 3.62; family solidarity (Peru high), 3.57.

It can be seen that both groups agree on class structure and class consciousness as a significant United States-Peruvian difference, with Peru regarded as highly stratified and class conscious. The difference in ratings on social acceptance and moral code shows that intercultural perceptions can vary according to important differences in respondents. Here, such factors as the age of the students and their experience in a Latin American university and in Peruvian family life must be taken into account. It is believed that the students were made more aware of differences in social acceptance because their youth and lack of status made it difficult to secure ready acceptance. Moreover, being North Americans, they would be accepted with reservations by many, if not most, students at San Marcos. They were aware of differences in the moral code and role definitions of men and women which could be observed both in the Peruvian families with whom they lived and at the university where they mingled with thousands of young people of both sexes.

It should be noted that on all of the items referred to—social acceptance, moral code and role definitions of men and women, class structure and class consciousness, civic participation and voluntary activity, and family solidarity—both groups of American judges agree that major differences occur. A comparison of Columns 5 and 6 in Table 64 demonstrates that all differences are in the same direction and in marked agreement. This comparison of replicated ratings produces high confidence in the validity of the scale items.

To establish the reliability of the scale two samples of respondents were asked to make test-retest ratings after a one-month interval, ranking the United States and Peru. The test-retest correlations for the fifteen items are given in Table 65. They range between .70 and .97— sufficiently high to establish confidence in the reliability of the scale.

TABLE 65. *Test-retest Coefficients for Two Samples of Respondents Ranking the United States and Peru*

ITEMS	35 AMERICAN STUDENTS IN THE UNITED STATES		21 AMERICAN ADULTS LIVING IN LIMA	
	U.S.	PERU	U.S.	PERU
1.	.91	.89	.94	.90
2.	.90	.86	.93	.91
3.	.95	.79	.90	.83
4.	.91	.84	.95	.88
5.	.94	.92	.91	.95
6.	.80	.80	.83	.85
7.	.88	.81	.89	.90
8.	.87	.86	.85	.88
9.	.91	.90	.95	.95
10.	.80	.75	.84	.80
11.	.89	.78	.93	.82
12.	.94	.70	.91	.85
13.	.91	.78	.87	.90
14.	.96	.85	.97	.95
15.	.89	.74	.94	.82

Application of the Scales

A MOST COMPELLING QUESTION is the extent to which a Latin American civilization may exist. A hypothesis may be set forth that respondent exposure to two or more Latin American cultures will demonstrate that any two countries in Latin America are more like each other in cultural patterning than any Latin American country is like the United States.

If this hypothesis could be shown true, then the affirmation of a ubiquitous Latin American civilization might be demonstrated empirically. Certainly, this hypothesis straddles the question "Does Latin America exist?" The intellectuals of the Latin American nations continue to wrestle with this question. All observers agree that the differences are many, but some, like George Pendle, affirm that all the 22 independent nations have a pervasive Spanish heritage. They note that all occupy a vast contiguous territory and—except for Portuguese Brazil—share a common language.

THE SEARCH FOR EVIDENCE OF A LATIN AMERICAN CIVILIZATION. Ideally, all Latin American countries should be rated on the international cultural scale items. A small exploration is shown in Table 66 where a comparison of ratings of Peru and Argentina are compared with ratings of the United States. Columns 1, 2, and 3 indicate the mean ratings given to each scale item for the United States, Peru, and Argentina. The raters of the United States and Peru were the 21 North Americans living in Lima who were described earlier. The raters of Argentina were 15 Argentines living in the United States and Argentina. Columns 4, 5, and 6 show differences between means as first Peru and Argentina, then Peru and the United States, and finally Argentina and the United States are compared. If the hypothesis holds, the differences between Peru and Argentina should be less than those between either Peru or Argentina, and the United States.

One index for such a determination is the grand mean difference of all ratings shown at the bottom of columns 4, 5, and 6. Here it can be seen that the difference between Peru and Argentina is indeed lower (1.27) than that between Peru and the United States (2.93) or Argentina and the United States (1.95). The findings suggest, however, that Argentina may share many characteristics with the United States since many of the differences between these two countries (shown in Column 6) are smaller than those between Peru and Argentina (shown in Column 4). Argentina is more like the United States on eight items and more like Peru on seven items. Table 67 is a compilation of the patterned similarities among the three nations. Here Peru is shown to be more similar to Argentina than to the United States on *all* scale items. Argentina is more similar to Peru on social acceptance, family solidarity, class structure and class consciousness, labor's orientation to the prevailing economic and social system, consensus over general philosophy and objectives of the society, civic participation and voluntary activity, and the definition of the role of private and public ownership of property.

"Latin American civilization" has its deepest roots in these seven scale areas where Argentina is more similar to Peru than to the United

TABLE 66. *Mean Ratings for the United States, Peru, and Argentina and the Difference between Means of Peru and Argentina, Peru and the United States, and Argentina and the United States*

SCALE ITEM	MEAN RATINGS OF			DIFFERENCES BETWEEN MEANS OF		
	U.S. (N = 21) (col. 1)	Peru (N = 21) (col. 2)	Argentina (N = 15) (col. 3)	Peru and Argentina (col. 4)	Peru and the U.S. (col. 5)	Argentina and the U.S. (col. 6)
1. Social acceptance	1.66	4.48	3.18	1.30	2.82	1.52
2. Health	1.38	4.66	2.93	1.73	3.28	1.55
3. Trust	1.75	4.86	3.27	1.59	3.11	2.02
4. Personal security	2.33	4.95	3.50	1.45	2.62	1.17
5. Family	5.42	1.85	2.71	.86	3.57	2.71
6. Child	1.33	4.43	2.80	1.63	3.10	1.47
7. Moral code	2.00	4.90	2.75	2.15	2.90	.75
8. Religion	4.57	2.05	3.66	1.61	2.52	.91
9. Class	5.00	1.38	3.07	1.69	3.62	1.93
10. Consensus	1.57	4.57	3.92	.55	3.00	2.35
11. Labor	5.33	3.10	2.69	.41	2.23	2.64
12. Democracy	1.42	3.66	2.81	.85	2.24	1.39
13. Work	1.52	4.76	3.07	1.69	3.24	1.55
14. Civic activity	1.19	4.81	3.58	1.23	3.62	2.39
15. Private property	1.19	3.29	3.58	.29	2.10	2.39
GRAND MEAN DIFFERENCE OF ALL RATINGS				1.27	2.93	1.95

States. Here is a context holding a belief in a wide mixture of private ownership and public ownership, labor poised in an antagonistic position to the prevailing economic and social system—a society splintered with differing ideological conflicts, but with a high family solidarity within an extended kinship system. Civic participation and voluntary activity is only moderate; class consciousness prevails; and social acceptance is reserved. These traits have special significance since Argentina can be thought of as a test case. It is highly Europeanized. Its population contains large numbers of English, German, and Italian. The Indian population is very small. Argentina ranks second among Latin American countries in per capita gross national product. If any

TABLE 67. *A Comparison of Pattern Similarities betweeen Peru, Argentina, and the United States*

Patterns on which Peru is more similar to Argentina than to the United States (col. 1)	Patterns on which Argentina is more similar to Peru than to the United States (col. 2)	Patterns on which Argentina is more similar to the United States than to Peru (col. 3)
1. Social acceptance	Social acceptance	
2. Health standards		Health standards
3. Concern and trust		Concern and trust
4. Personal security		‡Personal security
5. Family solidarity	§Family solidarity	
6. Independence of child		Independence of child
7. Moral code		*Moral code
8. Religion		†Religion
9. Class structure	Class structure	
10. Societal consensus	‡Societal consensus	
11. Labor's orientation	†Labor's orientation	
12. Democracy		§Democracy
13. Work and achievement		Work and achievement
14. Civic activity	Civic activity	
15. Role of property	*Role of property	

* Item ranks first in similarity.
† Item ranks second in similarity.
‡ Item ranks third in similarity.
§ Item ranks fourth in similarity.

of the Latin American countries is on the periphery of Latin American civilization, it may be Argentina. Yet having said that, it may be that the items showing similarity with Peru are the essential links in the common "Latin American civilization."

THE SEARCH FOR IBERO-LATIN AMERICAN CIVILIZATION AND THE ROOTS OF ANGLO-AMERICAN CULTURE. In the summer of 1968 the research was extended to Spain and England, the so-called mother countries of Latin America and North America respectively. The design called for the application of the 15 scales to two comparable panels of knowledgeable judges in each country. In Spain 17 Spaniards who had lived in the United States for at least one year rated Spain and the United States; similarly 17 Americans who had lived in Spain for at least one year rated Spain and the United States. Judges were interviewed in Madrid, Barcelona, and Seville in order to include any regional variations. In England a similar design was followed; 15 Spanish judges and 15 North American judges were interviewed in London and Bristol.

Does an Ibero-Latin American civilization exist? A complete answer to this question will require a comparison of Spain with all Latin American countries. Research is projected to fulfill this demand. However, with available data, Spain can now be compared with Peru and Argentina. The data are comparable since they were gathered by the same researcher with the same scales and under the same conditions. It should be remembered, however, that the data on Peru and Argentina were gathered in 1965 and 1966 respectively. Table 68 compares Spain with Peru, Argentina, and the United States. Except for Peru, the ratings shown are those of citizens of the rated country who were living there. The American judges were living in Spain at the time of the study.

TABLE 68. *Mean Ratings for Spain, Peru, Argentina, and the United States and the Differences between These Countries**

SCALE ITEM	Spain (N = 17)	Peru (N = 21)	Difference	Spain (N = 17)	Argentina (N = 15)	Difference	Spain (N = 17)	U. S. (N = 17)	Difference
1. Social acceptance	3.1	4.5	1.4	3.1	3.2	0.1	3.1	1.8	1.3
2. Health	3.2	4.7	1.5	3.2	2.9	0.3	3.2	1.9	1.3
3. Concern	4.1	4.9	0.8	4.1	3.3	0.8	4.1	2.8	1.3
4. Personal security	2.2	5.0	2.8	2.2	3.5	1.3	2.2	3.9	1.7
5. Family	2.3	1.9	0.4	2.3	2.7	0.4	2.3	4.6	2.3
6. Child	4.5	4.4	0.1	4.5	2.8	1.7	4.5	1.7	2.8
7. Moral code	4.6	4.9	0.3	4.6	2.8	1.8	4.6	2.3	2.3
8. Religion	2.6	2.1	0.5	2.6	3.7	1.1	2.6	4.8	2.2
9. Class	2.1	1.4	0.7	2.1	3.1	1.0	2.1	5.0	2.9
10. Consensus	5.0	4.6	0.4	5.0	3.9	1.1	5.0	1.8	3.2
11. Labor	2.3	3.1	0.8	2.3	2.7	0.4	2.3	5.7	2.4
12. Democracy	4.6	3.7	0.9	4.6	2.8	1.8	4.6	1.3	3.3
13. Work	4.0	4.8	0.8	4.0	3.1	0.9	4.0	2.0	2.0
14. Civic activity	4.8	4.8	0.0	4.8	3.6	1.2	4.8	1.5	3.3
15. Private property	3.1	3.3	0.2	3.1	3.6	0.5	3.1	2.3	0.8
GRAND MEAN DIFFERENCE OF ALL RATINGS			0.75			0.96			2.22

* Ratings of the United States were made by 17 Americans living in Madrid, Barcelona, and Seville. Except for Peru, all ratings in this table were made by citizens of the country rated who were living in that country.

The comparison of Spain and Peru was expected to show a close similarity since it is widely believed that Peru is especially characterized by its historical legacy of Spanish culture. Our earlier study had shown that Peru was indeed characterized by a distinctive pattern in which each scale rating contrasted significantly with that of the United States. The comparison of Spain and Argentina was expected to show a high degree of similarity, but less than for Spain and Peru due to the Western influences from modern Europe which have impressed themselves upon Argentina. The comparison of Spain and the United States was expected to show striking differences in most of the scales. These differences were perceived as crucial to the hypothesis specifying Anglo-Saxon and Hispanic societary patterns in North and South America.

The findings reveal that the expected similarities and differences appear. Peru and Spain are very similar in patterning with the exception of personal security and protection of property. In this pattern, Spain demonstrates a much higher confidence in personal security and protection of property. Spain is rated higher in personal and community health standards. But with these exceptions the two countries are shown to be very much alike on the patterns and norms tested. Note that the grand mean of all differences is .75, or less than one point on the six point scales.

Argentina and Spain show a high similarity on most scales. However, Argentina exhibits a higher commitment to a belief in democracy, a more single code of morality and common role definitions for men and women, and greater independence for the child. The grand mean of all ratings is .96, still less than one point on the six point scale.

The seven scale areas where the closest similarity had been detected earlier between Peru and Argentina again show a very high similarity in the comparisons of Spain with Peru and Argentina. The deepest roots appear to be the fairly rigid class structure and high class consciousness, low civic participation, belief in a wide mixture of private and public ownership of property, labor poised in an antagonistic position to the prevailing economic and social system, a society splintered with differing ideological conflicts, but with a high family solidarity within an extended kinship system. Social acceptance is reserved.

Spain, in contrast to the United States, shows differences of more than one in all scales except for definition of private property, where the difference is just under one. The grand mean of all differences is 2.22. This is two and one quarter points on the six point scales.

These findings strongly suggest that the scales are tapping significant patterns and norms and that an Ibero-Latin American civilization is real and that its presence as a set of patterns and norms may be measured in quantitative units. A contrasting Anglo-American culture is indicated but not demonstrated. The challenge to identify such a culture pattern set the objective for the research measurement sought in England.

Does an Anglo-American civilization exist? Can the roots of North American civilization be found in England? These questions invite a comparison of England and the United States. A close similarity was expected based on historical facts alone. What was not known was how the cultural patterns and norms would be rated and whether a sharp, contrasting pattern could be found between England and Spain. A comparison was made on the 15 original scales and five new scales. The new scales were developed to capture patterns which had seemed to be of highest importance as a result of previous studies. These patterns include standards of honesty and integrity of government officials; political influence of foreign enterprise on host government; encouragement of foreign enterprise; degree of nepotism in organizational life; and degree of expected reciprocity in favors and rewards. These scales are shown on the next page with the defining elements of each interval. These scales are now included in the total battery and were applied in all interviews in Spain and England. It is believed that the battery now represents the most significant patterns and norms which distinguish the ethos or societary character of a national society. It is believed that they can now be universally applied.

It will be recalled that a marked difference between Spain and the United States has already been demonstrated. Now Table 69 shows the comparison between England and the United States and Spain. In each comparison the ratings were made by citizens of the country being rated. The ratings of the United States were made by American citizens living in London and Bristol, England.

The findings show a high similarity between England and the United States with the exception of a presumed freer social acceptance in the United States and the higher commitment in the United States to private property. The other 18 scales are in close correspondence and affirm an identity of cultural patterns that we call Anglo-American civilization. The grand mean of all differences is .95, or less than one point on the six point scales.

The comparison of England and Spain shows many contrasts and many similarities. Major differences occur on independence of the child, definition of religion, societal consensus, labor's orientation to the society, belief in democracy, civic activity, honesty of government officials, nepotism, and reciprocity. The grand mean of all differences is 1.50.

It will be recalled that the comparison of United States with Spain (Table 68) revealed a grand mean difference of 2.22. This suggests that America stands further away from Spain than does England from Spain. Interestingly, Peru may be considered as retaining more of a traditional Hispanic culture than does modern Spain. Arranging all

SCALE OF INTERNATIONAL PATTERNS AND NORMS EXTENDED

16. STANDARDS OF HONESTY AND INTEGRITY OF GOVERNMENT OFFICIALS

1	2	3	4	5	6
	Government officials at all levels have a high standard of honesty and integrity. Violations are prosecuted vigorously and punished with appropriate penalties.		Government officials are generally honest but there are differences in the honesty of officials at different levels. Violations do occur and are prosecuted. The certainty of detection and the severity of penalty varies according to differing practices.		Government officials at all levels commonly engage in various kinds of corrupt practices. Most violations are seldom prosecuted. Occasionally token prosecutions are made when abuse becomes excessive.

17. POLITICAL INFLUENCE OF FOREIGN ENTERPRISE ON HOST GOVERNMENT

1	2	3	4	5	6
	Foreign enterprise has marked political influence on major economic and political policies of the nation. It can resist attempted nationalization of its own enterprises and enforce favorable trade and political relations.		Foreign enterprise does have significant political influence over certain economic conditions of its special concern, but it has no real influence over political policy and process within the host country.		Foreign enterprise has no real influence over national policies—economic or political. Host government may enforce strict control over all foreign enterprise but often permits foreign enterprise to operate within same set of guidelines as domestic firms.

18. ENCOURAGEMENT OF FOREIGN ENTERPRISE

1	2	3	4	5	6
	All foreign enterprise is strongly encouraged to invest and operate businesses of all kinds throughout the country.		Selected forms of foreign investment are encouraged. Use of foreign management personnel may be discouraged.		Foreign investment and operation of enterprise is discouraged by official and unofficial means.

19. DEGREE OF NEPOTISM IN ORGANIZATIONAL LIFE

1	2	3	4	5	6
	Family members of owners, managers, clerical, and manual workers are given preferential and sometimes privileged opportunities for employment in all types of organizations.		Family members of owners, managers, and professionals are given priority within organizations owned or managed by their relatives.		Merit and training is the sole basis for selection of all persons in all types of organizations.

20. DEGREE OF EXPECTED RECIPROCITY IN FAVORS AND REWARDS

1	2	3	4	5	6
	Pattern of expected reciprocity in favors prevails in regard to economic or political support given to individual or group. Personal basis of contact is encouraged and reciprocity is expected by a returned favor (or gift) in near future.		Reciprocity is expected only in specific situations when both parties have a written or oral agreement to exchange political and social support for services rendered.		No pattern of expected reciprocity prevails in economic or political life. Favors or special gifts for service and business rendered is regarded as self-serving and "wrong."

TABLE 69. *Mean Ratings for England, the United States, and Spain and the Differences between These Countries**

SCALE ITEM	MEAN RATINGS England (N = 15)	U.S. (N = 15)	DIFFER- ENCE	MEAN RATINGS England (N = 15)	Spain (N = 17)	DIFFER- ENCE
1. Social acceptance	4.0	1.4	2.6	4.0	3.1	0.9
2. Health	3.1	2.0	1.1	3.1	3.2	0.1
3. Concern	2.0	2.6	0.6	2.0	4.1	2.1
4. Personal security	2.1	3.5	1.4	2.1	2.2	0.1
5. Family	2.9	3.4	0.5	2.9	2.3	0.6
6. Child	2.1	2.5	0.4	2.1	4.5	2.4
7. Moral code	3.4	2.4	1.0	3.4	4.6	1.2
8. Religion	4.6	3.6	1.0	4.6	2.6	2.0
9. Class	3.1	4.7	1.6	3.1	2.1	1.0
10. Consensus	2.1	2.4	0.3	2.1	5.0	2.9
11. Labor	4.0	5.0	1.0	4.0	2.3	1.7
12. Democracy	2.1	2.2	0.1	2.1	4.6	2.5
13. Work	3.1	2.2	0.9	3.1	4.0	0.9
14. Civic activity	3.1	2.2	0.9	3.1	4.8	1.7
15. Private property	3.3	1.2	2.1	3.3	3.1	0.2
16. Honesty of government officials	1.3	1.8	0.5	1.3	3.5	2.2
17. Political influence	5.3	5.0	0.3	5.3	3.8	1.5
18. Encouragement of private enterprise	2.3	1.7	0.6	2.3	2.5	0.2
19. Nepotism	4.0	5.0	1.0	4.0	1.5	2.5
20. Reciprocity	5.0	4.0	1.0	5.0	1.5	3.5
GRAND MEAN DIFFERENCE OF ALL RATINGS			0.95			1.5

* Ratings of the United States were made by 15 Americans living in London and Bristol, England. All other ratings shown in the table were made by citizens of the country rated who were living in that country.

of the countries according to their similarity the order would be as shown with their grand mean differences indicated.

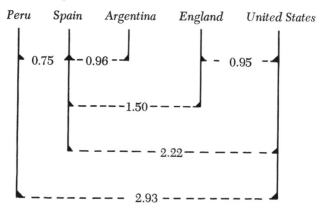

PART V

Future Research Requirements
of Comparative Study

THIS PART REVIEWS EXISTING COMMUNITY POWER STUDIES *and examines the research problems of international studies. Three principal types of variation are recognized: variation in institutionalized power, variation in community social structures, and variation in issues. Specific design and methodological problems are discussed.*

Five future research requirements are set forth and suggestions for research advances are proposed. The requirements center about a broader conceptualization of community power, the measurement of the solidarity of top leaders, the mapping of inter-institutional linkages, the measurement of collective institutional and organizational power, and the measurement of fluidity in community power structures.

CHAPTER 15

THE CUTTING EDGE OF COMPARATIVE

COMMUNITY POWER RESEARCH

COMPARATIVE COMMUNITY RESEARCH refers to a comparison of two or more communities. These communities may be located in the same country or in different countries. We may speak of the first type as intra-national and the second as international. In each case comparative community design opens possibilities not available in the study of a single community.

The possibility of studying communities with varying power structures is an intriguing challenge to the community researcher. In the United States there is opportunity to find different institutional power arrangements. One thinks of the possible dominance of the church in Salt Lake City; government in Washington, D.C.; business in Wilmington, Delaware; or education in university towns such as Ann Arbor, Michigan; Ames, Iowa; East Lansing, Michigan; State College, Pennsylvania; and Pullman, Washington. Yet most studies have not exploited this variety of institutional bases. There are a number of reasons for this, but the most important is that almost all studies have demonstrated that either business or government represents the most powerful set of institutions in influencing community decision making. Business was shown to be of dominant influence in Atlanta, Georgia;[1] Salem, Massachusetts;[2] Dallas, Texas;[3] El Paso, Texas;[4] and many others. Political parties and government were shown to be of most influence in New Haven, Connecticut;[5] Syracuse, New York;[6] Oberlin, Ohio;[7] and others. The most militant forces in American life today are centered about ra-

Institutional Sector with High Influence	National Manifestations
Business	U.S.A., Belgium, West Germany, Japan
Government	Soviet Russia, Yugoslavia, England, Egypt
Labor	England, U.S.A., Sweden, Australia, West Germany, France
Military	Dominican Republic, Haiti, Formosa, Turkey, Greece
Religion	Spain, India, Argentina
Society and Wealth	Kuwait, Saudi Arabia
Independent Professions	Argentina, Peru
Education	England, Soviet Russia, U.S.A., Japan
Political Parties	Soviet Russia, Egypt, Peru
Mass Communication	U.S.A., England, Russia, Japan
Recreation	Monaco (commercialized recreation)
Social Welfare	Sweden, England, U.S.A.
Culture and Art	Austria, France, Japan, U.S.A.

FIGURE 25. *High Influence of Institutional Sectors in Various Nations of the World (Tentative Estimates)*

cial and anti-war elements. Incorporating these forces into community power theory constitutes a new challenge. There is much to learn in the United States, but the researcher must go to other countries to learn more about the range of power structures.

International power structure designs open new opportunities. For such research we need a power typology of world cities, but we do not have one. We can begin by identifying nations where we may expect institutional differences. Figure 25 attempts to set out a heuristic chart— a related set of countries matched to specific institutional sectors with high influence. Until more knowledge is available the community power researcher must make tentative judgments and then proceed.[8] From American studies we know most about the community power patterns generated by business and government but little about world communities where power is concentrated in other institutional sectors. American researchers are especially lacking in knowledge of community life influenced by powerful and cohesive military and religious sectors. Multiparty systems and organized labor movements antagonistic to the prevailing social system are relative unknowns to contemporary American experience. In the United States the challenge of domestic Communist and other radical parties is slight.

Comparative Analysis of Community Power Structures

RECENT FINDINGS from a large research project based on studies of community power structures in a group of southwestern United States and

Mexican cities have been reported by Charles P. Loomis and his associates.[9] These findings make a substantial confirmation of the domination of businessmen in community decision making. In Table 70, the occupations of key influentials are given for El Paso, Denver, Tucson, Las Cruces, San Diego, McAllen, C. Juarez, Tijuana, Seattle, Bristol, and Atlanta and show the following distribution: business and finance, 63 percent; government, 11 percent; independent professions, 7 percent; mass communication, 7 percent; education, 5 percent; religion, 3 percent; welfare and culture, 2 percent; agriculture, 2 percent; labor, less than 1 percent.

Nine out of the eleven cities reported at least one financier among the key influentials, with a total of 30 (almost a quarter) being named in all. Both of the relatively specialized categories of manufacturing and merchandising were represented in at least eight cities. The merchants (including both wholesale and retail) produced slightly over one fifth of the key influentials. Manufacturers, who were almost one sixth of all key influentials were not represented in Tucson and Las Cruces. This may be explained by the relative absence of manufacturing in these cities.

Lawyers were among the key influentials in seven of the cities, ranking them next to businessmen in frequency of choice. It may be that the lawyer is becoming an effective link between business and other sectors of the community. Mayors were chosen in five of the eleven cities; other governmental officials and political leaders were chosen nine times in four cities. While it may be argued that the hierarchical structure of local government makes it likely that the mayor will be most often chosen from among governmental officials, the fact that mayors were not chosen as key influentials in six of the cities suggests the need for further exploration of the place of government in the community power structure.

Labor is notably lacking representation in the influence structure in all communities except Bristol. Agriculture, which is represented only in Las Cruces, has three of the thirteen persons listed; one of these is at the very top of the Las Cruces list. Religion, education, society and wealth, welfare, and cultural leaders have only scattered representation.

Recently John Walton summarized 33 studies dealing with 55 communities.[10] He examined the communities to discover the nature of the community characteristics, methods employed, type of issues studied, and the nature of the community power structure.[11] Table 71 shows that communities ranging from less than 10,000 to more than 100,000 population have been studied. Columns 17 and 18 show that 35 communities have been studied by the reputational (one- or two-step) approach, four communities by the decision-making approach, and 10 communities by

TABLE 70. *Institutional Identity of Key Influentials in Eleven Cities*

Institutional Categories	Seattle[a]	Bristol[a]	Atlanta[b]	Denver[c]	San Diego[d]	El Paso[e]	Tucson[f]	McAllen[g]	Las Cruces[h]	C. Juarez[i]	Tijuana[j]	Total
Business												
Finance	4	—	1	5	4	3	3	7	—	2	1	30
Merchant	3	—	3	2	3	—	5	4	3	1(1)[k]	5	29
Manufacture	1	3	2	1	2	2	—	1	1	2(3)[k]	4	19
Transportation and Utilities	—	—	3	1	—	—	—	—	1	—	—	5
Government												
Political	2	—	—	—	—	—	—	—	—	4	—	6
Mayor	1	—	1	—	—	1	—	—	—	1	1	5
Other Government	—	—	—	—	—	1	—	—	—	1	1	3
Independent Professions												
Lawyer	1	1	2	—	1	1	—	1	1	—	—	8
Physician	—	2	—	—	—	—	1	—	1	—	—	4
Education	—	2	—	1	—	—	1	—	2	—	—	6
Religion	—	1	—	—	—	—	—	—	—	1	—	2
Communications	—	—	—	1	2	3	2	—	1	—	—	9
Agriculture	—	—	—	—	—	—	—	—	3	—	—	3
Welfare and culture	—	2	—	—	—	—	—	—	—	—	—	2
Labor	—	1	—	—	—	—	—	—	—	—	—	1
TOTALS	12	12	12	11	12	11	12	13	13	12	12	132

[a] Studied by D. C. Miller.
[b] Studied by Floyd Hunter.
[c] Studied by Robert C. Hanson.
[d] Studied by Aubrey Wendling.
[e] Studied by R. Clyde McCone and Eugene C. Erickson.
[f] Studied by Edward Spicer and James Officer.
[g] Studied by Frank and Elizabeth Nall.
[h] Studied by Sigurd Johansen and Laiten L. Carmien.
[i] Studied by William V. D'Antonio.
[j] Studied by L. Vincent Padgett and Orrin E. Klapp.
[k] Alternative classification of politics.

a combination of methods. Governmental issues and nongovernmental issues have received attention an equal number of times, as shown in Columns 23 and 24.

The community power structures have been classified as: pyramidical—monolithic, monopolistic, or a single concentrated leadership group; factional—at least two durable factions; coalitional—fluid coalitions of interest, usually varying with issues; and amorphous—absence of any persistent patterns of leadership. The pyramidical power structure appears 19 times; factional, 17; coalition, 14; and amorphous, 5 (Columns 25, 26, 27, 28).

Comparative design provides an opportunity to test hypotheses under either similar or different sets of conditions. When similar selection criteria are satisfied, common relationships may be predicted for the communities. When the commuities are selected so that they differ in some desired characteristic (for example, population), the variation in relationships under study may be determined. If many variables are held constant by the types of cities selected, the tests of relationship between any two variables can be made with increasing rigor.

The range of variation in world communities provides the arena for investigation. The community power researcher does not lack for test sites. What he must do, if his study is to be most fruitful, is define the cutting edge in the research field. This means he must take the available theory and research, formulate hypotheses, and apply designs that probe for new knowledge. He must try to relate his work to that of others or, at least, define operational variables that can be replicated in future work. The usefulness of his work will depend on the extent to which the investigation makes more precise the relationships between variables, the breadth of the area in which his theory yields predictions, and the additional lines of research it suggests.

Principal Variables for Design of Comparative Studies

THE FIRST IMPORTANT DETERMINATION in comparative power research is the identification of those variations that are most important in identifying relationships with community power. In designing comparative studies the researcher can choose among three principal types of independent variables: variation in institutionalized power sectors of the community, variation in community social structure, and variation in issues. In the present state of knowledge, each of the types is equally promising.

VARIATION IN INSTITUTIONALIZED POWER. If the institutional base is truly the origin of social factors which generate the unique character

TABLE 71. Comparative Outline of Studies of Community Power Structure*

Column key:
1. Region
2. <10,000
3. 10,000–50,000
4. 50,000–100,000
5. >100,000
6. Industrialized
7. Non-industrialized
8. Diversified Economy
9. Narrow Economy
10. Absentee Ownership
11. Increasing Population
12. Stable Population
13. Heterogeneous Population
14. Homogeneous Population
15. Integration
16. Cleavage
17. Reputational
18. Two-step
19. Positional
20. Decision-making
21. Combined
22. Case Study
23. Non-governmental
24. Governmental
25. Pyramidal
26. Factional
27. Coalitional
28. Amorphous
29. Leadership Group (N)

Community	1	2	3	4	5	6	7	8	9	10	11	12	13	14	15	16	17	18	19	20	21	22	23	24	25	26	27	28	29
1. Regional City	S				X	X		X				X	X			X	X	X					X		X				40
2. Loraine	NC†								X						X		X									X		X	
3. Red Wing	NC		X					X				X		X			X					X				X			
4. Big Town	S					X		X				X	X			X	X	X					X		X			X	75
5. Community A	NC			X		X		X				X		X			X	X			X		X		X				25
6. Bakerville	S					X		X						X			X	X				X	X			X			69
7. Bennington	NE					X		X			X			X				X					X						59
8. Pacific City	W				X			X	X	X	X			X	X		X	X	X				X	X	X				47
English City									X		X			X			X	X					X	X					35
9. Cibolia	NC					X		X						X		X	X								X				76
10. Seattle	W				X				X	X	X				X			X		X		X	X		X		X	X		5
11. Springdale	NE	X					X				X			X								X	X						415
12. New Haven	NE				X		X				X		X				X		X	X			X	X			X		61
13. El Paso	S		X		X		X				X		X				X			X			X			X	X		60
C. Juarez					X				X				X				X						X				X		30
14. Tia Juana	W	X							X		X		X				X						X						16
15. Northville									X					X		X	X	X					X		X				
16. Miami (Dade County)					X	X					X						X					X	X					X	
17. Sanford	S						X				X			X			X						X				X		
Amory	S						X				X			X			X						X				X	X	
Algona	S						X				X			X			X						X				X		
Gretna	S						X				X			X			X						X			X			
Milton	NC						X				X			X			X						X				X		
Norwood	NE						X				X			X			X						X				X		
18. Service City	W					X		X							X		X							X			X	X	
19. Syracuse	NE				X			X			X	X				X		X			X				X			X	X	
20. Syracuse	NE				X			X			X	X				X		X			X				X			X	X	
21. Dixie City	S					X		X									X					X		X			X		
22. Community A	NC		X	X		X		X			X	X			X		X							X			X		49
23. Cerebrille	NC		X	X		X		X			X	X			X		X					X		X			X		49
24. Burlington	S		X			X		X	X		X	X	X	X		X	X	X					X		X				16

Community	Region	>10,000	10,000–50,000	50,000–100,000	>100,000	Industrialized	Non-industrialized	Diversified Economy	Narrow Economy	Absentee Ownership	Increasing Population	Stable Population	Heterogeneous Population	Homogeneous Population	Integration	Cleavage	Reputational	Two-step	Positional	Decision-making	Combined	Case Study	Non-governmental	Governmental	Pyramidal	Factional	Coalitional	Amorphous	Leadership Group (N)
25. Watertown	S				X		X	X						X			X	X						X		X				74
Centralia	S				X		X	X						X			X	X						X		X				61
26. Orange Point	S						X						X			X							X	X		X	X			
Floriana	S	X					X						X			X							X	X			X			
Center City	S		X									X	X			X							X			X				
Eastborne	S	X					X		X			X											X	X		X	X			
Westborne	S						X		X		X												X	X			X			
Dorado	S										X												X	X			X			
Hiberna	S								X														X		X					
Estiva	S																						X		X					
27. Dallas	NC	X				X								X			X	X	X					X	X				67
28. Wheelsburg	NE	X			X		X				X			X				X	X					X					78
29. Edgewood	NE	X					X			X	X		X					X						X		X			36
Riverview	S					X		X	X									X						X	X				35
30. Midway County	S					X		X	X					X			X	X			X			X			X	20
River County	S						X										X	X			X			X	X			38
Beach County	S						X					X					X	X			X			X				18
Southern County	S						X														X			X				8
31. Atlanta	W				X	X		X		X	X			X			X	X			X		X		X		X	133
32. Farmdale	W	X					X	X	X		X		X				X	X			X		X					14
Oretown	S			X		X		X			X						X	X			X		X		X		X	38
Petropolis	S			X		X		X			X		X			X	X	X			X		X				X	61
Metroville	S		X			X							X			X				X	X							41
33. Oberlin	NC	X																						X		X			
TOTALS		10	13	11	17	25	19	24	16	8	24	12	25	22	6	15	27	25	4	4	10	14	26	26	19	17	14	5	

* Adapted from John Walton, "Substance and Artifact: The Current Status of Research on Community Power Structure," *American Journal of Sociology,* LXXI (January 1966), 431–32. The community in the first study is Atlanta, Georgia; the eighth study refers to Seattle, Washington and Bristol, England.

of the community power structure (as postulated in the Miller-Form community power system model), then some 13 institutional sectors must be examined in communities where they may be dominant. Major power variations have been found repeatedly around such social institutions as business, government, and political parties. There is every reason to believe that much new knowledge may be gained by further examination of relatively unexplored sectors such as society and wealth, education, mass communication, labor, religion, military, social welfare, independent professions, culture and art, and recreation.

Our confidence in this approach is based on the belief that each institutional sector incorporates a different set of consensual values. These values are expressed by the professionals and workers in each sector. Often, as in religion, they are shared by large numbers of laymen in that sector.

Many of the values are inculcated in the training of the professional; others grow out of experience and personal investment in the work of the sector. All sectors may be likened to special interest groups. They struggle for increased power or prestige and they defend their values when attacked. They marshal monetary resources, leadership, votes, or moral persuasion according to their capacity. Their rise or decline in power affects the total institutional structure. When a given sector rises to dominance, it brings its goals and values to bear and the total institutional structure is shaped into new form and direction.

The principal problem in studying this kind of variation is locating communities which have the desired institutional dominance. The sociologist must often solicit the help of political scientists, historians, and anthropologists to find appropriate test communities.

VARIATION IN COMMUNITY SOCIAL STRUCTURE. It is widely believed that variations in community social structures produce variations in the type of power structure. Significant variables that have been proposed include the degree of stability in community life, the orientation of community leaders, the community's economic foundations, the relations between the community and other political systems, and the dynamics of population growth.[12] In Chapter 2 a list of variables related to the economic, governmental, and social bases of the community were set out as those most directly influencing the community power structure.

Seasholes has utilized factor analysis data to identify six independent variables having a bearing on the type of influence structure a given community has. They are size, maturity, median income, income homogeneity, industrialization, and isolation.[13] He suggests a study design as shown in Figure 26. Seven towns are chosen in a manner that permits systematic investigation of the six community characteristics. By pairing towns that differ in only one of six characteristics, tentative conclusions may be drawn about the effect of these variables on types of influence structure. He points out that a universe of 65 cities and towns was used to assemble the matrix so that one factor could be varied as others were held constant.

SIZE	high	high	high	high	low	low	low
HOMOGENEITY	low	low	low	high	high	high	high
INDUSTRIALIZATION	high	low	low	low	low	low	low
MATURITY	high	high	high	high	high	high	low
INCOME	low	low	high	high	high	high	high
ISOLATION	low	low	low	low	low	high	high
	Waltham, Lynn, Cambridge	Somerville, Revere, Malden, Brookline	Newton	Watertown, Quincy, Milton, Melrose, Medford, Everett, Dedham, Belmont, Arlington	Saugus, Winchester	Swampscott	Wenham, Westwood, Wayland, Walpole, Sharon, Reading, Lynnfield, Lincoln

FIGURE 26. *The Matching of Seven sets of Towns in Pairs so that Six Community Variables may be Manipulated One at a Time while Holding All Other Variables Constant (after Seasholes).*

Seasholes proposes that the dependent variables composing an influence structure are issue area specialization, consensus, social class homogeneity, cosmopolitanism, formality, and location. *Issue area specialization* refers to the extent to which individuals do or do not appear on more than one list of influentials—that is, the list of school, transportation, land use, and "general" influentials. *Consensus* refers to the extent to which leaders agree with each other on issues in general and on issues in three important issue areas. *Socio-economic status homogeneity* refers to the extent to which leaders are drawn from the same social class. *Cosmopolitanism* refers to the extent to which leaders are oriented toward the metropolis as a whole, as against their own city or town. *Formality* refers to the extent to which leaders hold government office. *Location* refers to the extent to which leaders reside in the city or town in which they are considered influential.[14]

Hypotheses are then formulated by Seasholes relating the independent variables of community social structure to the dependent variables of the influence structure. Figure 27 shows a hypothetical pattern of relationships awaiting test. Note, for example, how population size is

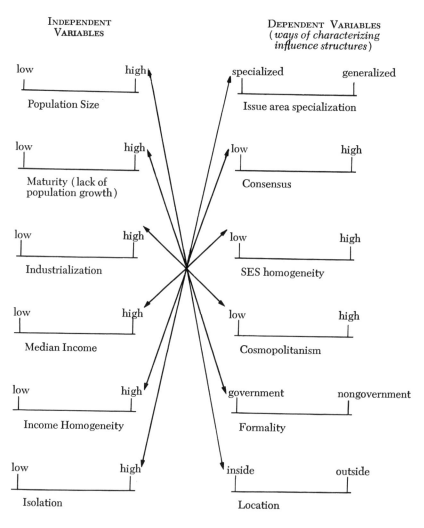

FIGURE 27. *Theoretical Framework Representing Hypothesized Relations between Independent Community Variables and Dependent Variables of Community Influence Structure (after Seasholes).*

presented. The set of hypotheses states: the greater the size, the greater the issue area specialization; the greater the size, the lower the consensus; the greater the size, the more likely that leaders are non-governmental.

Walton, in his summary of studies dealing with power structure of 55 communities, tests the relationship of some demographic and economic characteristics of communities. He hypothesized that socially integrated heterogeneous populations have less concentrated power structure; the more industrialized the community, the less concentrated will be the power structure; communities with a high proportion of absentee ownership tend to have less concentrated power structures; the more diversified the economic base, the less concentrated the power structure. He found that social integration showed some association with less concentrated power structures. Economic variables reflecting patterns characteristic of increasing industrialization are moderately associated with less concentrated power structures.[15]

Presthus and Clark have each set forth a list of propositions for test.[16] These initial efforts to establish relationships will undoubtedly continue. What we observe now are the beginnings of a systematic body of knowledge.

VARIATION IN ISSUE. Another set of designs for comparative analysis revolves around variations in issues. Barth and Johnson have suggested a typology of issues which involve five dimensions: unique-recurrent; salient-nonsalient to leadership; salient-nonsalient to community publics; effective action possible-effective action impossible; local-cosmopolitan.[17] Generalizations concerning the decision-making processes in American communities will be expedited by comparing the way in which different types of issues are settled by different types of decision makers in different types of communities. The aim is to hold one factor constant and allow the other factors to vary. Some of the important axes of comparison are described here.[18]

Similar issues in a range of communities. This is a research design in which the issues are similar but other factors vary. It is especially appropriate when applied to issues which appear in most communities; e.g. school levy proposals, elections, fluoridation referenda.

Similar influentials on a variety of issues. Issues and communities vary but the influentials are the same. This design is especially appropriate to indicate how the content of an issue affects the outcome of a decision, holding influentials constant.

Similar communities with a variety of issues. This is a design which compares communities. It requires a typology of communities based on such criteria as size, economic base, or type of power model. This design is especially appropriate to indicate how the content of an issue affects the outcome of a decision, holding community variables constant.

Factorial designs permit comparison of a more complicated sort, varying systematically a number of factors. Thus, we may compare similar communities on similar issues and diverse issues, holding issues constant in some comparisons and varying them in others.

Numerous studies have now been made that utilize these designs in whole or in part.[19]

A National Sampling Frame for Comparative Community Power Studies

Rossi has proposed the most ambitious design yet formulated for community power study. His proposal recognizes that it is rarely possible for the individual social scientist to undertake studies which encompass more than a very few communities unless he is content to use data already collected. Data on political decision making and the composition of community leaders are ordinarily not available and the researcher must gather these data. Continuity and generalization are greatly impeded by these conditions. His proposal to surmount these difficulties rests on the establishment of a national network of social scientists, each to be available part-time to collect data on a uniform basis from a sample of 200 American cities of over 50,000 population. These social scientists would collect locally available statistics and other documentary materials, reconstruct histories of community actions, interview local elites, etc. Local representatives of such a network would be responsible for setting up a panel of informants in their communities and collecting from them information about and judgments concerning the communities in question. Every study made with this technique would constitute part of an on-going "panel study" of American cities. All data would be placed in a permanent set of archives, thus making the data from each study available to the social science community.[20]

This proposal gives an indication of the scope of comparative design desired for both national and international study. It expresses the requirements for continuity and generalization needed to advance knowledge in community power. This design awaits financing and implementation. Meanwhile, the state of theory and methodology sets the limits for research progress for all community power research, whether it be single-community or comparative, national or international. It is not possible here to review the many contributions to theory and knowledge in the field. What can be set out is a brief history of the methodological advances. These are quite limited and their specification is perhaps the single best definition of the cutting edge of community power research.

THE CUTTING EDGE OF METHODOLOGY

THE FOLLOWING INVENTORY of methodological advances sets the limits for operational research.

1952—Robert Lamb reports on a quick documentary method (use of Rand McNally's *International Bankers Directory* and *Poor's Register of Directors and Executives*) to locate economic dominants in a community. (*Human Organization*, Vol. 11, no. 2, 29–32.)

1953—Floyd Hunter applies sociometry techniques to identification of leaders and organizations involved in community decision making; a method of tracing issues is developed using interview and informant methods to locate role of upper and lower limits personnel in institutional and associational units of the community.

1957—James S. Coleman outlines stages in issue controversies which provide a framework for analyzing issues. (*Community Conflict*, Glencoe, Ill., 1957.)

1957–58—Raymond Wolfinger employs gate-keeper approach by observing struggle over charter proposal in office of the mayor of New Haven. (See Robert A. Dahl, *Who Governs?* 1961.)

1957—Delbert C. Miller develops a prediction technique for determining issue outcome. (Proceedings of the Pacific Sociological Society, *Research Studies of the State College of Washington*, June 1957.)

1958—Samuel Stouffer reports his quick (Q) method of identifying reputational leaders. (See Form and Miller, *Industry, Labor, Community*, 1960.)

1959—Floyd Hunter describes use of roll-up questions in interviewing. (*Top Leadership, U.S.A.*, 1959.)

1959—E. A. T. Barth and Stuart D. Johnson present a typology of social issues. (*Social Forces*, Vol. 38, No. 1, 1959.)

1959—Robert C. Hanson reports refinement of the Miller prediction technique and success in predicting accurate percentage outcomes of two issues in Denver, Colorado. (*American Sociological Review*, Vol. XXIV, October 1959.)

1960—Thomas F. Thompson employs gate-keeper approach by observing in office of mayor Cary, Indiana. ("Public Administration in the Civil City of Gary, Indiana," doctoral thesis, Indiana University.)

1960—Irwin T. Sanders presents short method of identifying top influentials in a community social profile for local action programs. (*American Sociological Review*, Vol. XXV, No. 1, 1960.)

1961—Robert A. Dahl reports techniques for analyzing decisions in different issue areas to determine the distribution of influence among participants; documentary approach reveals historical change of incumbents in mayor and city council positions. (*Who Governs?*)

1961—Peter H. Rossi and Robert A. Dentler describe methods of tracing influences of citizen participation upon decisions made within renewal planning process. (*The Politics of Urban Renewal*, Glencoe, Ill., 1961.)

1962—William V. D'Antonio and Eugene C. Erickson develop evaluation techniques for appraising the reputational method in comparative and longitudinal studies. (*American Sociological Review*, Vol. XXVII, June 1962.)

1963—Charles M. Bonjean describes technique for identifying visible, concealed, and symbolic leaders. (*American Journal of Sociology*, Vol. LXVIII, May 1963.)

1963—Linton C. Freeman and associates report on a comparison of leaders located by four procedures: participation in issues, social activity, reputation, and formal position. (*American Sociological Review*, Vol. XXVIII, October 1963.)

1964—Robert Presthus presents intensive comparison of key leaders identified by issue and reputational techniques. (*Men at the Top*, New York, 1964.)

1964—José Luis de Imaz applies documentary techniques to longitudinal studies of elites in Argentina. (*Los Que Mandan*, Buenos Aires, 1964.)

1964—Robert E. Agger, Daniel Goldrich, and Bert Swanson study "manifest" and "latent" leaders in a comparative four community design. (*The Rulers and the Ruled*, New York, 1964.)

1965—Howard J. Ehrlich and Mary Lou Bauer discover relationship between reputation for community leadership and frequency of citation in local and metropolitan newspapers. (*American Sociological Review*, Vol. XXX, June 1965.)

1966—William A. Gamson reports that reputation for influence is highly associated with activity on issues in study of 54 issues in 18 New England communities. (*American Journal of Sociology*, Vol. LXXII, September 1966.)

This inventory of methodology is not complete, but it does reflect the major resources upon which the community power researcher now draws. Both methodology and theory leave much to be desired. Existing knowledge is fragmentary and often contradictory. But the steps that must be taken are clear. Some requirements will be described.

REQUIREMENTS FOR FUTURE RESEARCH

A Broader Conceptualization of Community Power and the Accompanying Structure. No future step is more important than broadening the concept of community power. The concept of community power as political decision making and its methodology as issue analysis is valuable but very limiting. This concept emphasizes the dynamic and transitory movement of power arrangements as issues are debated in the community. It fails to tap fully the *structure* of influence and power which molds opinion and exerts a covert as well as an overt manifestation of that structure. In Chapter 1 a broader concept of community power was introduced and defined as the network of influences that bear upon all decisions that have a general effect upon the community. Community decisions of general importance occur around issues, projects, status and power allocations in voluntary, political, and governmental organizations, in work organizations, and in decisions over land use.

No community power research has yet focused around such a broad concept, and as a result the total base of community power has not yet been found. In that base, positional, reputational, and issue-decisional leaders play independent and overlapping roles. The degree of leadership overlap is no longer important as a test of validity. What is important is the manner in which each category of leadership functions. It is well known that reputational leaders tend to avoid involvement in issues and prefer to associate with noncontroversial projects. It is well known that positional leaders play important roles in the status and power allocations within their own organizations. They can establish personnel and other policies which have a large effect on the community or they can practice an isolation policy which alters role relationships throughout their firms. It is well known that real estate interests are important in land-use decisions but little research has been undertaken since Everett C. Hughes made his study in the 1920s.[21] The leaders who are influential in the status and power allocations within voluntary, political, and governmental organizations have seldom been studied. The need now is to utilize all methods of leadership, organizational, and institutional identification and relate them to the broader conception of community power. The Miller-Form system model of community power structure points in that direction. The use of the reputational method to examine leaders, organizations, and institutions and establish their relative influence is an example of a search in depth. Similar efforts should be made with the issue and positional techniques. Newspaper, questionnaire, and documentary analysis will serve as directly complementary tools.

The Measurement of Solidarity of Top Leaders and their Decisionmaking Relationships. No problem in community power analysis is more difficult than attempting to establish the decision-making relationships of top leaders. Research and understanding have been greatly impeded by the term "elite." If any part of our conceptual or methodological apparatus should have a decent burial (to paraphrase Wolfinger) it is this misleading term. It implies a high solidarity and a consensus on goals and values that is ordinarily absent in most communities. A much better strategy is to seek out that "pool" of leaders who play influential roles, to ascertain their common and diverse interests, and to appraise their degree of solidarity as a unit or in cliques. The structure of the top influentials can be observed in the interpersonal relations of people who initiate major community policy—including land-use decisions; undertake the direction of major community projects and influence status and power allocations in voluntary and political organizations; and play veto roles in major projects and issues. Since direct observation is time-consuming and much activity is concealed from public view, indirect methods must be utilized. A considerable number of these are available but no systematic approach has yet been devised. In Chapters 6 and 12 various methods are introduced in the study of decision-making cliques in Seattle, Bristol, and Lima. What emerges is a network that is fragmentary, transitory, and elusive. Unsubstantiated hearsay and opinion are abundant. Some solid activity of leaders can be documented such as common and overlapping participation in business directorships, social clubs, civic projects, and in professional organizations. But these participations require interpretation and this is not easy to accomplish because hearsay evidence can intervene.

Focused interviews of from one to two hours yield the best results when these interviews are held with the top influentials and selected informants. Sometimes informants who are important position leaders and have had dealings with top influentials feel free to describe the decision-making relationships which transpired. Two patterned groupings have generally emerged to characterize top influential structures: a general pattern of fluid coalition among the influentials about most issues, with activity ranging from involvement to quiet support, veto, and inactivity; clique relationships observed around a set of specific situations, especially on an issue involving a special interest—threatened tax increase, school bond levy, threatened change of government, right-to-work bill threatening labor, and so on.

Research progress in the measurement of the solidarity of top leaders requires an awareness of these diversities in power arrangements and the most careful and skilled collection of relevant data. New tools of research are not foreseeable. The researcher must do a better job with what he has.

The Mapping of Interinstitutional Linkages.   Interinstitutional linkages are especially important as two or more institutional sectors find that their interests are drawn together. In modern industrial life business and government have become ever more closely interlocked. Indeed, C. Wright Mills in the *Power Elite* claimed that big business, big government, and big military are a ruling triumvirate in the United States, sharing common interests, intermeshing leadership, and maintaining a common ideology. His ideas invited a hundred critics, but all agreed on the difficulty and importance of identifying the intricate character of the interinstitutional linkages between business, government, and military. In England, the cry of "Establishment" evokes visions of a tight coalition of family, education, government, and business. In Latin America, the cry of "Oligarchy" raises the specter of the Catholic Church, landholders, and the military in a conspiracy to maintain the status quo against all efforts to achieve social change.

Discovering the "truth" in these allegations about coalitions is a giant undertaking in macro-sociology. The mapping of interinstitutional linkages poses on the macro level what the determination of decision-making relationships among top influentials raises on the micro level.

Hunter undertook the task of ascertaining institutional linkages in his study, *Top Leadership, U.S.A.* His book can be used as one model for analysis. He relied heavily on interviews with top leaders in all parts of the United States, and he mapped their interrelations through contacts, participation in national policy interests, and their specific roles in relation to government.

In this research, the study of Lima forced recognition of the alleged coalition of Catholic Church, large landholders, and military leaders. The numerous efforts to discover interlinkages are reported in Chapter 12. The search was first directed at finding some "key" that would reveal the interrelations. The successive topics chosen for study were the old families, the list of large landholders, the members of the President's cabinet, the political party leaders, the principal government leaders, the economic dominants (such as bankers, investment, and real estate holders), the chief religious leaders, the chief military leaders, the social clubs, the joint chiefs of staff, the homes of key leaders, cocktail parties, and finally father-son chains. While much was learned, no one can recommend a "shotgun" strategy. But no alternative is yet clear. The determination of bases of power for leaders as established by the ratings of top leaders is a promising tool. The study of overlapping economic, government, social, familial, religious, and military identities is impor-tant. Such study provides questions for interpretation. Focused inter-views with top influentials and informants can provide that interpreta-tion, although it becomes more and more clear that no one in a large city knows even the top of the power structure in its entirety. Any strategy to secure such a total picture must be a planned piecemeal operation in which one informant describes a part that must be fitted to other parts as they are received from other especially vantaged informants.

The Measurement of Collective Institutional and Organizational Power. Nothing has been made more clear in this study than the great gap that now exists in the understanding of collective institutional and organizational power. There was a tendency in earlier studies to dismiss the power of labor, religion, and the military when no key influentials were identified with these sectors. However, the rating of institutions and organizations for their influence quickly revealed that the collective power of labor, religion, and the military often ranks very high. When it is taken as a given that community power rests on a *structure*, it is not difficult to accept the importance of collective orga-nizational power. Future community power research will most cer-tainly seek to assess and relate this type of power. It has been demon-strated that the reputational approach can be applied to the rating of institutions and organizations, assessing their relative influence. Addi-tional appraisal might well follow Dahl's suggestion that power poten-tial rests on resources, willingness to use the available resources, and the efficiency of their use.

Leaders may come and go but organizations carry within them re-sources that must be reckoned with. This is especially true if their po-tential is high. Good examples are the military with its coercive potential and labor with its political strength and economic weapons such as the strike. The moral legitimization or negative sanctioning of the church can be vital on many issues. The worldwide impact of the Roman Cath-olic Church on birth control provides a case in point.

The Measurement of Fluidity in Community Power Structures. Current research reveals the presence of many models varying from

the one-man rule to a situation where there is a high degree of frag-
mentation of power, with no single person or group in control of community decisions.

The writer now proposes that an operational scale of the mono-
lithic-pluralistic continuum can be achieved. Three factors are essential
to such a determination: representation of institutional sectors by key
influentials, solidary character of top influentials, and strength of political parties. Each factor is believed to bear a strong relationship to the
fluidity of the power structure and would be capable of operational
measurement. The number of institutional sectors represented by key
influentials is a crude but useful index of the institutional fluidity of the
structure. The solidary character of top leaders can be classified into
four types ranging in degree of fluidity. The most fluid is an amorphous
type in which there is an absence of any persistent pattern of leadership.
A coalitional type is a fluid coalition of leaders which varies according
to issues. A factional type contains at least two durable factions. A highly
solidary type with a single concentrated leadership group is the most
rigid.[22] Political parties can be observed in three significant combinations: two strong parties or coalitions; one strong party and others weak;
or all weak. Two strong opposing parties reflect the operation of
countervailing power and suggest that strong labor and government
segments are represented in the community power structure. At the very
least, issue outcome is often indeterminate and a fluid condition is maintained under a strong two-party system. In the case of an unbalanced
situation of one strong party and many weak parties, or with all parties
weak, a more rigid community power structure is indicated. It is postulated that the three factors, institutional representation, solidary character of top influentials, and strength of political parties, are highly predictive of the degree of fluidity within the total power structure. The
schema assumes a society in which political forces can be marshaled
and expressed in free elections.

Figure 28 shows how a 24-point scale can be developed specifying
high fluidity at one pole and high rigidity at the other. Each power
structure can be identified by first classifying it under its proper representation of institutional sectors—broad, medium, or narrow. It can
then be successively subclassified according to the solidary character
of the top influentials and the strength of the political parties. The final
classification places it in its proper position on the scale. Tentative estimates have been made for the cities described in this monograph and
are inscribed on the figure. Since Cordoba was ruled by decrees of
the military junta it is not included.

The scale obviously requires considerable refinement. When this

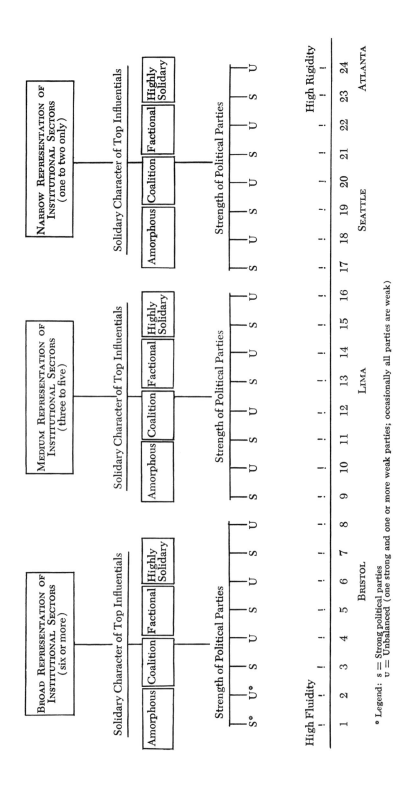

FIGURE 28. *Schema for Quantification of Fluidity in Community Power Structures*

has been achieved, much of the controversy over the character of pluralism can be reduced. It is hoped that terms like monolithic and pluralistic can be discarded as too crude for research purposes. A more precise grading of power structures opens up the possibility of working with quantitative variables in the study of most relationships. This is one of the advanced goals toward which research is now drawn. Up to now, a community power structure has been a single complex of qualitative characteristics derived after laborious research. It must become a quantitative variable which is more quickly determined and amenable to quantitative manipulation. The goal is not near but it is visible.

APPENDIX I

Patterns of Research Craftsmanship

THE RANGE OF COMMUNITY POWER ANALYSIS by its intrinsic nature is so broad that it is easy to become absorbed in the many intriguing leads that direct the researcher to such institutional sectors as business and finance, political parties, church, military, society and wealth, education, mass communication, and others. The researcher must exercise great restraint, and choose carefully a few hypotheses that seem most significant. In comparative study, especially where one study is to follow another, it is necessary to freeze a central part of the design. A decision, once made, fixes the comparative features of the work. There is seldom an opportunity to go back to the field site and gather the data which the researcher may wish to have at a later time. Each investigation, moreover, offers an opportunity to introduce a new hypothesis or supplementary studies. The early stage of a study, especially in a new culture, should be exploratory. The possibility of exploiting some unique feature of the community should be seized.

The study of power structure and decision-making processes draws the researcher into a search for institutional and organizational linkages, and the character of the larger social system. The patterns, norms, and values of the society must be understood and related to decision making. For this reason it is imperative that the investigator live in the site community for at least one year. He should begin at once to read the newspapers and magazines and establish a file of issues, problems, leaders, organizations, and power processes. He should attend conferences and forums, make contacts with the United States Embassy (or the consulate in a smaller city), and join any social organizations which will bring him valuable contacts. In Lima I joined the Lima Football and Cricket Club, a British-operated social club open to Americans, Peruvians, and other nationalities. It is important to participate fully in the daily life of the community. One's children can be a natural point of contact with children and parents in the host culture. Neighbors, the maid, new friends, the doctor, the dentist, storekeepers, school teachers, all have something to contribute to better understanding of institutional life in the strange, new culture. The community power researcher must organize his experiences to learn what he needs to know about a new society. From the first days in the site city, he begins the appraisal of the economic, social, and governmental base of the nation and community. He must seek out the libraries, government agencies, and private institutes for documentary materials. The framework for comparative analysis described in Chapter 2 was used to make these assessments in all the four site cities. This framework leads to the analysis of community power itself. The system model of community power is based on the assumption that the most important starting point is in the relative distribution of power exercised by different institutions in the nation and local community. One of the first tasks is to find knowledgeable persons in each of the institutional sectors who can help assemble names of leaders and organizations that are of high influence in the community. The first interviews with these knowledgeable judges can be most fruitful if the researcher is ready to ask meaningful questions as a judge makes his selections. Such contacts may provide new research leads.

The assessment of the many leads rests upon a judgment of the fruitfulness of a suggested hypothesis. The value of a hypothesis is determined by its capacity to move research forward toward a fuller understanding of the similarities and differences in power structures and processes under varying conditions. It is always assumed that the general purpose of international comparative research design is to utilize cities throughout the world in order to take advantage of the full range of institutional power distributions.

The attempt to move into world cities soon involves the researcher in the barriers of language. For myself, the investigations in South America required study of the Spanish language, in which I had no previous training. Three university courses, five tutors, and three years of part-time study were necessary for my preparation. On this base I was finally ready to accept a Fulbright appointment providing me with an opportunity to teach courses in Spanish at the Universiy of San Marcos in Lima. In both Cordoba and Lima my identification with the national university was very important in giving a legitimacy and sponsorship to the research. The American and British citizens living in these cities were a source of assistance. Many are in business, education, government, and the professions. They can greatly assist in arranging contacts with nationals, many of whom they work with daily. Members of the Peace Corps can arrange contacts in the barriadas, educators can provide entry to the middle class, and businessmen to upper classes.

The reservoir of specialists attached to the United States Embassy is another rich resource for the community power researcher. In Lima there are more than 650 persons listed in the directory of the Embassy. Among the most useful are the economic, political, public information, labor, military, and cultural officers. I found them most useful in interpreting my collected data. I employed focused interviews seeking answers to puzzling questions raised by the study. I found that Embassy officials could designate their appropriate counterparts in the government agencies of the host country. I turned to these Peruvian officials to broaden the perspective of the same data that had been put before American observers. I found that comparative interpretations are a valuable component of comparative research design.

APPENDIX II

Lima Leadership Schedule*

ISSUES AND PROBLEMS

Note that there are two types of issues and problems.

      i. Problems of principal importance for Lima

      ii. National problems with repercussions in Lima

Please indicate three problems or issues from the list that you believe are the most important.

Problems of Principal Importance for Lima

Indicate three in order of importance: 1, 2, 3.

1. Improvement of transport and traffic movement.
2. Improvement and maintenance of roads and streets.
3. Improvement or elimination of slum housing.
4. Control of crime and delinquency.
5. Control of street vendors.
6. Planning and zoning of Lima.
7. Problems of sanitation, sewage, and water.
8. Abolition of the system of proportional representation of the political parties as a method for electing municipal councilmen.
9. Improvement of public markets.
10. Containment of corrupt practices among city officials.

National Problems with Repercussion in Lima

Indicate three in order of importance: 1, 2, 3.

1. Increase of agrarian reform.
2. Nationalization of oil in Brea and Pariñas
3. Improvement of telephone services.
4. More housing for the city.
5. Rapid industrial development.
6. Completion of the marginal highway.
7. Abolition of politics in the universities.
8. Control of inflation.

  * This interview schedule is very similar to those used in Seattle, Bristol, and Cordoba

9. Control of growth of population.
10. Elimination of contraband.
11. Reform of primary and secondary education.
12. Reduction of labor problems.
13. Containment of obstructionist tactics by opposition parties.
14. Containment of corrupt practices among officials of the national government.
15. Reform of the national tariff structure.

Leaders in Lima

Please look at the following list of persons that live and work in Lima. Indicate your acquaintance with each and whether you have worked on any committees with him in the past three years.

NAME OF LEADER	Do NOT KNOW	HAVE HEARD OF	KNOW LITTLE	KNOW WELL	KNOW SOCIALLY (may visit in his home or meet at club)	WORKED ON COMMITTEES WITH HIM DURING PAST 3 YEARS
1. Juan Mejia Baca						
2. Augusto Tamayo Vargas						
3. Guillermo Griffiths Escardo						
[etc.]						

Selection of Most Powerful Leaders of Lima

Look again at the list of persons who live and work in Lima. Without taking into account what you may think of them and of their ideas, please select 15 persons from the list that are the *most powerful* in regard to the initiation, support, or vetoing of acts that have influence in matters which have a general effect upon the city. Add names of your own choosing if they do not appear on the list. (1) Place names of the selected leaders below and (2) indicate the principal bases of their power and influence. (3) Indicate in which issues or projects they have participated actively in recent years. Use as reference the list of issues and problems if you desire.

Types of Power or Influence

1. Economic Power
2. Political Influence
3. Governmental Authority
4. Moral and Religious Persuasion
5. Social Prestige
6. Means of Communication

7. Specialized Knowledge or Skill
8. Military Support
9. Well liked or esteemed person
10. Superior Qualities of Leadership

NAME OF CHOSEN LEADERS	TYPES OF POWER										PROJECT OR ISSUE IN WHICH HE PARTICIPATED MOST
	1	2	3	4	5	6	7	8	9	10	
1.											
2.											
[etc.]											

Selection of Civic Leaders of Lima

Civic leaders are those that (1) have influence (2) work for community betterment and (3) cooperate with other leaders. Select 15 persons from the list of Lima leaders that can best provide influence for a civic matter which requires wide public support. Place the names of these leaders below, indicate bases of influence, and issue or project in which he participated.

NAME OF LEADERS CHOSEN	TYPES OF POWER										PROJECT OR ISSUE IN WHICH HE PARTICIPATED
	1	2	3	4	5	6	7	8	9	10	
1.											
2.											
[etc.]											

Leadership Schedule

Whom do you regard as the chief community spokesman for:
Business merchants   _____
Military   _____
Manufacturers   _____
Bankers   _____
Labor   _____
National University   _____
Society and Wealth   _____
Social welfare   _____
Local government   _____
Religion   _____
Political party or coalition in power
  (APRA-Odrista)   _____

Opposition party or coalition (Popular Action-Christian
  Democratic) _____

Best local contact man with city officials (besides local members of
  legislature) _____

Best local contact man with federal officials in Lima (besides
  legislators) _____

Culture and art _____

Local newspapers _____

Doctors _____

Lawyers _____

Public school teachers _____

To what persons should the community turn for leadership—
  When the economic welfare of the community is threatened?

  _____

  When a civic project needs to succeed?

  _____

  When political influence or power is needed?

  _____

Organizations

Which of these organizations would you select as the most influential in
getting things done in the community. Add other organizations of you wish.
Rate:

> *1—most influential*
> *2—influential*
> *3—less influential*

National Agrarian Society
APRA Party
National Corporation of Merchants
Confederation of Workers of Peru
La Prensa (Newspaper)
Chamber of Commerce
Board of National Assistance
El Comercio (Newspaper)
Associated Electric Enterprisers
International Petroleum Company
Lions Club of Lima
Rotary Club of Lima
National Institute of Planning
Federation of Housing Cooperatives of Peru
Popular Action Party
Caritas (Magazine)

Peruvian League for Fight Against Cancer
National Federation of Educators of Peru
Reiser and Curioni (industrial firm)
Christian Democratic Party
Odrista Party
Action for Development
North American Committee for Peru

Institutions

Kindly rank the institutional sectors for their relative strength and influence in getting things done and in influencing the nation and the city when issues and projects are debated.

Rank for Peru from 1 to 13 and then rank for Lima.

PERU	INSTITUTIONAL SECTORS	LIMA
	Religion	
	Government	
	Culture and art	
	Business and finance	
	Labor	
	Social welfare	
	Society and wealth	
	Independent professions (medicine, law, and engineering)	
	Education	
	Political parties	
	Military	
	Mass communication (newspapers, magazines, radio, TV)	
	Recreation (parks, beaches, playgrounds)	

We are not interested in how you stand for or against issues (or projects), but what major issues before Lima—either immediately past or current—have you been interested in?

_____

Kindly select an issue in which you have taken part:
Issue (or project) _____
Were you contacted on this issue? ___ ___
                                       yes   no

How were you contacted?   Personal call_____
                              By phone_____
                              Private luncheon_____
                              Committee meeting_____
                              Informal, chance meeting_____
                              Other (specify) _____

Did you contact others?   ___   ___
                          yes   no
How did you contact others? Personal call_____
                              By phone_____
                              Private luncheon_____
                              Committee meeting_____
                              Informal, chance meeting_____
                              Other (specify) _____

Kindly think about the way the various institutional sectors come into this issue. There are two things we would like to know:

(1) How important the issue is to each sector;
(2) If important or very important, the stand of the sector: for; against; split on the issue.

Institutional Sectors	IMPORTANCE			STAND		
	Very Important	Important	Not Important	For	Against	Split
Religion						
Government						
Culture and art						
Business and finance						
Labor						
Social welfare						
Society and wealth						
Independent professions						
Education						
Political parties						
Military						
Mass communication						
Recreation						

What persons and organizations are working *for* the issue or project? *Against?*

(Refer to lists of people and organizations. Add others not listed.)

Fᴏʀ   Aɢᴀɪɴsᴛ

Thinking only of the groups which are *against*, which of the following arrangements best describe the situation as you see it?
Check here

_____1. The groups which are against are going it alone; that is to say, there is little cooperation among them.

_____2. Some of the important groups are cooperating but others have remained independent.

_____3. Practically all of the important groups and individuals are united and share resources and leadership in their efforts to defeat the issues.

What about the different groups of people who are *for?*
Check here

_____1. Are they working independently?

_____2. Some cooperation.

_____3. United in their activities.

Now we would like to consider only the top community leaders in Lima. Which of these four alternatives is the case?
Check here

_____1. All of the top leaders here are for the issue or project.

_____2. All of the top leaders are against the issue or project.

_____3. There is a split among top leaders on this issue.

_____4. None of the top leaders have taken a stand on the issue.

Depending on your response to the last question we want to ask your estimate about top influential activity.

Leaders *for* it:

_____1. Not supporting it at all publicly.

_____2. Are giving contributions but not making speeches or otherwise publicly active.

_____3. Supporting it very actively with contributions, speeches, and public appearances.

Leaders *against* it:

_____1. Are not fighting it at all.

_____2. Are giving contributions, but are not publicly active.

_____3. Are very active with contributions, speeches, and public appearances.

Functional Groups

In your opinion what groups are the most important for assuring the support for a project or issue that is of general concern to the community?

Group	Key persons in the group

Cliques

It is often said that religious, political, business, and military leaders work closely together in groups and make the big decisions which affect the community. Is this true or false?

True_____   False_____   Why?

NOTES

PREFACE

1. Claire W. Gilbert, "Some Trends in Community Politics: A Secondary Analysis of Power Structure Data from 166 Communities," *Southwestern Social Science Quarterly*, XLVIII (December 1967), 373–83. See also Roland J. Pellegrin, "Selected Bibliography on Community Power Structure," ibid., 451–66. John Walton selected 33 studies dealing with 55 communities as those capable of comparative analysis in his "Substance and Artifact: The Current Status of Research on Community Power Structure," *American Journal of Sociology*, LXXI (January 1966), 430–34.

2. Norman E. Whitten, Jr., "Power Structure and Socio-cultural Change in Latin American Communities," *Social Forces*, XLIII (March 1965), 320–29. Cf. Francine F. Rabinovitz, "Sound and Fury Signifying Nothing?: A Review of Community Power Research in Latin America," *Urban Affairs Quarterly*, III (March 1968), 111–22.

3. Exceptions include William V. D'Antonio and William H. Form, *Influentials in Two Border Cities* (Notre Dame, Ind., 1965); Orrin E. Klapp and L. Vincent Padgett, "Power Structure and Decision-Making in a Mexican Border City," *American Journal of Sociology*, LXV (January 1960), 400–06.

4. Obviously, the researcher must take into account that community variations occur and are sometimes major factors.

5. Walton has shown that there are certain correlates of power structure types and possible biases associated with particular research methods. See his "Substance and Artifact," 430–38, and "Discipline, Method, and Community Power: A Note on the Sociology of Knowledge," *American Sociological Review*, XXXI (October 1966), 684–89.

1. THEORETICAL POSITIONS, OPERATING ASSUMPTIONS, AND METHODOLOGICAL DECISIONS

1. "The Sixteen Faces of Power" (dittoed, Bureau of Applied Social Research, Columbia University, 1964). Cf. his "The Concept of Power: Some Overemphasized and Underrecognized Dimensions," *Southwestern Social Science Quarterly*, XLVIII (December 1967), 271–86.

2. Abraham Kaplan, *The Conduct of Inquiry* (San Francisco, 1964), 52.

3. Ibid., 87.

4. "Community Decision Making," *Administrative Science Quarterly*, I (March 1957), 425.

5. Peter H. Rossi, "The Study of Decision Making in the Local Community" (mimeo, University of Chicago, August 1957), 18–19. Cf. a later paper by Rossi, "Theory, Research, and Practice in Community Organization," in *Social Science and Community Action*, ed., Charles R. Adrian (East Lansing, 1960). Robert A. Dahl, "The Analysis of Influence in Local Communities" (duplicated, May 1959) lists money and credit, control over jobs, control over the information of others; social standing, knowledge and experience; popularity, esteem, charisma, legality, constitutionality, officiality, ethnic solidarity, and the right to vote.

6. Rossi, "Community Decision Making," 406–11.

7. See especially Floyd Hunter, Ruth C. Schaffer, and Cecil G. Sheps, *Community Organization* (Chapel Hill, N.C., 1956), 37–39.

8. Charles M. Bonjean, "Community Leadership: A Case Study and Conceptual Refinement," *American Journal of Sociology*, XLVII (May 1963), 672–88.

9. Delbert C. Miller and James Dirksen, "The Identification of Visible, Concealed, and Symbolic Leaders in a Small Indiana City: A Replication of the Bonjean-Noland Study of Burlington, North Carolina," *Social Forces*, XLIII (May 1965), 548–55.

10. Aaron Wildavsky, *Leadership in a Small Town* (Totowa, N.J., 1964), 336–37.

11. Ibid., 315.

12. Rossi, in "Theory and Method in the Study of Power in the Local Community," a paper presented to 1960 annual meeting of American Sociological Association, August 1960, reports that "it is much harder to see how the issue decisional approach will produce data that will lend themselves to systematization."

13. William H. Form and Delbert C. Miller, *Industry, Labor, and Community* (New York, 1960), Chapters 14 and 18.

14. Rossi, "Theory and Method in the Study of Power in the Local Community," 37–38.

15. Many persons who associate Floyd Hunter with the reputational method of community power study sometimes forget that he employed a wide variety of techniques. An examination of his three books, *Community Power Structure* (Chapel Hill, N.C., 1953), *Community Organization*, and *Top Leadership, U.S.A.* (Chapel Hill, N.C., 1959), reveals the wide range of techniques available to the community power researcher. The list that follows was drawn from his work. *Newspapers*: "Over a period of eighteen months newspapers . . . were clipped of items bearing on the subject of power." *Notes of random thought* "occurring to the writer as hypothetical." *Documents relating to political activities* "were classified." *Personal correspondence* and other documents "which seemed to have a bearing on the problem were edited and classified." *Preparation for interview* "Schedule of questions that would yield data pertinent to power alignments and dynamics

within a given community." *A method for identification of community leaders*: "Lists of leaders occupying positions of prominence in civic organizations, business establishments, University bureaucracy, office holders in politics, and persons prominent socially and of wealth status were secured." *Judges used for selection of top influentials*: "person who had lived in the community for some years and who had a knowledge of community affairs." *Interviewing*: "schedules were used in interviewing top influentials." *Social and ecological placement of top influentials*—occupations, offices, meeting places, residential areas occupied: "To locate power in Regional City, it is necessary to identify some of the men who wield power, as well as to describe the physical setting in which they operate." *Biographical analysis* "drawn from personal observation, from news accounts of the men, from data given by them in interviewing, and from things said about them by other people." *Sociometric analysis*: "Through analyzing the mutual choices made by those interviewed, it will be shown that there is an esprit de corps among certain top leaders. . . ." *Clique analysis*: "All interviews with leaders helped to fill in some of the gaps —to lend credence to the fact that there are structural relations among members of the leadership group." *Issue analysis*: "All informants were asked the question: 'What are the two major issues on projects before the community today?' . . . The Plan of Development has been a controversial project in the community—for some ten years. Upper and lower limit leaders interested in policy making are shown. Understructure personnel can be identified by code numbers and role played. The isolation of policy matters and projects flowing from top policy decision is, in the opinion of the writer, one effective way of approaching the tricky problem of action research. . . . Every man in Regional City could conceivably be placed in relation to his actions or lack of action concerning the Plan of Development." *Analysis of the power structure of a subcommunity*: "The method turning up policy determining leadership within the Negro community was the same as used in the larger community, but in this subcommunity, Negro judges were used—seven of them, to give a basic list of leaders who might be questioned on leadership patterns." *Historical analysis of local, state, and national policy interrelations*: "Notes were taken from newspapers . . . and interviews to find historic patterns." *Sociological analysis of role of individual in the organized community*: Using "books and articles, such as Arthur Hillman, *Community Organization and Planning*; Robert Brady, *Business as a System of Power*; Morris Opler, 'Social Science and Democratic Policy'; C. Wright Mills, *White Collar*, etc." *Direct experience and observation*: "Floyd Hunter lived and worked in Regional City for many years before undertaking his study. He held the position of Executive Director of the Atlanta Community Planning Council (1943–48) which gave him an opportunity to observe men and organizations for a five-year period before his research." *Historical analysis of the community*: "The staff felt that the summer should be spent in gathering data on historic Salem, the ways in which Salem had faced community problems in the past, and in general, to determine leadership patterns and practices." *Participant observation*: "Mrs. Hunter intensively studied the Polish community in order to relate organized activity of this group to other ethnic groups and to the community as a whole." *Questionnaire* was "sent to Leaders of 106 organizations to (1) judge the power and influence of their own and other policy making associations, (2) give names of five national leaders considered to be of top influence in national policy-making." *Roll-up interviewing*: "The process of questioning was cumulative. One accumulates questions as well as data through interviewing, questions that cannot be anticipated at the beginning of the study. They may not be important enough to try to get information about them from everyone seen, and a few answers may satisfy the research requirement of objectifying findings by getting answer from others rather than coming to purely subjective conclusions." *Telephone panel* "was used to follow policy in the making."

For still more methodological implementation, see Hunter's list of 21 methodological steps taken in the study *Top Leadership, U.S.A.*, xv–xvi.

16. Charles M. Bonjean and David M. Olson, "Community Leadership: Directions of Research," *Administrative Science Quarterly*, IX (December 1964), 278–300.

2. A FRAMEWORK FOR COMPARATIVE ANALYSIS OF COMMUNITY POWER STRUCTURES

1. Floyd Hunter, *Community Power Structure* (Chapel Hill, 1953), 29.
2. Robert A. Dahl, "Leadership in a Fragmented Political System: Notes for a Theory," paper presented at the Conference on Metropolitan Leadership held at Northwestern University, April 1960, or see Roscoe C. Martin et al., *Decisions in Syracuse* (Bloomington, Ind., 1961), 5–9.

3. SEATTLE AND BRISTOL: *A Comparison of Community Power Structures Contrasting Private Enterprise and Democratic Socialist Political Ideologies*

1. Bryan Little, *The City and County of Bristol* (London, 1954).
2. Cf. Howard R. Bowen, *Social Responsibilities of the Businessman* (New York, 1953), especially Chapters 8 and 9; William H. Whyte, Jr., *Is Anybody Listening?* (New York, 1952), Chapter 1.
3. Robert S. Lynd and Helen M. Lynd, *Middletown in Transition* (New York, 1937); Floyd Hunter, *Community Power Structure* (Chapel Hill, N.C., 1954); James B. McKee, "Status and Power in the Industrial Community: A Comment on Drucker's Thesis," *American Journal of Sociology*, LVIII (January 1953), 364–70; Robert A. Dahl, *Who Governs? Democracy and Power in an American City* (New Haven, Conn., 1961); Roscoe C. Martin et al., *Decisions in Syracuse* (Bloomington, Ind., 1961); Robert Presthus, *Men at the*

Top: A Study in Community Power (New York, 1964); Robert E. Agger, Daniel Goldrich, and Bert E. Swanson, *The Rulers and the Ruled: Political Power and Impotence in American Communities* (New York, 1964); Roland J. Pellegrin and Charles H. Coates, "Absentee-owned Corporations and Community Power Structure," *American Journal of Sociology*, LXI (March 1956), 413–17; Donald W. Olmsted, "Organizational Leadership and Social Structure in a Small City," *American Sociological Review*, XIX (June 1954), 273–81; Floyd Hunter, Ruth C. Schaffer, and Cecil G. Sheps, *Community Organization* (Chapel Hill, N.C., 1956); W. V. D'Antonio and W. H. Form, *Influentials in Two Border Cities* (Notre Dame, Ind., 1965).

4. Robert S. Brady, *Business as a System of Power* (New York, 1939); Floyd Hunter, *Top Leadership, U.S.A.* (Chapel Hill, N. C., 1959); C. Wright Mills, *White Collar: The American Middle Classes* (New York, 1951), and *The Power Elite* (New York, 1956); Karl Mannheim, *Freedom, Power, and Democratic Planning* (New York, 1950); Arnold Rose, *The Power Structure: Political Process in American Society* (New York, 1967).

5. Terry N. Clark, "Power and Community Structure: Who Governs, Where, and When? *The Sociological Quarterly*, VIII (Summer 1967), 291–316; Presthus, *Men at the Top*, 405–33; William H. Form and Delbert C. Miller, *Industry, Labor, and Community* (New York, 1961), 637–78.

6. Cf. Albert J. Reiss, Jr., "Some Logical and Methodological Problems in Community Research," *Social Forces*, XXXIII (October 1954), 51–57; Gordon W. Blackwell, "A Theoretical Framework for Sociological Research in Community Organization," *Social Forces*, XXXIII (October 1954), 57–64; Conrad W. Arensberg, "The Community Study Method," *American Journal of Sociology*, LX (September 1954), 109–24. The theory and concepts used in this chapter were developed jointly with William H. Form of Michigan State University. See Form and Miller, *Industry, Labor, and Community*.

7. Employment in manufacturing, wholesaling, and retailing is less than 60 percent, 20 percent, and 50 percent respectively of total employment in these activities. See Chauncey D. Harris, "A Functional Classification of Cities of the United States," *Geographical Review*, XXII (January 1943), 86–89.

8. A valuable test of this technique has been reported in John M. Foskett and Raymond Hohle, "The Measurement of Influence in Community Affairs," *Research Studies of the State College of Washington*, XXV (June 1957), 148–54. Cf. Carol E. Thometz, *The Decision Makers: The Power Structure of Dallas* (Dallas, 1963), 42–47.

9. A test of the significance of the difference between the proportions of business representation among key influentials in Seattle and in Bristol showed that the difference was significant at the .02 level. No statistically significant difference was found between the proportion of key influentials in Seattle and Atlanta, although the direction toward increased business representation in Atlanta among its key influentials is indicated. The two lawyers in Atlanta are corporation lawyers. If they were classified as business, Atlanta's business

representation would be 92 percent, and a significant upward difference between the two cities would be shown.

10. Bosworth Monck, "How to Make a Captain in Industry," *The Listener,* LIII (January 13, 1955), 57. Cf. C. J. Adcock and L. B. Brown, "Social Class and the Ranking of Occupations," *British Journal of Sociology,* VIII (March 1957), 26–32.

11. While there is a high overall similarity in prestige positions given to the occupational structures of the United States and Great Britain, significant differences do occur within the structure. Cf. Robert W. Hodge, Donald J. Treiman, and Peter H. Rossi, "A Comparative Study of Occupational Prestige," in *Class, Status, and Power,* ed., R. Bendix and Seymour M. Lipset (New York, 1966), 318. For the comparison between the United States 1963 NORC prestige scores and matching titles in Great Britain, a coefficient of determination r^2 of .83 is reported. The unexplained variance is important because of the differences in cultural values affecting businessmen, government officials, and intellectuals.

12. Peter H. Rossi, "The Organizational Structure of an American Community," in *Complex Organizations,* ed., Amatai Etzioni (New York, 1961), 302.

13. Rose, *The Power Structure,* 485.

4. Positional, Reputational, and Issue-Decisional Leaders in Seattle and Bristol

1. Robert O. Schulze and Leonard U. Blumberg, "The Determination of Local Power Elites," *American Journal of Sociology,* LXIII (November 1957), 290–96.

2. Ibid., 292.

3. *Communism, Conformity, and Civil Liberties* (Garden City, N.Y., 1955). Cf. Linton C. Freeman, *Patterns of Local Community Leadership* (Indianapolis, 1968).

4. Cf. F. A. Stewart, "A Sociometric Study of Influence in Southtown," *Sociometry,* X (February, August 1947), 11–31, 273–86.

5. *Community Organization* (Chapel Hill, N.C., 1956), 37–39.

6. Cf. Arthur J. Vidich and Joseph Bensman, *Small Town in Mass Society* (Princeton, N.J., 1958), 112: "The pervasiveness of political discussion is of special significance when one notes that it is focused on personalities rather than on issues, and that it continues in the presence or absence of issues. Issues, then, are not an essential ingredient of village politics."

7. From Form and Miller, *Industry, Labor, and Community,* 531–32.

8. Presthus, *Men at the Top,* 147–48. Linton Freeman reports an overlap of 33 percent between issue and reputational leaders studied in Syracuse, New York. See his "Locating Leaders in Local Communities," *American Sociological Review,* XXVIII (October 1963), 791–98.

9. Nelson W. Polsby, "Three Problems in the Analysis of Community Power," *American Sociological Review,* XXIV (December 1959), 796–803.

10. William A. Gamson, "Reputation and Resources in Community Politics," *American Journal of Sociology,* LXXII (September 1966), 123.

5. The Seattle Business Leader

1. "The Nine Hundred," *Fortune,* XLVI (November 1952), 132–35, 232–36. For its report *Fortune* took the three highest paid men in each of 250 largest industrial companies, 25 largest railroads, and 25 largest utilities.

2. The list of names was assembled in order to communicate with business leaders regarding a program of economic education offered by the University of Washington at the request of the Chamber of Commerce.

3. Cf. W. Lloyd Warner and James C. Abegglen, *Occupational Mobility in American Business and Industry, 1928–1952* (Minneapolis, 1955), 42.

4. Ibid., 30. Cf. Warner and Abegglen, *Big Business Leaders in America* (New York, 1955), 59–83, 177–95.

5. There is no disposition to follow the pattern of previous research as reported by Arnold M. Rose. "In comparing their results to those obtained by other methods, and by accepting concurrence of results as validation of their method, reputational researchers have implicitly denied the special competence their method is supposed to possess." *The Power Structure: Political Process in American Society* (New York, 1967), 267.

6. Decision-Making Cliques and Power Structures in Seattle and Bristol

1. Floyd Hunter, *Community Power Structure* (Chapel Hill, N.C., 1953); John M. Foskett and Raymond Hohle, "The Measurement of Influence in Community Affairs," *Research Studies of the State College of Washington,* XXV (June 1957), 148–54. Robert O. Schulze and Leonard U. Blumberg, "The Determination of Local Power Elites," *American Journal of Sociology,* LXIII (November 1957), 290–96; Peter H. Rossi, "Community Decision Making," *Administrative Science Quarterly,* I (March 1957), 415–43; Delbert C. Miller, "The Seattle Business Leader," *Pacific Northwest Business,* XV (February 1956), 5–12; Robert A. Dahl, *Who Governs?* (New Haven, Conn., 1961), 330–40.

2. Sociometric analysis is most commonly employed. For a brief statement of various methods of analysis see Charles H. Porter and Charles P. Loomis, "Analysis of Sociometric Data," in *Research Methods in Social Relations,* ed., Marie Jahoda, Morton Deutsch, and Stuart Cook (New York, 1951), Part II, 561–86.

3. Hunter, *Community Power Structure*, 79. Cf. M. Kent Jennings, *Community Influentials: The Elites of Atlanta* (New York, 1964), 155–68.

4. Roland J. Pellegrin and Charles H. Coates, "Absentee-Owned Corporations and Community Power Structure," *American Journal of Sociology*, LXI (March 1956), 413–19.

5. Floyd Hunter, Ruth C. Schaffer, and Cecil G. Sheps, *Community Organization* (Chapel Hill, N.C., 1956), 27–37.

6. Rossi, "Community Decision Making"; Robert O. Schulze, "Economic Dominants in Community Power Structure," *American Sociological Review*, XXIII (February 1958), 3–9.

7. James B. McKee, "Status and Power in the Industrial Community: A Comment on Drucker's Thesis," *American Journal of Sociology*, LVIII (January 1953), 369.

8. Dahl, *Who Governs?*

9. Peter H. Rossi and Robert A. Dentler, *The Politics of Urban Renewal* (Glencoe, Ill., 1961).

10. Edward C. Banfield, *Political Influence* (Glencoe, Ill., 1961).

11. Roscoe C. Martin et al., *Decisions in Syracuse* (Bloomington, Ind., 1961).

12. Linton C. Freeman et al., *Local Community Leadership* (University College of Syracuse University, 1960).

13. Norton Long, "The Local Community as an Ecology of Games," *American Journal of Sociology*, LXIV (November 1959), 251–61.

14. Joan Henning Criswell, "Sociometric Methods of Measuring Group Preferences," *Sociometry*, VI (No. 4, 1943), 398–408.

15. Scores were allocated as follows: Business, 1 point for each directorship of business other than own, with 2 points for each board chairmanship or ownership of another business. Social, civic, and professional areas were each marked for every organization listed according to the number of categories marked for "attend regularly" (1 point), "committee member" (2 points), "officer" (3 points).

16. Sidney Siegal, *Nonparametric Statistics for the Behavioral Sciences* (New York, 1956), 96–104.

17. In a letter to the writer, August 2, 1956, Floyd Hunter says: "I think I may have quoted and used the term 'crowds or cliques' rather broadly in the Regional City study, but it still has meaning for me. In several cities I have been in recently, it appears, too, that some of the corporate groups may be reluctant to 'bind themselves into reciprocal quid pro quo agreement,' but many such groups have followers identified with them that make up a 'crowd' in the minds of others in the community. It is a term that might be tightened up, however, and your findings cannot be dismissed lightly."

18. Delbert C. Miller, "Industry and Community Power Structure," *American Sociological Review*, XXIII (February 1958), 14.

19. This is well documented in Schulze, "Economic Dominants in Community Power Structure," 7–9. However, the withdrawal of "economic dominants" exhibited in Cibola was not demonstrated in Seattle or Bristol.

20. Dahl, *Who Governs?*, 11.

21. See Form and Miller, *Industry, Labor, and Community*, 441–43, 657–66.

7. THE PREDICTION OF ISSUE OUTCOME: *The Right-to-Work Initiative in Seattle*

1. This theory as shown in the next few pages was developed jointly with William H. Form of Michigan State University.

2. I am indebted to Stuart D. Johnson of Humboldt State College (California) for assistance in conducting some of the major interviews.

3. Selected excerpts from Robert C. Hanson, "Predicting a Community Decision: A Test of the Miller-Form Theory," *American Sociological Review*, XXIV (October 1959), 662–71.

4. Lists of names of "knowledgeable" persons were secured during initial guided interviews with five long-time residents of the area. The potential respondents were selected from these lists. The suggested names included persons holding positions in formal organizations in the community, officers and executive secretaries of major voluntary associations, various council and board members from the various sectors, etc.

5. A "don't know" response to the initial question was treated as equivalent to a "not important" response, i.e., the second question was not asked.

6. The probability of 18 of 36 responses falling in one of three response categories by chance alone is less than 5 in 100.

7. The probability of 12 of 36 responses occurring by chance alone in one of 5 response categories is less than 5 in 100.

8. It is interesting, though not quite valid, to compare these results with those obtained in a "poll among a scientific cross-section of voters in all parts of the state," conducted by Research Services, Inc. for *The Denver Post*. The following results were reported in the October 15 issue of the paper on the "right to work" proposal: Against—38 percent; For—35 percent; Undecided—27 percent. The report noted that the "against" vote was higher in Denver, but no figures were cited. The right-to-work proposal failed in the state as a whole by a 3 to 2 ratio, roughly 60 percent against to 40 percent for. A previous poll, reported in the September 12 issue of *The Denver Post*, disclosed that 51 percent of voters questioned in "Colorado cities" would vote against right-to-work. Figures for the Denver area were reported as 55 percent against, 28 percent for, and 17 percent undecided. In the same article, results of an early March poll were mentioned which indicated confusion among voters over "right to work" and "union shop." Voters then were in favor of both, with 56 percent of Denver voters saying they *favored* "right to work," evidently not understanding that the "right to work" amendment would prohibit union shops.

9. The October 15 poll cited in footnote 8 included the question: "Which of the five amendments of the Colorado constitution to be voted on in Novem-

ber are you familiar with now?" Of those questioned, 56 percent were familiar with the right-to-work amendment and only 23 percent with the civil service amendment over the state as a whole. On the civil service amendment, voters at this time were reported to be 34 percent for, 10 percent against, and 56 percent undecided. No figures were given for Denver. The poll failed to predict direction since the civil service amendment was rejected in the state as a whole by a slight margin, about 52 percent against and 48 percent for.

10. On the right-to-work proposal, there were 16 "don't knows" on the degree of importance question (see Table 78, Column 4); on the civil service proposal, there were 24 "don't knows" on the same question.

11. Delbert C. Miller, "Town and Gown: The Power Structure of a University Town," *American Journal of Sociology*, LXVIII (January 1963), 432–43, reports a test made in Bloomington, Indiana which required the vote of the city council for passage or defeat of an urban renewal project. Total scores were derived using Hanson's method, which yields 91 percent for and 9 percent against. The city council approved the project after a stormy six-and-a-half-hour public hearing. The strong resistance was organized by a small minority group which fought aggressively against the urban renewal project. A historical record with a social analysis of this issue is Grafton D. Trout, Jr., "The Bloomington, Indiana Controversy over Urban Renewal," January 15, 1962 (mimeo, Sociology Department, Indiana University).

12. Miller and Form addressed themselves to such questions and developed a more powerful theory. See *Industry, Labor, and Community*, Chapter 11.

8. CORDOBA AND LIMA: *The Research Setting*

1. Richard W. Patch, "The Peruvian Elections of 1962 and their Annulment," *American Universities Field Staff Reports Service* (West Coast South America Series, IX, No. 6), 17. See also George Pendle, *A History of Latin America* (Baltimore, 1963), 217–26.

2. William H. Form and William V. D'Antonio, *Influentials in Two Border Cities* (Notre Dame, Ind., 1965).

3. Orrin E. Klapp and L. Vincent Padgett, "Power Structure in Decision-Making in a Mexican Border City," *American Journal of Sociology*, LXV (January 1960), 400–06.

4. This work (New York, 1964) is a comparative study of social classes in Querétaro, Mexico, and Popayán, Colombia.

5. For the best cross-cultural urban bibliography see R. Lorenz, P. Meadows, and W. Bloomberg, *A World of Cities* (Syracuse Cross Cultural Project, Publication No. 12, Syracuse University, 1964). Cf. *Social Science Research on Latin America*, ed., Charles Wagley (New York, 1964), 243–89.

6. *Two Cities of Latin America*, 2.

7. "Power Structure in a Venezuelan Town: The Case of San Cristóbal," paper read to the American Sociological Association, San Francisco, August 1967.

8. *Los Que Mandan* (Buenos Aires, 1965).

9. *Elites in Latin America*, ed., Seymour Lipset and Aldo Solari (New York, 1967).

9. Cordoba, Argentina under the Military Junta

1. That this study could be done at all is a tribute to the faculty and students of the Institute of Sociology of the University of Cordoba. Prof. Alfredo Poviña, the director of the Institute, is one of the best known and respected men in the community and his name brought support to the research. The careful counsel of Prof. Juan Carlos Agulla, Dr. Eva Chamorro, and Dr. Alfredo Critto guided the writer over trouble spots and opened many doors. I am indebted to them for much helpful advice and support and to the following graduate students for research assistance: Daisy N. de Cassabella, Maria del C. Carceglia, Nélida Chacón, Carlos C. Ceballos, Ernesta Dadomo, Marta Degoy, Rosa Dejtiar, Emiliano Endrek, Ivo Ferrari, Lucía Garay, Marta Giménez, Ignacio Justiniano, Susana Manzano, María Oviedo Bustos, Lucía Proto, Carmen O. Ramírez, Enrique Saforcada, Maria O. de Yardarola, and Victorio Schillizzi.

2. A majority of these graduate students had received a Doctor of Laws degree, and most of them held professional and managerial positions in the city.

3. When all 44 positional leaders are compared with the 37 reputational leaders, a 40-percent overlap is found. It will be noted that there appears to be greater overlap among the key influentials. Seven of the top reputed leaders hold important official positions as defined by the schedule. The reputed leaders ranking from 11 through 20 hold only three of the top official positions.

4. An 83-percent agreement was obtained between the expert panel and the top influentials on those 12 issue-decisional leaders selected by the panel as most active in two or more issues.

5. William A. Gamson has reported striking new evidence of the general participation of reputational leaders in issues. "Reputation and Resources in Community Politics," *American Journal of Sociology*, LXXII (September 1966), 128.

6. The coefficient of agreement is described in Charles C. Peters and Walter Van Voorhis, *Statistical Procedures and Their Mathematical Bases* (New York, 1940), 201; or, see John H. Mueller and Karl F. Schuessler, *Statistical Reasoning in Sociology* (Boston, 1961), 275–76.

7. Wording suggested by Dr. Alfredo Critto as most appropriate in the cultural setting.

8. Ernest Havemann and Patricia Salter West, *They Went to College* (New York, 1952).

9. Juan Carlos Agulla has interpreted the decline of the traditional aristocracy in Cordoba. See his *Eclipse de Una Aristocria,* Ediciones Líbera. Centro Argentino por la Libertad de la Cultura, Buenos Aires, 1968.

10. COMMUNITY POWER PERSPECTIVES AND ROLE DEFINITIONS OF NORTH AMERICAN EXECUTIVES IN CORDOBA

1. Records show that most of the stock is owned by the Republic of Argentina and private Argentine investors, but control is firmly American.

2. For versions in Spanish see Delbert C. Miller, Eva Chamorro, and Juan Carlos Agulla, "La Estructura del Poder de Una Ciudad Argentina," *Cuadernos* (University of Cordoba), XXVI (October 1964), 29–49. Also by the same authors, *De la Industria al Poder* (Buenos Aires, 1966); Juan Carlos Agulla, "Poder, Comunidad y Desarrollo Industrial: La Estructura del Poder en Una Comunidad Urbana en Desarrollo: Córdoba," *Aportes* (October 1966), 80–105.

3. Dr. Eva Chamorro assisted in interviewing and supplied data from her study of attitudes toward industrialization in Cordoba; Professor Juan Carlos Agulla and the graduate students of the Institute of Sociology provided interviewing assistance and careful guidance in interpretation of results.

4. In South America home visitation is not common outside of the extended family. To "know socially" often means to meet at lunch or at formal receptions.

5. A Guttman analysis reveals that no single dimension dominates the attitudinal responses. Group interviews show that diverse reactions are evoked by the words "all foreign capitalists," "foreign businesses," and "North American executives." Errors averaged about 30 percent on each item. (A maximum of only 15 percent is allowable to qualify for unidimensionality.) The analysis indicates that any future effort to construct Guttman scales in these areas must separate each of the connotations expressed above.

6. Robert H. Scholl, "International Business and the Community" (Standard Oil Company of N.J., New York, 1963).

11. LIMA, PERU: *Center of Embattled Political Parties*

1. Basic documents included *Vademecum del Inversionista* (Banco de Crédito del Perú, Lima, 1965–66); *Guía Administrativa, 1966* (Librería Studium, Lima).

2. Carlos Malpica, *Los Dueños del Perú* (Fondo de Cultura Popular, Lima, 1964).

3. I am indebted to the advanced students of sociology in the University of San Marcos for their assistance in interviewing and assembling the pre-

liminary list of leaders and organizations most influential in the community life of Lima.

4. This was the first study in which it seemed necessary to take precautions about the interviewing of top influentials. I felt that as a Fulbright grantee I must be careful not to bring that program into political conflict over my research. Embassy officials felt particularly concerned because some top influentials, especially certain political leaders, were antagonistic toward the United States. The environment for social research when conducted by a North American must be considered sensitive. A North American with any official or quasi-official connection with the United States government must be especially aware of possible repercussions in the press and other agencies of the community. The problem of conducting research in a sensitive or hostile research environment has been carefully described by Robert E. Ward et al., *Studying Politics Abroad: Field Research in Developing Areas* (Boston, 1964). The following events were current at the outset of the interviewing stage: Project Camelot, a now well-known social research project sponsored by funds from the U.S. Department of Defense, had just aroused a storm of opposition in Chile and rumors were rife that a similar project was planned or already under way in Peru. A set of bitter clashes between the army and Communist guerrillas was proceeding in the mountains. A cabinet had been brought down with charges that its members were "soft" on Communism. The nationalization of the oil fields of the Standard Oil Company was the hottest political issue in Peru. It was feared any research which would probe into this issue would appear to be inspired by special interests. Bombings had occurred outside the American-owned Crillon Hotel in the center of Lima and at the Sears, Roebuck and Co. store, and bombings or bombing attempts had been made at all three Peruvian-North American cultural centers of Lima and Callao.

5. Two other expert panels confirmed these rankings with a high degree of agreement. One was composed of ten faculty members selected from the University of San Marcos and Catholic University and a second was composed of forty advanced sociology students at the University of San Marcos. A coefficient of agreement was calculated for the top influentials and the two expert panels with a coefficient of .85. It can be concluded that there is relatively high agreement in judgments.

6. The rank order given for Lima shows a high agreement between the top influentials and the faculty and advanced student panels, with a coefficient of agreement of .86.

7. These positions are the result of some important conditions. All of them represent positions occupied by Peruvians. There are important positions in some foreign companies and hotels, but it is almost necessary that the owner or chief executive of the company be a Peruvian. Large real estate holders present a problem. No one can be sure which person fits the position as largest real estate holder. As pointed out earlier, almost all landholders are heavily committed to industry and finance also. The top three were selected as the largest real estate holders. Similarly, it was necessary to select the top three

investment houses, the top three department stores, etc. The size of the city tends to produce a multiple number of units of approximately the same large size. The top three is an arbitrary determination. Another consideration is the fact that Lima is a capital city and many national offices must be represented since they also play a large role in city affairs. This is especially true in the highly centralized national government which prevails. See Allen Austin, *Estudio Sobre el Gobierno Municipal del Perú* (ONRAP, Lima).

8. For a Peruvian account of militarism see Víctor Villanueva, *El Militarismo en el Perú* (Lima, 1962).

9. *Peru* (Pan Amercian Union, Washington, D.C., 1964), 7.

10. Lawrence C. Lockley, N. H. Lockley, and Winston Templ, *Guía Económica del Perú* (Instituto Peruano de Administración de Empresas, Lima, 1966), 159.

11. Malpica, *Los Dueños del Perú*, 61–62.

12. Albert O. Hirschman, *Journeys Toward Progress* (Garden City, N.Y., 1965), 377–78.

13. Ibid., 276–97.

14. Lockley et al., *Guía Económica del Perú*, 73.

12. Decision-Making Cliques and Power Blocs in Lima

1. Francisco Luis Quesada, *Las Estructuras Sociales* (2nd ed., Lima, 1965), 201–26; Roberto Maclean y Estenos, *Sociología del Perú* (National University of Mexico, Mexico City, 1959), 101.

2. *Mensaje al Perú*, 1955.

3. Víctor Villanueva, *El Militarismo en el Perú* (Lima, 1962), 154.

4. Maclean, *Sociología del Perú*, 657.

5. Karl M. Schmitt and David D. Burks, *Evolution or Chaos* (New York, 1963), 203.

6. "Fernando Belaúnde Terry and Peruvian Politics," in *Latin American Politics*, ed., Robert D. Tomasek (New York, 1966).

7. "Oligarquias y Establecimiento," *Visión* (Mexico City, December 9, 1966), 19.

8. Excerpts from an address by Rockefeller to the Latin American Press Association, Lima, Peru, October 27, 1966. Reported in Lima *Peruvian Times*, October 28, 1966.

9. It is interesting to observe that the current land reform edict of the military rulers (1969) has brought the National Agrarian Society (large land holders) into intense conflict with the military authorities.

13. Comparative Analysis of the Four Cities

1. Form and Miller, *Industry, Labor, and Community*, 441–46.

2. Cf. Peter H. Rossi, "The Organizational Structure of an American Community," in *Complex Organizations*, ed., Amatai Etzioni (New York, 1961), 302.

3. Morris Janowitz, "Military Elites and the Study of War," *Conflict Resolution*, I (March 1967), 9–18.

4. Bruce M. Russett et al., *World Handbook of Political and Social Indicators* (New Haven, Conn., 1964), 155–56.

5. Ibid. A comparison can be made between the United States and the United Kingdom. Ibid., 245.

14. The Role of Values in International Decision Making: *Anglo-American versus Latin American Differences*

1. *Who Governs?* (New Haven, Conn., 1961), 83–84.

2. Hunter, *Community Power Structure*, 248.

3. Ibid., 243.

4. *Men at the Top* (New York, 1964), 149.

5. Ibid., 428.

6. "Power and Values in Trans-Community Relations," in *Current Trends in Community Studies*, ed., Bert E. Swanson (Community Studies, Inc., Kansas City, Mo., 1962), 72.

7. Ibid., 76.

8. Ibid., 77.

9. Gabriel A. Almond and Sidney Verba, *The Civic Culture* (Princeton, N.J., 1963), 313.

10. Rossi, "The Organizational Structure of an American Community," in *Complex Organizations*, ed., Amatai Etzioni (New York, 1961), 302.

11. Bosworth Monck, "How to Make a Captain in Industry," *The Listener*, LIII (January 13, 1955). Cf. C. J. Adcock and L. B. Brown, "Social Class and the Ranking of Occupations," *British Journal of Sociology*, VIII (March 1957), 26–32.

12. Aníbal Ismodes Cairo, *Sociología* (Lima, 1964), 382–86.

13. Harold Fallding, "A Proposal for the Empirical Study of Values," *American Sociological Review*, XXX (April 1965), 223–33; William J. Wilson and F. Ivan Nye, "Some Methodological Problems in the Empirical Study of Values," *Washington Agricultural Experiment Station*, Bulletin No. 672 (Washington State University, Pullman, July 1966); Almond and Verba, *The Civic Culture*; Handley Cantril, *The Pattern of Human Concerns* (Ithaca, N.Y., 1965); Sister Marie Augusta Neal, *Values and Interests in Social Change* (New York, 1965); David Horton Smith and Alex Inkeles, "The OM Scale: A Comparative Socio-Psychological Measure of Individual Modernity," *Sociometry*, XXIX (December 1966), 353–77; Joseph A. Kahl, *The Measurement of Modernism: A Study of Values in Brazil and Mexico* (Austin, Texas, 1968).

14. I am especially indebted to Professors James Morris and William F. Whyte of Cornell University for their assistance. Kathleen Whyte was also helpful. Professors Aníbal Ismodes Cairo, José Mejía Vaca, and Manuel Román de Sirgado of the University of San Marcos and Catholic University at Lima made many helpful suggestions. My research assistant in Peru, Patricia Frankman, made all Spanish translations of the scales. My research assistant in the United States, Judson Yearwood of Panama, carried out a large part of the statistical analysis.

15. Roberto Maclean y Estenós, *Sociología del Perú* (National University of Mexico, 1959), 646–51.

16. William F. Whyte, "Imitation or Innovation? Reflections on the Institutional Development of Peru," paper read to a conference sponsored by the Peruvian Ministry of Education, Institute of Peruvian Studies, Lima, August 12, 1965.

17. George Pendle, *A History of Latin America* (Baltimore, 1963), 225.

18. These students from five different states were in their junior year in college when they were selected to go to Lima. They were fluent in Spanish, lived with Peruvian families, and attended San Marcos University.

15. THE CUTTING EDGE OF COMPARATIVE COMMUNITY POWER RESEARCH

1. Floyd Hunter, *Community Power Structure* (Chapel Hill, N.C., 1953).

2. Floyd Hunter, Ruth C. Schaffer, and Cecil G. Sheps, *Community Organization* (Chapel Hill, N.C., 1956).

3. Carol E. Thometz, *The Decision Makers: The Power Structure of Dallas* (Dallas, 1963).

4. William D'Antonio and William H. Form, *Influentials in Two Border Cities* (Notre Dame, Ind., 1965).

5. Robert A. Dahl, *Who Governs?* (New Haven, Conn., 1961).

6. Roscoe C. Martin et al., *Decisions in Syracuse* (Bloomington, Ind., 1961).

7. Aaron Wildavsky, *Leadership in a Small Town* (Totowa, N.J., 1964).

8. Fred R. von der Mehden, *Politics of the Developing Nations* (Englewood Cliffs, N.J., 1964), 54–64, 118, 127.

9. W. D'Antonio, W. H. Form, C. P. Loomis, and E. C. Erickson, "Institutional and Occupational Representations in Eleven Community Influence Systems," *American Sociological Review*, XXVI (June 1961), 444–46.

10. John Walton, "Substance and Artifact: The Current Status of Research on Community Power Structure," *American Journal of Sociology*, LXXI (January 1966), 430–38. Cf. Claire W. Gilbert, "Community Power and Decision-Making: A Quantitative Examination of Previous Research," in Terry N. Clark, *Community Structure and Decision-Making: Comparative Analysis* (San Francisco, 1968).

11. The studies outlined in Table 71 are as follows: (1) Hunter, *Community Power Structure*; (2) James B. McKee, "Status and Power in the Industrial Community: A Comment on Drucker's Thesis," *American Journal of Sociology*, LVIII (January 1953), 364–70; (3) Donald W. Olmstead, "Organizational Leadership and Social Structure in a Small City," *American Sociological Review*, XIX (June 1954), 273–81; (4) Roland J. Pellegrin and Charles H. Coates, "Absentee-owned Corporations and Community Power Structure," *American Journal of Sociology*, LXI (March 1956), 413–19; (5) George Belknap and Ralph Smuckler, "Political Power Relations in a Mid-West City," *Public Opinion Quarterly*, XX (Spring 1956), 73–81; (6) Alexander Fanelli, "A Typology of Community Leadership Based on Influence and Interaction Within the Leader Sub-system," *Social Forces*, XXXIV (May 1956), 332–38; (7) Harry Scoble, "Leadership Hierarchies and Political Issues in a New England Town," in *Community Political Systems*, ed., Morris Janowitz (Glencoe, Ill., 1961), 117–45; (8) Delbert C. Miller, "Decision-making Cliques in Community Power Structures: A Comparative Study of an American and an English City," *American Journal of Sociology*, LXIV (November 1958), 299–310; (9) Robert O. Schulze, "The Bifurcation of Power in a Satellite City," *Community Political Systems*, 19–80; (10) William J. Gore and Robert L. Peabody, "The Functions of the Political Campaign," *Western Political Quarterly*, XI (March 1958), 55–70; (11) Arthur J. Vidich and Joseph Bensman, *Small Town in Mass Society* (Princeton, N.J., 1958); (12) Robert A. Dahl, *Who Governs?* (New Haven, Conn., 1961); (13) William H. Form and William V. D'Antonio, "Integration and Cleavage among Community Influentials in Two Border Cities," *American Sociological Review*, XXIV (December 1959), 804–14; (14) Orrin E. Klapp and L. Vincent Padgett, "Power Structure and Decision-making in a Mexican Border City," *American Journal of Sociology*, LXV (January 1960), 400–06; (15) Ted C. Smith, "The Structure of Power in a Suburban Community," *Pacific Sociological Review*, III (Fall 1960), 83–88; (16) Edward Sofen, "Problems of Metropolitan Leadership: The Miami Experience," *Midwest Journal of Political Science*, V (February 1961), 18–38, and Thomas J. Wood, "Dade County: Unbossed, Erratically Led," *Annals of the American Academy of Political and Social Science*, CCCLIII (May 1964), 64–71; (17) Ernest A. T. Barth, "Community Influence Systems: Structure and Change," *Social Forces*, XL (October 1961), 58–63; (18) Robert C. Stone, "Power and Values in Trans-Community Relations," in *Current Trends in Comparative Community Studies*, ed., Bert E. Swanson (Kansas City, Mo., 1962); (19) Linton C. Freeman et al., *Local Community Leadership* (Syracuse, N.Y., 1960); (20) Roscoe C. Martin et al., *Decisions in Syracuse* (Bloomington, Ind., 1961); (21) Jackson M. McClain and Robert Highsaw, *Dixie City Acts: A Study in Decision Making* (Birmingham, Alabama, 1962); (22) David A. Booth and Charles R. Adrian, "Power Structure and Community Change: A Replication Study of Community A," *Midwest Journal of Political Science*, VI (August 1962), 277–96; (23) Delbert C. Miller, "Town and Gown: The Power Structure of a University Town," *American Journal of*

Sociology, LXVIII (January 1963), 432–43; (24) Charles M. Bonjean, "Community Leadership: A Case Study and Conceptual Refinement," *American Journal of Sociology*, LXVIII (May 1963), 672–81; (25) Ivan Belknap and John Steinle, *The Community and Its Hospitals* (Syracuse, N.Y., 1963); (26) Gladys M. Kammerer et al., *The Urban Political Community: Profiles in Town Politics* (Boston, 1963); (27) Carol Estes Thometz, *The Decisionmakers: The Power Structure of Dallas* (Dallas, 1963); (28) Donald A. Clelland and William H. Form, "Economic Dominants and Community Power: A Comparative Analysis," *American Journal of Sociology*, LXIX (March 1964), 511–21; (29) Robert Presthus, *Men at the Top* (New York, 1964); (30) Ralph B. Kimbrough, *Political Power and Educational Decision Making* (Chicago, 1964); (31) M. Kent Jennings, *Community Influentials: The Elites of Atlanta* (New York, 1964); (32) Robert E. Agger, Daniel Goldrich, and Bert E. Swanson, *The Rulers and the Ruled* (New York, 1964); (33) Aaron Wildavsky, *Leadership in a Small Town* (Totowa, N.J., 1964).

12. Sethard Fisher, "Community Power Studies: A Critique," *Social Research*, XXIX (Winter 1962), 449–66.

13. Bradbury Seasholes, "Patterns of Influence in Metropolitan Boston," *Current Trends in Comparative Community Studies*, ed., Bert E. Swanson, 65. David Rodgers, "Community Political Systems," ibid., 47, lists seven variables that he regards as most significant. He agrees with Seasholes by listing population size and degree of industrialization. In addition, he lists heterogeneity of population, differentiation of polity from kinship and economic system, scope of local government, political parties, and unionization.

14. Seasholes, "Patterns of Influence in Metropolitan Boston," 66.

15. John Walton, "Substance and Artifact: The Current Status of Research on Community Power Structure," *American Journal of Sociology*, LXXI (January 1966), 430–38. Cf. Irving A. Fowler, "Local Industrial Structures, Economic Power, and Community Welfare," *Social Problems*, VI (Summer 1958), 41–51. Cf. Claire W. Gilbert, "Community Power and Decision-Making."

16. Presthus, *Men at the Top*, 405–33; Terry N. Clark, "Power and Community Structure: Who Governs, Where and When?" *The Sociological Quarterly*, VIII (Summer 1967), 291–316.

17. Ernest A. T. Barth and Stuart D. Johnson, "Community Power and a Typology of Social Issues," *Social Forces*, XXXVIII (October 1959), 29–32.

18. Peter H. Rossi, "Community Decision Making," *Administrative Science Quarterly*, I (March 1957), 438–39.

19. Among these are: Dahl, *Who Governs?*; Rossi and Dentler, *The Politics of Urban Renewal*; Edward C. Banfield, *Political Influence*; Roscoe C. Martin et al., *Decisions in Syracuse*; Linton C. Freeman et al., *Local Community Leadership*; Presthus, *Men at the Top*; Robert Agger et al., *The Rulers and the Ruled*; Aaron Wildavsky, *Leadership in a Small Town*; M. Kent Jennings, *Community Influentials* (Glencoe, Ill. 1964); D'Antonio and Form, *Influentials in Two Border Cities*.

20. Peter H. Rossi, application proposal prepared in 1965, National Opinion Research Center, University of Chicago. Current activities are described by Terry N. Clark, *Community Structure and Decision-Making: Comparative Analysis*, 463–71.

21. "A Study of a Secular Institution: The Chicago Real Estate Board" (doctoral thesis, University of Chicago, 1928).

22. John Walton, "Substance and Artifact," 430–38, was successful in classifying 55 power structures into these categories. Cf. Rossi, "Power and Community Structure," *Midwest Journal of Political Science*, IV (November 1960), 390–401.

INDEX

unions, Bristol's and Seattle's compared, 34; and Seattle's right-to-work initiative, 86–88; *see also* labor

United States, culture compared with Argentina's and Peru's, 249–51; culture compared with England's and Spain's, 254–56; culture compared with Peru's, 234–56; rating scale for measuring culture norms, 234–56; value systems of, 228–30; *see also* Atlanta; Seattle

upper class in 4 world cities, 226

validity tests, of international rating scales, 235–37, 243–44; prediction of issue outcome as a, 90–91, 98–99; by replication tests, 246–48; selection and application of, 18

value systems, in Argentina, 230–31; concept of, 234; in Great Britain, 230; in Latin American countries, 231–33; of Lima, 175–76; in Peru, 230–31; role in international decision making, 228–56; scaling instrument for measuring, 233–56; in underdeveloped countries, 231–33; in United States, 228–30

Verba, Sidney, 229

visible leaders, 10

voluntary community activity, in Cordoba, 126–27; definition of, 217, 219; and free enterprise system, 228; by influentials, 39, 54, 69–71; international rating scale for, 241–42, 248; in Lima, 153–54, 201; participation in U.S. as compared with other countries, 229–31; role in 4 world cities compared, 208–12; by Seattle business leaders, 61–64; *see also* organizations

Walton, John, 261, 269

Warner, W. Lloyd, 58

Whiteford, Andrew H., 106

Whitten, Norman E. Jr., xvii

Whyte, William F., 234

Wiese, Augusto, 185

Wildavsky, Aaron, 10

work, international scale for rating belief in, 241; Peru's and U.S.'s views on, 245–46; *see also* occupations

workers of Lima, 172–73